Celebrating Sensitives

What We Can Learn From
Historical Sensitive Persons
about being an Empowered Empath

Dr. Rev. Laura Palmer, PhD

Mechanicsburg, PA USA

Published by Sunbury Press, Inc.
Mechanicsburg, Pennsylvania

www.sunburypress.com

Copyright © 2024 by Dr. Rev. Laura Palmer, PhD.
Cover Copyright © 2024 by Sunbury Press, Inc.

Sunbury Press supports copyright. Copyright fuels creativity, encourages diverse voices, promotes free speech, and creates a vibrant culture. Thank you for buying an authorized edition of this book and for complying with copyright laws by not reproducing, scanning, or distributing any part of it in any form without permission. You are supporting writers and allowing Sunbury Press to continue to publish books for every reader. For information contact Sunbury Press, Inc., Subsidiary Rights Dept., PO Box 548, Boiling Springs, PA 17007 USA or legal@sunburypress.com.

For information about special discounts for bulk purchases, please contact Sunbury Press Orders Dept. at (855) 338-8403 or orders@sunburypress.com.

To request one of our authors for speaking engagements or book signings, please contact Sunbury Press Publicity Dept. at publicity@sunburypress.com.

FIRST SUNBURY PRESS EDITION: November 2024

Set in Adobe Garamond | Interior design by Crystal Devine | Cover by Victoria Mitchell | Edited by Gabrielle Kirk.

Publisher's Cataloging-in-Publication Data
Names: Palmer, Laura, author.
Title: Celebrating sensitives : what we can learn from historical sensitive persons about being an empowered empath / Dr. Rev. Laura Palmer, PhD.
Description: First trade paperback edition. | Mechanicsburg, PA : Sunbury Press, 2024.
Summary: Being Sensitive can be hard. Celebrating Sensitives offers tools and techniques from Historic Sensitive Persons. Historic figures from Monet to Dr. Martin Luther King Jr. to President Lincoln teach us how to be Sensitive and impactful on our world. Learn how being Sensitive helped these Historic Sensitive Persons become the people we know today.
Identifiers: ISBN 979-8-88819-214-6 (softcover).
Subjects: SELF-HELP / Personal Growth / General | SELF-HELP / Spiritual | SELF-HELP / Self-Management / Stress Management.

Designed in the USA
0 1 1 2 3 5 8 13 21 34 55

For the Love of Books!

This book is dedicated to
all Highly Sensitive Persons,
past, present, and future.

You are important to the development of humanity,
and we are grateful for all of you!

Thank you!

Contents

Acknowledgments vii

PART I: THE HIGHLY SENSITIVE PERSON *1*
    Chapter 1: The Highly Sensitive Person Character Trait 3

PART II: THE HISTORICAL SENSITIVE PERSONS *21*
    SECTION 1: RELIGIOUS FIGURES AND ARTISTS 23
        Chapter 2 – Saint Hildegard von Bingen 23
        Chapter 3 – Frederick Douglass 29
        Chapter 4 – Claude Monet 33
        Chapter 5 – Dr. Reverend Martin Luther King, Jr. 37

    SECTION 2: INVENTORS AND INNOVATORS 43
        Chapter 6 – Florence Nightingale 43
        Chapter 7 – George Washington Carver 48
        Chapter 8 – Nikola Tesla 52

    SECTION 3: LEADERS 56
        Chapter 9 – Abraham Lincoln 56
        Chapter 10 – Harriet Tubman 62
        Chapter 11 – Ulysses S. Grant 67
        Chapter 12 – Eleanor Roosevelt 70
        Chapter 13 – Princess Diana 76

    SECTION 4: THE LESS THAN LOVING HISTORICAL SENSITIVE PERSONS 85
        Chapter 14 – Niccolo Machiavelli 85
        Chapter 15 – Rasputin 91
        Chapter 16 – Joseph Stalin 98
        Chapter 17 – Adolph Hitler 101
        Chapter 18 – J. Edgar Hoover 106
        Chapter 19 – Historical Sensitives in Review 114

PART III: BEING AND THRIVING AS A HIGHLY SENSITIVE PERSON 121

Chapter 20 – Physical care 123
Chapter 21 – Emotional Care 146
Chapter 22 – Mental Care 160
Chapter 23 – Energetic Care 176
Chapter 24 – Spiritual Care 188
Chapter 25 – Soul Curricula and Why Highly Sensitive Persons Should Care about Self-Care? 197
Chapter 26 – Conclusion 221

Bibliography 227
Notes 229
Index 242
About the Author 245

ACKNOWLEDGMENTS

This book was not written in a vacuum. My fingers may have typed these words, but it is the result of nearly twelve years of reading countless books and articles as well as an infinite number of long conversations with friends and family. I would like to express my eternal gratitude to Carol Snyder, AnneMarie Rossi, Autumn Brooks, Kami Blackwell Lichtenberg, and Dusty Deal, without whom this collection of words would not have been possible. Thank you all for your support, belief in me, and listening to me drone on and on about this stuff. And of course, to all the authors whom I cite, without their hard work and research, my work would not have possible. And to Dr. Elaine Aron who identified the Highly Sensitive Person and has offered support and understanding for all of us, thank you! Lastly, I thank the people at Sunbury Press who took my mental meanderings and made them physical, especially my editor Gabrielle Kirk, who made my words more polished and professional.

PART I

The Highly Sensitive Person

PART I

The Highly Sensitive Person

CHAPTER 1

The Highly Sensitive Person Character Trait

The Sensitive Revolution

Hello and welcome to the wonderful world of Sensitives! While the entire world may not be sensitive, and being a Sensitive can be a bit of a bumpy ride, I have good news—the best news possible. The world is evolving to be more sensitive. We are in the midst of a Sensitive Revolution.

Look around, and you'll see sensitivity everywhere. From compassion for animals and our planet to Sensitivity classes. From food sensitivity labels to laundry detergent designed especially for sensitive skin. From people being held responsible or even fired for their insensitivity to people fighting for equality. Yes, we are everywhere.

I believe that is why we are experiencing such a tumultuous time. There are people who are afraid of evolving, of changing, and are lashing out like a stubborn, grumpy old grandfather. While the world is moving toward more compassion and consideration, some are kicking and screaming against it.

I consider those kickers and screamers to be similar to the tale of the "Stone Child" in Clarissa Pinkola Estés' book *Warming the Stone Child*. She tells the story of an orphan who has nothing but a large stone, nearly as big as the orphan. The orphan uses this stone for everything from a chair to food (as flavor in soup) to a pillow at night. The orphan lugs this heavy stone everywhere, desperately holding onto it for dear life. However, unbeknownst to the orphan, the stone is actually holding the orphan back, slowing the orphan down, and sucking the life energy out of the orphan. If the orphan would only drop the stone, the orphan would discover a whole new world of possibilities and opportunities—one that is much lighter and easier.

PART I : THE HIGHLY SENSITIVE PERSON

Everyone has some stones they are clinging to—some outdated behaviors or habits that are no longer useful to them. It is the rare human who realizes this and works to release, evolve, and change; you may be one of those rare humans, a highly sensitive human. The majority of humans remain in their old patterns, ways, and beliefs because they are comfortable, easy, and safe. These are the humans who are currently hurting and lashing out. Many are attempting to stop change and move society back toward yesterday by desperately holding onto what they know is comfortable and safe. But time marches on, and so does change. Our time in history is an opportunity for true change, evolution, and a sensitive revolution. It really is an exciting era.

We have the opportunity, as a society, to become more kind, more heart-based, more sensitive. I believe it is the Highly Sensitive Person who will lead the charge and usher in this Sensitive Revolution. It is important to understand the Highly Sensitive Person trait, the pros and cons, the pluses and minuses, and possible challenges and benefits.

To better understand the HSP trait and the good things it brings, here is a poem I wrote a few years ago.

The Weird Kids - A Letter to Sensitive Kids Everywhere
By Laura Palmer
(As Published in the compilation book *Creating Love*
edited by Jeannette Folan)

A Weird Kid sees what no one else sees.
A Weird Kid talks to the Dogs and the Trees.

A Weird Kid can feel when someone is sad.
A Weird Kid knows when someone was bad.

A Weird Kid may hurt and not know why.
Maybe a sad soul has just passed them by.

A Weird Kid feels that they don't quite fit.
So in a corner they quietly sit.

A Weird Kid's not happy when music is loud.
A Weird kid hates being in a big crowd.

A Weird Kid watches as the world goes by.
A Weird Kid may be called Sensitive and Shy.

Weird Kids are Smart, Geeks & Nerds.
We stay far away from the thundering herd.

We process things deeply, so quick and so much.
We feel every feeling, all in a bunch.

While you may feel like you're a bit weird,
I'm here to tell you, my sweet little dear.

You are special. You have a great gift.
This whole world, You can help shift.

You carry a great and innate power.
Every year, every month, every day every hour.

You have a purpose, a path, and a light
That is very well hidden, far out of sight.

YOU're greatly needed to help and to heal.
YOU have the ability with all that you feel.

YOU remember the lessons learned from the past.
Some call you truly, YOU're an EMPATH!

Strangers don't know you have this great power.
They'll TRY to push you and make you cower.

Breathe, 4 counts in and 4 counts out.
Just try it and feel what it's all about.

Make a close friend, with whom you can share
Your abilities and fears, someone who cares.

For there's power in numbers,
This much is true,

> With support and comfort
> You can be your true you.
>
> So play with your gift, whatever it be.
> Practice, experiment, walk confidently.
>
> You are the change for which most of us strive.
> YOU have what they search for all of their lives.
>
> You are wonderful, this much is true.
> But stay being you. Be true to you.
>
> So help heal this world, as you are meant to,
> Help those around you.
> Be You through and through!

Ah! Doesn't it feel wonderful to think you could help, that you are part of the solution? Doesn't it feel uplifting to know you are unique, talented, and intuitive? Doesn't it feel glorious to believe you are a divine being created for good? Yes, by golly, you are!

Being sensitive can be wondrous but also challenging. I hope this collection of words helps you notice and focus on the wondrous moments. I hope to offer some ideas, techniques, and tools to springboard you to new heights on this amazing journey we will take together. We will walk back through history with an eye for Sensitivity and see what our Historical Sensitive Persons still have to teach us. You will have an opportunity to learn more about yourself, see yourself in some amazing historical people, and learn some eye-opening reasons to take good care of yourself and suggestions for achieving healthy self-care.

The Basics of the HSP

In 1996, Dr. Elaine N. Aron published her book entitled *The Highly Sensitive Person*. Since then, many others have followed: *The Highly Sensitive Person In Love*, *Making Work Work for The Highly Sensitive Person*, and *The Highly Sensitive Child*. Her work is a great help to many who struggle to live in a non-sensitive world and acts as a launching pad for many others. I, personally, have studied and taught about the HSP characteristics for over 10 years, and I continue to learn new traits daily.

When I came across the book in 1998, it was already in its second printing. I felt like Dr. Aron was speaking directly to me. I was enthralled. Over the years of living a typical lifestyle, I came to forget her book and the Sensitive within me. In the spring of 2012, a friend asked me to help her with her dissertation about Highly Sensitive Persons, and it all came rushing back. I learned not only was I a Highly Sensitive Person, but also an empath; I could feel someone else's physical pain, which explained why I felt so poorly most of my life. As I continued to learn more about highly sensitive persons (HSPs), I was simultaneously learning more about history and realized how my American public, general education was riddled with holes and one-sided facts. One morning, the two topics came together for me. It seemed so natural. It was more of a "duh huh" moment than an "aha" moment. I thought, "Well, of course! Of course, there have been Sensitives throughout history. HSPs didn't magically appear when Dr. Aron's book was published." Once this light was turned on, I began to identify key HSP traits in many historical figures. This work focuses on only a handful.

What intrigued me most was that even though these historical figures had HSP traits, they impacted history and our lives today, seemingly diametrically opposed to the HSP trait. As an introverted HSP, I tend to shy away from contact and conflict, but these people practically ran toward it. This was so contradictory to what I had learned and experienced about HSPs that I needed to learn more about what made them the heroes and fighters they were.

After emptying my local library of thick biography after thick biography, I concluded that my concept—and possibly many others' concepts—of the HSP is very narrow and pigeonholes us into specific archetypes, which, as HSPs, we naturally accept. But the truth is that HSPs are more than quiet shy little servants. WE MAKE HISTORY!

The purpose of this work is to investigate history makers and see if they may have been Highly Sensitive Persons. By highlighting our Historical Sensitives we can see that although many HSPs appear to be shy and nerdy wallflower types, they can tap into their inner Leader, Champion, and Game-Changer archetypes to make a significant and positive difference in the world. With this in mind, I hope to inspire you as an HSP to follow your instincts, create change, and improve the world.

PART I : THE HIGHLY SENSITIVE PERSON

Apologies and Warnings

The Bible verse Matthew 7:7 says, "Seek and ye shall find." With my research, I sought and therefore have found. While I attempted to remain neutral in my findings, they may have been slanted toward, or interpreted by, my zeal and excitement for discovering historical HSPs. Therefore, if you feel I have overstepped or concluded incorrectly that these historical people are heart-based, caring HSPs, I heartily apologize.

History is rarely nice and neat; it can be downright brutal. Every day, we learn more and more facts about the people of our history. We discover that our historical heroes may not have been as perfect as we once thought but rather more fully human, complete with faults. Some of these historical figures may be controversial in their actions and impact on history. My attempt here is merely to prove their sensitivity, not to judge, condone, or condemn their actions.

I assume you, the reader, are likely to be a Highly Sensitive Person yourself. For this reason, we will not be delving into the details of the time or events of the historical person's life. Rather, we will focus, whenever possible, on their early years for hints of their core character before they became historical.

HSPs can quite easily project ourselves into someone else's shoes; it's the core of our character. Should this work become too challenging or emotional for you to read, I again apologize and recommend you take your time, perhaps read in small increments, or skip a section entirely.

Introduction to the HSP

Being an HSP is similar to being the Princess in Hans Christian Andersen's 1835 fairy tale "The Princess and the Pea." Even though the Princess sleeps on top of countless mattresses, she is so sensitive that she can't find comfort—she can feel the pea beneath the bottom mattress. In the fairytale, it is this sensitivity that makes her desirable. A modern genre depicting HSPs is the Superhero comic books and movies; a group of mutant humans who have special powers learn how to control and use their special abilities to defeat the villain. HSPs are superheroes. Or if you prefer Gary Zukav's description in his book, *The Seat of the Soul*, HSPs are the next step in human evolution.[1]

Being an HSP certainly has its blessings and challenges. I have wondered if I would make a good politician. I carefully consider others' perspectives, which I believe is enlightening and perhaps even required in the job description. But I also hedge and change my mind often, sometimes never making a solid decision. For this reason and others, I find being an HSP exhausting. I can only imagine how frustrating it is to be a non-HSP in an HSP's world. (That would be quite a turnaround.)

Dr. Aron's work

Dr. Aron's book, *The Highly Sensitive Person*, and website, HSPerson.com, discuss her research findings and identify a previously un-termed characteristic trait, the Highly Sensitive Person. An HSP is a person who is easily overwhelmed and emotional, processes everything deeply, and is sensitive to the subtleties of their environment. Her research surmises the HSP character trait is found in approximately 20% (some say as high as 35%) of the population, with 70% of these being introverted and evenly split between genders.

Characteristics of the Highly Sensitive Person

Dr. Aron's book and website offer a self-test to help you identify if you are an HSP. The HSP character trait can be briefly summed up with the acronym DOES.

- D - Depth of processing
- O - Overstimulation
- E - Emotional or empathic
- S - Sensitive to subtleties in their environment

Let's briefly look at each characteristic to better understand the HSP trait. Since being Sensitive to the subtleties in our environment is key to being an HSP, we will begin in reverse order.

SENSITIVITY TO SUBTLETIES

This is the crux of the HSP trait, which is why we are beginning here. HSPs are constantly, consciously or otherwise, "reading the room." We can walk into a room and feel the energy, the emotion. We can feel the emotional, energetic remnants of an argument or a tender moment. Another term for this ability is claircognizant, meaning we have "clear knowing" or "clear sensing." Some of us would argue that what we pick up is anything *but* clear.

Being claircognizant can sometimes be scary. We know something but don't know why or how we know it. And what we know can be unsettling. For example, many HSPs reported unsettling feelings and dreams in the weeks and months leading up to 9/11. With very little detail or helpful information to act upon, most reported understanding the messages only after the event occurred. Conclusively, HSPs can feel dread, impending disaster, or doom and have no idea how to alleviate or stop the occurrence, and therefore feel frustration and ineptitude.

EMOTIONAL OR EMPATHIC
Since HSPs are claircognizant, we can easily pick up someone else's emotions or energy, empathize with someone—especially a loved one—and provide comfort. Traditionally, we are the people who are described as "hysterical," "irrational," "embarrassingly emotional," or "high-strung." An HSP can become easily overwhelmed, emotional, and unable to handle everything they are picking up from others if they do not take time for themselves to recharge, cleanse, and ground themselves. If left unchecked, HSPs can develop serious physical issues, usually within the nervous system (i.e., multiple sclerosis or fibromyalgia).

OVERSTIMULATION
Since HSPs are busy "reading the room" and picking up energy from others, their nervous systems can become overstimulated and easily tired, requiring time to recharge. The basic function of the nervous system is to detect "environmental changes that impact the body and work in tandem with the endocrine system to respond to such events."[2] The Better Health Channel defines the function of the nervous system as a communicator for the body, both internally and externally, stating, "The nervous system helps all the parts of the body to communicate with each other. It also reacts to changes both outside and inside the body. The nervous system uses both electrical and chemical means to send and receive messages."[3] HSPs become overwhelmed easily because we are picking up (reading) subtleties in our environment with sights, sounds, and smells, making us jumpy or startled easily.

DEPTH OF PROCESSING
This characteristic, depth of processing, implies an HSP may not be quick-witted but rather someone who will think of a comeback hours or even days later. HSPs can "read a room" but also take the time to process, what they are "reading" or picking up. We ask ourselves all kinds of questions, such as, "What did they mean by that?" "Their mouth said one thing, but their body language said something different; what does that mean?" Sometimes we can process so much, considering all the varying angles and perceptions, that we generally overthink everything. Therefore, we can find it difficult to make a decision.

Now that you know more about the character trait, let's briefly sum up the Highly Sensitive Person traits with some keywords you may want to keep in mind when reading about our selected historical figures.

- Shy or awkward, especially in social settings or with potential intimate partners
- Strong imagination or rich inner life
- Loves learning and reading
- Highly intelligent
- Loves nature and/or animals
- Tends to tire easily or require time for themselves
- Not interested in material things
- Low tolerance for physical pain
- Chronic health issues, such as migraines, stomach issues, or fatigue
- Compassionate and caring
- Likely inherited and increasing over generations (therefore we can also look to the parents of the historical person for HSP traits)

One thing I absolutely love most about the Highly Sensitive Person is that it is a character trait. It is found in 20% of all species residing on this globe. This trait crosses species, cultures, genders, races, religions, and lifestyles. Being an HSP is the best example of being human. We are not found in just one race, one gender, or one culture. As we will see, we are found in ALL the races, genders, and cultures.

Dr. Aron's Further Findings

Many other studies have found over 100 species with the HSP character trait (Yippee!). On her self-titled website, Dr. Elayne Daniels writes that the HSP character trait offers an "evolutionary advantage as a survival strategy." She continues to theorize that since HSPs of any species are more responsive to their environment and can sense danger more easily, the HSP trait "provides a survival strategy of being observant before acting." This wait-and-see tactic "assists a species in continuing to evolve." Dr. Daniels concludes that this strategy is "only beneficial if found in a minority."[4]

When reading Dr. Daniels' article, initially, I was elated. Finally, theoretical proof that we Sensitives are pivotal, desired, and even necessary to the species. Then, I questioned, "But why must we remain a minority?" Upon further pondering, I realized HSPs, as Dr. Daniels writes, are wonderful at waiting and seeing, but we need a little push on actually doing. How many projects have you spent time planning, thinking about, and organizing but hesitated to take the first step in actually doing them? How many half-started projects do you have in your closet? (Personally, I can't count that high or don't want to.) This wait-and-see attitude is wonderful, but if we were the majority of the species, things might never get done. The species also needs those active non-HSPs to take our ideas and assist in making them happen.

Personally, there have been a few times in my life when I waited too long and missed out on an opportunity. I researched and researched to find the perfect kitchen appliance, only to discover my chosen appliance had been discontinued (Ugh!). Or the puppy I finally decided would make a good addition to the family had already been adopted (Good for them, but . . .). Coupons expire, things are purchased, and the world turns, all while we weigh the pros and cons trying to decide what we want.

FMRI and Neurodivergent

Dr. Aron and her team performed another study in which they used fMRIs (Functional Magnetic Resonance Imaging) to track the neuropathways of HSPs and non-HSPs. The results showed HSPs have a different pattern of thought; our process is more in-depth than that of non-HSPs, proving Sensitives are indeed different neurologically from the "norm" and, by this definition, are neurodivergent.

The term "neurodivergent" may connote feelings of terror, psych wards, and looney bins. But the term is simply defined by the Oxford dictionary simply as "Not neurotypical." Yes, this may lead to other diagnoses. I know a few HSPs who have been diagnosed as highly functioning Autistic, ADD, or ADHD. But when they informed me, my response was, "Of course; you're highly sensitive."

To my Sensitive mind, being "not neurotypical" is a good thing. It means you think differently than the status quo. It means you have the potential to rethink old, worn-out ways of doing things and bring forward fresh new ideas to help society evolve. You may invent a new material to replace plastic. You may develop an idea that revolutionizes the way we travel, work, or eat. We will see how Historical Sensitives make great and impactful inventors. We will see how thinking neurodiverse-ly can bring about change and ease people's lives. When looked at from that perspective, being different is really very exciting.

Spectrum of Sensitivity

For the research and professional community, Dr. Aron termed the character trait as Sensory Processing Sensitivity or SPS. Prior to her work and even up to today, people were "diagnosed" with Sensory Processing Disorder (SPD) or other terms. This diagnosis concludes something is "wrong" with the person, implying a "cure" is needed. Peeking at the symptoms of Sensory Processing Disorder and comparing them to the HSP traits, one can theorize that people diagnosed with SPD may be HSPs, just with more physical sensitivity to sights, sounds, and smells, and might highly benefit from some protection and cleansing techniques.[5]

In January 2018, Dr. Aron and her team published a paper entitled "Dandelions, tulips, and orchids: evidence for the existence of low-sensitive, medium-sensitive, and high-sensitive individuals." This paper suggests that rather than a binary, an either/or trait (either you're an HSP or non-HSP) there is instead the "existence of three . . . groups," and she termed this newly identified middle sensitive group "tulips" in keeping with her previously established flower metaphor, naming HSP orchids and non-HSP dandelions. Dandelions are the least sensitive and heartiest, able to grow and bloom in any condition, even in the cracks of sidewalks. Orchids require a more defined and ideal environment to thrive. Tulips are a happy medium between the two flowers, being less fragile than orchids but more sensitive than dandelions. The paper concludes that some people are orchids, highly sensitive, while the majority are tulips, with medium sensitivity, and a substantial minority (approximately 20%) are dandelions, characterized by a particularly low sensitivity.[6]

Since we orchids require the perfect positive environment in which to flourish and understand that the world is not a perfect place, orchids tend to feel something is "wrong" with them and therefore comprise 80% of counseling patients.[7]

These findings reveal a Spectrum of Sensitivity. Rather than a binary HSP/non-HSP trait, it suggests a sliding scale of sensitivity. We can now consider sensitivity to be less like a light switch and more like a barometer, going up and down for each person, with some people higher while others are lower on the sensitivity scale.

Sensitive Strivers

Some have posited that HSPs can be Type A personalities—those high-achieving people who use others' energy to spur them on to higher heights. Melody Wilding, a licensed social worker, author, and "executive and leadership coach for smart, sensitive high-achievers who are tired of getting in their own way," is one such person.[8] Through her coaching and research work, she coined the term "Sensitive Strivers," defining her term as "a high-achiever who is also more sensitive to their emotions, the world, and the behavior of those around them."

This term and her work are very exciting and imply a broader definition of the HSP, one that includes ambition, power, and a drive for success, some qualities we will see in our Historical Sensitives.

The Different Ways the HSP Trait May Present Itself

TYPICAL ARCHETYPES OF HSP CHARACTER TRAIT
In 1919, Carl Jung was the first to develop and define the psychological concept of Archetypes as "idealized or prototypical models of a person, object, or concept."[9] The concept of archetypes has broadened since Dr. Jung's day. He developed 12 archetypal characters, while others, like Caroline Myss, have expanded the idea and importance of archetypes in her book *Sacred Contracts*. Perhaps more colloquially understood as "characters," archetypes are common roles or parts humans play in the game of life. Some humans play the role of Hero, Explorer, Jester or Prince or Princess, Librarian, or Detective.

If we combine Dr. Aron's work with that of Caroline Myss' expanded archetypes, we can find some common archetypes for HSPs.

GEEK/NERD/SAGE
You may have been called various things as an HSP, such as geek, nerd, or bookworm. These are common and considered derogatory names for the archetypes The Student, The Scholar, and The Sage. (Personally, I love being called a geek or nerd, but then I'm weird and an HSP.) Many HSPs love to read, perhaps because we can escape to a safe and faraway place. HSPs love learning, perhaps because we enjoy the bigger, deeper questions, or perhaps because we are intelligent and typical out-of-the-box answers are frustrating and boring. Consider the characters Dr. Sheldon Cooper and Dr. Leonard Hofstadter in the television show, *The Big Bang Theory*. Sheldon and Leonard are absolutely Highly Sensitive Persons; they are brilliant, shy, and introverted. These characters, while exaggerated for comedic effect, typify the archetype Nerd, or the more nicely termed Scholar, and sum up the typical Highly Sensitive Person.[10]

CAREGIVER/NURTURER/HOST

Because HSPs are empathetic, we are naturally great Caregivers, Nurturers, or Hosts, sometimes to our own detriment. We love to make sure others are comfortable and have everything they need. An extroverted HSP will flit around a party, ensuring that everyone enjoys themselves and has enough to drink and eat. Of course, once the party is over, the HSP will promptly drop into bed exhausted. While gender roles are currently changing, the Mother archetype typifies HSPs, regardless of the person's gender.[11]

HERMIT

Because HSPs are so sensitive to the subtleties of our environment, we "pick up" on things. When combined with our ability to deeply process, we may take on other people's energies, worries, and cares. Since others' energies are often overwhelming, we tire very quickly and require naps or alone time, pointing to the archetype of the Hermit. Hermits love being alone, searching for higher meanings.

But the key to the Hermit—which most people forget, especially HSPs—is that they bring light to the world. Yes, we may go away and hide for a bit, but we must return with newfound ideas and information. The trick for the HSP is to get out of hiding and bring forward our light. Sometimes the Hermit is forced upon us in the form of a physical ailment. As a result, many unaware HSPs experience life-long illnesses, typically in the form of stomach issues, fibromyalgia, or migraines.[12]

ARTIST

Perhaps the best archetype that exemplifies the HSP is the Artist. Like Artists, HSPs can be moody, emotional, or grumpy, usually because we have picked up someone else's energy. HSPs see the world differently; consider Pablo Picasso and his perspective-breaking work. HSPs like to be alone, and some, like Clarissa Pinkola Estés in *Mother Night* suggests, must create.[13]

HEALER/MYSTIC

Other common archetypes for HSPs are Healers, Mystics, and Redeemers. HSPs who are higher on the Spectrum of Sensitivity, namely empaths, intuitives, and psychics, will naturally lean toward the ultimate caregiving character, one of spiritual and religious positions. We have already identified HSPs' love of caring for others; tending to another's soul and spirit is equally important, if not more so. Therefore, we should include religious figures in our historical search.[14]

THE INTROVERT

While the Introvert is not an archetype per se, it is the basis for many of the typical HSP archetypes, namely the previously mentioned Scholar, Hermit, and Mother. You may think to yourself, "The HSP character trait sounds a lot like the Introvert personality type." And you would be right. The two overlap quite a bit. 70% of HSPs are introverted (we don't have a percentage of how many introverts are HSPs yet). I have yet to meet an introvert who is not an HSP (but I'm biased and see Sensitivity everywhere). Being an HSP goes much further and deeper, in my opinion, than the Introvert. As we have seen, an HSP's physiology is different, and our genes are different. We have more mirror neurons than non-HSPs. Our nervous systems are more sensitive to our surroundings. Being a Sensitive means being aware of and caring for your environment.

ATYPICAL ARCHETYPES: HSP CHARACTER TRAIT

The purpose of this work is to find non-traditional archetypes in historical HSPs. Therefore, let's take a moment to find out what these may be.

LEADER

The Leader archetype is defined as someone who is "active rather than passive," charismatic, and wants to change the world for the better. A Leader can evoke a vision and inspire others to believe in that vision while following the Leader to achieve it.

REBEL

The Rebel archetype sees injustice or inequality and works to make things right by speaking out or taking action. Rebels have a unique perspective, produce creative new ideas, and are risk-takers. They like their independence, rejecting the status quo. They may have their own sense of right and wrong and are highly sensitive and informed about current issues. Variations on this archetype include Activist, Freedom Fighter, and Innovator. Given the Rebel's creativity, one can view the Rebel as an Artist using different mediums for their creations.

KNIGHT/CHAMPION

The Champion or Knight Archetype fights for all the right reasons—a righteous fighter fighting for justice and equality—think Lancelot in Arthur's Knights of the Round Table or Superman. The Knight is not a leader but rather a servant, a typical HSP archetype, who fights for their Master, or Lord, and a "noble cause," sometimes to such a focused point they forget about taking care of themselves. (Ok, so maybe it's not such an atypical HSP archetype.)

The Champion is similar to the Knight but has a more peaceful strength. Champions are idealist leaders who typically have a more democratic form of leadership, allowing ideas to come from others. They are Champions for a Cause. They are great at expressing themselves, charismatic, and good networkers. Consider Dr. Martin Luther King Jr. or Gandhi.

THE CHARISMATIC

While I was doing my research for this work, I asked many friends for their ideas on historical figures. "Could Che Guevara have been a Sensitive?" I asked. My friend, after pondering, answered, "Hmmm, he was definitely a Charismatic." I nearly responded, "A charismatic could be a Sensitive" but as a classic Sensitive, I kept my mouth shut and went to my library for more information. It turns out that indeed, the Charismatic can be a Sensitive, with many of their qualities being similar. The combination of the two may be why some people are in history books.

The Charismatic can be defined as someone who is self-aware, confident, and competent. People admire the Charismatic and want to be around them, sometimes clamoring to be near them. There are a few characteristics of both the Charismatic and the HSP that overlap, energetically warm and good listeners being two of them.

"Warm" people are approachable, trustworthy, and optimistic. A person's warmth is interpreted as caring and loving. It is a person's warmth that draws others to them, admires them, and even follows them.

The Charismatic is an active listener who focuses on the speaker and really listens, giving the speaker time and space to express their thoughts or feelings. This makes the speaker feel like they are being paid attention to—they feel they matter.

The Charismatic trait is also known for humility, the ability to share the spotlight, and praise others. Being humble allows the Charismatic to treat everyone equally.

These skills, which define the Charismatic, can be learned by anyone, but they all come naturally to the HSP. Our energy feels comfortable and attractive to others. We naturally treat everyone with the same love and respect; it is part of who we are.[15]

TYPES OF HSP META-SKILLS

There is a myriad of ways being Sensitive can present itself. I call these extra abilities meta-skills, natural but hidden talents. You may recognize some of the terms. Judith Orloff's *The Empath Survival Guide* is a fantastic book for identifying your meta-skills; I highly recommend it. Since Dr. Orloff did such a wonderful job in her book, I will not go into depth but rather introduce you to the varying types of meta-skills.

CLAIRCOGNIZANT

I've already suggested HSPs are claircognizant. This clear knowing, or "gut feeling," is the core of being a Sensitive. Being claircognizant is the reason why, when you are listening and paying attention, you may choose a different route home, unwittingly missing the huge car accident on your usual route. It is the reason you are such a good friend and gift-giver. You just "know" they'll love it.

CLAIRSENTIENT

Clairsentient is similar to Claircognizant, but rather than knowing you feel instead. With both of these "Clairs," you get a "sense" of things. This can be very frustrating in a non-HSP dominant world, because you don't know why you feel it and you can't prove it. Both claircognizant and clairsentient are the baseline for HSPs, we all have this ability. It can be tricky to identify, but it can also be developed with awareness.

CLAIRVOYANT

There is a Clair for each of the senses, the most popular being clairvoyance. Clairvoyant is the term for the meta-skill of "clear seeing." For example, once you've found the perfect gift for your friend, you get a clear picture of your friend with your gift. Simply put, you get messages visually. Many artists, painters, and graphic designers lean toward being clairvoyant.

CLAIRAUDIENT

Clairaudient means you receive messages audibly, or you hear voices or phrases. (Incidentally, be careful who you tell this to; you could end up in an unwanted secure location.) When I hear messages, they are usually so out of the ordinary that they can only be from elsewhere. Please note: messages or signs will only be for your good. They will never tell you to do something unlawful or hurtful to yourself or anyone else. If you are hearing or experiencing those types of messages, reject them in very clear language. If you can't shoo the negative voices away, ask a professional of your choosing.

OTHER CLAIRS AND META-SKILLS

Those are the most common types of meta-skills, but there are also clairgustance (clear tasting) and clairsalience (clear smelling, which I call clair-smellient; it's more fun and easier to remember). There is a meta-skill for each of your senses. But you may have different, less common meta-skills, such as Kinesthetic Empathy, energetic knowledge from touching something or someone. Perhaps you pick up and experience someone else's physical or emotional pain. You know those times when "all of a sudden" you feel a sharp shooting pain somewhere? or "all of a sudden," you feel very, very sad? Kinesthetic Empathy.

Perhaps your meta-skills lean more toward the elements. Some Sensitives can feel great during a hailstorm or a blizzard. Some of us can feel an earthquake coming. Some of us are sensitive to the planets and their movements. Still others have a great passion for our planet or animals. Doreen Virtue calls these Elementals. Consider Greenpeace or the World Wildlife Foundation. These types of organizations, working to make the Earth healthy and balanced, are very likely founded and run by HSPs, working for the highest good. Or perhaps you are more like a Dreamer, who does most of your "good fighting" while sleeping.

Meta-skills can also combine to create a unique you. Maybe you are a clairvoyant with a passion to clean up Mother Earth. Or perhaps you are clairaudient and kinesthetic. I work well with energy, but a wild thing happens when I do a remote reiki session with a Sensitive. The information I receive comes in the form of the client's meta-skills. For example, when I'm working with an HSP with clairvoyance, I'll "see" the information as clear as day. But with a clairaudient HSP, I'll hear the information. With someone who is more emotional, I'll cry uncontrollably. Yes, I'm a weirdo, but we all are. We are Sensitive. That's my point.

PART II

The Historical Sensitive Persons

Now that you are more aware of the characteristics of the Highly Sensitive Person, many historical figures may spring to mind. Practically any artist's name you know—Van Gogh, Shakespeare, Mozart, and Maya Angelou—were all most likely highly sensitive. Out of respect for your time and resources, focus is required here. You are invited and encouraged to explore your favorite historical figures to find other Highly Sensitive Heroes.

SECTION 1 - RELIGIOUS FIGURES AND ARTISTS

The religious figure and artist are easy to view as Highly Sensitive Persons. I have come to believe that what was once termed the Artistic Temperament is our modern term for a Highly Sensitive Person. Let's dive into history to see some of my personal favorites and see the correlation.

CHAPTER 2

Saint Hildegard von Bingen

The Historical Hildegard von Bingen
Hildegard von Bingen was born in the year 1098 in a province of Germany. You may be most familiar with her illuminated manuscripts or her songs, but she also wrote books and founded not one but two abbeys. Her songs enjoyed a renaissance during the 1990s with a CD release of her Gregorian chants. One of the most prolific composers of chants from her era, she is one of the few to have written both music and lyrics. Fortunately, and amazingly, Régine Pernoud's biography, titled *Hildegard of Bingen: The Inspired Conscience of the Twelfth Century*, includes many of Hildegard's own words.

Being a spiritual child, her parents sent her to the Benedictine monastery in Disibodenberg at the age of eight, and she took her vows on All Saints Day, 1112. Professor Dorsey Armstrong reports in her Great Course titled *Great Minds of the Medieval World* that her parents were pious and poor, and Hildegard being the 10th child, they "donated" her to church in lieu of tithing.[1] After the death of her friend and mentor in 1136, Hildegard was voted Mother Superior by her peers. Viewing the unanimous vote as a sign of acceptance, Hildegard began sharing her visions and life's mission. She began writing, drawing, and traveling despite her considerable physical ailments. The Roman Catholic Church has had her listed as a saint for so long that no one really knows the actual date of her canonization. But on May 10, 2012, Pope Benedict XVI performed an "equivalent canonization" just to make sure. Saint Hildegard von Bingen died at the age of 81 on September 17, 1179, in Bingen am Rhein, an area within the then-Holy Roman Empire, now Germany.

The Sensitive Hildegard von Bingen

Hildegard von Bingen was a visionary, literally. Saint Hildegard writes of experiencing visions as early as the age of three. She describes seeing "such a light," saying her "soul was shaken by it; yet because I was a child, I could say nothing about it."[2] She continued to write that as she grew older, she realized she was different, and therefore she "concealed as much as [she] could the vision in [her] soul."[3]

Saint Hildegard's experience is a commonality throughout the ages. Many adult HSPs report seeing or hearing things during their childhood that, to them, are perfectly normal. Only when they discover that not everyone shares their abilities and that they are not normal do HSPs begin to conceal their gifts, just like Saint Hildegard. Hildegard was frightened to the point of not sharing her visions with anyone when her nursemaid did not see what she could see.[4] And with few exceptions, divulging her visions only to those she felt would understand and accept her, Hildegard kept "silence tranquilly."[5]

After her promotion to Mother Superior, a unanimous decision by all the nuns in her monastery, she felt safe enough to confess her visions and sufferings, but still only to a few. She would draw and dictate for hours, but she questioned if she should write to the current Pope regarding her feelings and visions, as she still feared being misunderstood and rejected. But the messages she received became so strong and clear that it was almost unbearable for her not to. Eventually, and thankfully, she did write, and the rest, as they say, is history.

Hildegard's hedging is consistent with the Sensitive character trait of humility. Classically, HSPs are humble. Some, if not most, struggle with healthy self-esteem and confidence, and it seems Hildegard was the same even with her clairsentience and clear (albeit painful) and straightforward knowledge. But overcome her self-esteem issues she did, and as such, she did many wonderful things.

Hildegard also experienced significant physical limitations and health issues, beginning in her early years and continuing throughout her life. One of her contemporaries described Saint Hildegard's physical challenges as so severe and continuous that "she was rarely standing up."[6]

Saint Hildegard seems to have experienced a battle within herself between the visions and the "multiple infirmities," refusing to divulge her experiences until she was "forced into the bed of suffering."[7] Personally, I have experienced this battle, questioning who to care for. There have been times in my life when I felt forced to choose between taking care of my body or someone else. Regardless of my decision, someone would be in pain—no easy choice, especially for a Sensitive. Often, I would choose to care for my body first, allowing me to care for others when I felt more rested and refreshed. Hildegard's illnesses would continue throughout her life. However, her visions were so strong and the messages so clear that she found strength in her faith to complete her mission of founding two abbeys.

As with many HSPs, Saint Hildegard was involved in many projects during her lifetime. Saint Hildegard was not only an Abbess but also a medical writer, composer, practitioner, philosopher, mystic, and visionary. Ms. Pernoud writes, regarding Hildegard's life between 1141 and 1151, of her numerous interests and hints that she may have been manic in her level of activity, which was "characteristic of her."[8] Many HSPs can be described as flighty, unable to focus on just one project but rather several tasks simultaneously either out of boredom or an abundance of energy—also a "symptom" of ADHD, ADD, and being on the "Spectrum" of Autism.[9]

The Impact of Saint Hildegard von Bingen's Sensitivity

Saint Hildegard von Bingen's writings are still published and read, and her chants are performed and listened to today. Her channeled drawings, in the form of illuminated manuscripts, are still published and can be viewed and contemplated. Today, she is studied and venerated both by feminists and metaphysical practitioners alike. She is held up as an example of perseverance and courage, as well as female leadership in the church during a time when women were considered second-rate citizens (at best). With the trend toward a more natural lifestyle, many still read and follow her writings on herbs and natural medicines.

But it was only once she felt accepted by her friends and peers, when she was in her Orchid Environment (see page 13), that she felt safe about her abilities and could truly be herself to become the Sensitive person we revere today.

My Opinions of Saint Hildegard von Bingen

Personally, I love Saint Hildegard honestly because of her name. The French version of her name, de Bingen, rolls off the tongue and bounces like Tigger, de bingen, de bingen, de bingen. While her name may be fun and bouncy, she was a very serious and stern person. She focused on her duties and mission and tried not to give in to her physical limitations. This must have taken tremendous amounts of mental strength and focus, something Sensitives tend to lack, but with practice and determination, like Hildegard, it can be achieved. With

Hildegard, we begin to see the possibilities and impact our mental strength can have on ourselves, our community, and indeed on our world and our future.

Saint Hildegard von Bingen was a leader and an innovator in the Catholic Church at a time when women were not considered to be capable of much of anything. Her faith led her to do many amazing and new things, sometimes all at once. Hildegard's possible mania points to her being both sensitive and an artist. When I was young and looking for a job, my resume included "multitasking" as a potential benefit to my employer. Looking back, I remember myself running around juggling multiple tasks, usually dropping a few in the process and often leaving tasks half-completed. I remember feeling constantly shaky and nervous. I chalked it up to needing food. My wiser older self recognizes now that while I did need food, I also needed to settle down, focus, and work on one task at a time. Someone once said to me, "Multitasking is doing many things badly." I believe it. With this simple quote in the back of my mind, I remember to focus, slow down, and concentrate on the single immediate task. I wonder if Hildegard would have benefited from this technique. Would it have slowed her down, thereby creating less? Or would it have helped her to create more? I wonder if Hildegard practiced more focus if it would have helped with her physical ailments as well.

When I imagine Saint Hildegard with her many projects, I see a woman flitting from project to project, filled with motivation and drive. We have mentioned how Sensitives can be overwhelmed by energy. For some, this energy is too much and can be draining and exhausting, causing us to rest, nap, and sleep. For others, we see prolific work, like Hildegard. As a Sensitive sleuth, I have found movement to be effective in releasing extraneous energy. One of my teachers, Granddaughter Crow, suggested I shake my hands to move the energy out of my body. Personally, I have found this technique very effective. When I "shake my tail feathers," or just "shake it off," I feel better, lighter, more focused, and relaxed. I wonder if Hildegard's prolific body of work in varied mediums was her way of releasing excess energy.

We also see in Saint Hildegard the influence of her environment. A visionary from her beginnings, Hildegard learned to keep quiet about her unusual experiences at a very early age, a practice she continued for about half her life. When she was voted Mother Superior, she took this to be a sign of acceptance and safety. The same building, the same people, different Hildegard. This is fascinating. One day, her environment felt confining; she was afraid to be her full self and kept her visions secret. The next day, her environment felt accepting and safe, and she was a blossoming orchid. The energy of the building didn't change. Presumably, the energy of her fellow nuns didn't change. It was the overt, obvious, and literal vote of confidence that affected Hildegard. This supports the claim that Sensitives must have overt positive support. Like an orchid, we need not only the appropriate environment but also obvious loving care.

Hildegard's experience could also point to a Sensitive's need to accurately identify the energy of the environment. By which I mean, it's possible that based on her previous experiences before entering the convent, Hildegard may have interpreted the environment of the convent as less supportive than it actually was. Hildegard's past may have clouded her ability to read her current environment accurately. At the convent, Hildegard may have always been surrounded by loving, supportive energy. Perhaps she kept her amazing self a secret more because of her past than her present. This points to the need for Sensitives whenever possible to identify traumas and process them early, close to the time of the trauma, rather than letting them fester and grow bigger and deeper. Spending some time with the trauma, shining light on the event, and processing the lesson of the event can be transformative for a Sensitive. This will enable us to remain in the present and read the current situation clearly and accurately.

Hildegard writes about her visions, specifically how the light she saw permeated everything:

> In this vision my soul, as God would have it, rises up high into the
> vault of heaven and into the changing sky and spreads itself out
> among different peoples, although they are far away from me in
> distant lands and places. And because I see them this way in my soul,
> I observe them in accord with the shifting of clouds and other created
> things. I do not hear them with my outward ears, nor do I perceive
> them by the thoughts of my own heart or by any combination of my
> five senses, but in my soul alone, while my outward eyes are open.[10]

Hildegard's words are fascinating to me. She describes a light spreading out over all different people and places and seeing everyone and everything as equal to the "clouds and other created things." She illustrates the concept that every living thing is divine. Everything is created and therefore is of the Creative Force, God-like in origin, and as such, all living things should be treated and loved equally, with respect and compassion, a practice most Sensitives attempt naturally. (I have converted her vision into a mediation available in Chapter 22, Mental Care.)

PART II : THE HISTORICAL SENSITIVE PERSONS

We are all "buddhas sitting at the feet of other buddhas," as Byron Katie writes in her book, *A Mind at Home with Itself*.[11] Sensitives can easily be described as Bodhisattvas, Buddhas in training, learning to love everyone equally as Divine beings. Sensitives are naturally loving beings. We want to help make our world a better place. We naturally hope there is goodness in everyone; I believe there is goodness in everyone (just as there is bad in everyone).

Sensitives love easily, but we can also pity easily. When we encounter someone who we believe is suffering, our hearts, our love, and our energy flow out to them. This can be construed as pity or a judgment based on our viewpoint or experience. But when we, like Hildegard and Byron Katie, meet and accept others wherever they are on their own path, see them as heavenly light, see them as Divine, with faith and love, then we are seeing them with love—pure love, true love.

CHAPTER 3

Frederick Douglass

The Historical Frederick Douglass
Mr. Frederick Douglass was born into slavery in Talbot County, Maryland, sometime around February 1818. His many achievements include being the author of "three classics of the genre," a speaker "of almost unparalleled stature," and an editor and abolitionist of "international fame."[1] He was a national leader of the abolitionist movement and, as such, a consultant to President Lincoln. Mr. Frederick Douglass died of a heart attack in Washington, DC, on February 20, 1895.

The Sensitive Frederick Douglass
Douglass possessed an "extraordinary memory" and ceaselessly wrote. He was highly intelligent with great powers of observation, impressing his contemporaries as "smart and curious beyond his years."[2] He had a "hustler's ability to learn," a term defined as the ability to use knowledge for "his own ends."[3] He used his extraordinary memory and imagination for good, writing in such a manner to bring vivid awareness to his cause—that of "universal and unconditional emancipation of my entire race"—to those previously unaware.[4]

Douglass was a natural talent with strong mental abilities, which he used to his advantage throughout his life. For Douglass, the mind was a person's greatest weapon. He exercised protection and preservation of his mind and body but found "self-control and mental protection to be much easier" than his body.[5] A technique handy for any Sensitive.

Douglass had the capability of "great love and compassion," but more interesting and telling of his sensitivity is his "desperate lifelong need" to be loved and cared for. Given his experiences, it is completely understandable that Douglass had trust issues.[6]

PART II : THE HISTORICAL SENSITIVE PERSONS

Douglass had a remarkable mind and a thirst for knowledge. Education was his "reason for living"[7] and his ability to remember with "all his senses" was his greatest tool.[8]

The 2021 PBS documentary titled *Becoming Frederick Douglass* describes Douglass as charismatic, eloquent, and educated. Over and over again, we will see Historical Sensitives described as such. The combination of charisma and Sensitive appears all throughout history. I believe, and we'll get more in depth later, that it is because we emit a loving and accepting energy with a higher vibration; others want to be near that energy level. It was his charisma that drew the public to him, and it was his eloquence, his honest and vivid writings and speeches that shocked the public into awareness.

Frederick Douglass controlled his message and image through his publications and photographs. He is thought to be the most photographed human of the 19th century. He loved the idea of photography, considering it to be one of the most influential inventions of his time, similar to the telegraph. He believed photographs showed the truth, conveying elegance, pride, and competence. When I look at one of the many photographs of Douglass, the first thing I notice is his brow, and how determined he was. But when I look into his eyes, I see love and compassion yearning to be released. Oh, how he yearned for equality for all humanity.

Much of Douglass' writings came from the Bible and his spirituality, using the Old Testament to align the struggles of the Hebrews with those of the African American people.[9]

One last image of Douglass I wish to leave you with. On August 12, 1841, in Nantucket, Douglass made his first public speech at an abolitionist convention. Douglass was 23 years old and just three years removed from slavery. Author Shomari Wills writes of this speech in *Black Fortunes*, "As he moved to the front of the room, audience members could see that he was shaking from stage fright." Douglass' speech was somewhat impromptu, attending the convention merely to stay updated on the issues. When asked to approach the stage "he was so overcome with fear that he could barely keep his feet underneath him." Mr. Douglass even "felt ill" but he "summoned all his willpower to keep his back straight and his limbs steady." His "voice trembled" and "stuttered" as he spoke of his experiences.[10]

This image of Douglass is contrary to everything I've thought about him. To describe Frederick Douglass as a young man with stage fright is indeed a different side, if not diametrically opposite, of this usually thought of strong and courageous person. This anecdote gives us a peek into who Douglass was before he became the man we think we know. This tid bit of history highlights and points directly to his Sensitivity. Douglass' early stage fright also proves to us Sensitives that we too, with practice and perseverance, can overcome our fears and become impactful on our world.

The Impact of Frederick Douglass' Sensitivity on History
Frederick Douglass' sensitivity is central to who he was and therefore pivotal to the abolitionist movement. His sensitivity contributed to his influence on Abraham Lincoln and the Emancipation Proclamation. Painting a vivid image of the struggle of enslaved people, Douglass moved people to realize the immorality of slavery. With his intelligence and education, he proved that the black man was indeed human and worthy of being treated as such. (It still stuns me that such things were required.)

Douglass' strength of sensitivity spurred him into action, wanting to right the wrongs of so many by changing laws, society, and beliefs.

My Opinions on Frederick Douglass
Ah, Fredrick Douglass. What a sweet and driven soul he was. His life experiences were so traumatic to him that he fought to do anything he could to make sure they didn't happen to others. He used his natural talent to work from his soul and conjure change. His natural intellect shone early and often. For example, as he played with the master's son as a young child, the son would be called to complete his studies. Noting how the son's intelligence grew, young Douglass quickly and correctly concluded that education was the key to changing lives.[11] A lesson he incorporated and practiced all his life. His intelligence, natural writing ability, and mental strength point directly to Douglass' sensitivity.

But it is his life's work, his soul's mission, and his passion to create an equitable world for all that really begin to tell the story of an HSP. When some Sensitives see injustice, it becomes their call to duty. For some of us, it is mistreatment of our planet. For others, it is seeing an animal malnourished. For yet others, it is the inequity of the social strata. But whatever the injustice, some Sensitives are incited to move heaven and earth to correct the imbalance. Douglass proves the adage "the pen is mightier than the sword." He used his words rather than his fists to complete his soul's mission—to fight the good fight and affect history and mankind.

I find it very interesting that Douglass died of a heart attack. I have long been intrigued by a person's dis-ease and their sensitivity, wondering if there was somehow a connection. My grandmother died of a heart attack, and I know she never processed her grief over the death of her son, thus carrying all that emotion and energy on her heart and possibly causing her death. My instinct and intellect wonder if the Sensitive Frederick Douglass felt the traumas of so many so deeply that it affected his health. Certainly, his work as an activist was heart-based, and it is easy to conclude that he put his heart and soul into his work. Perhaps so much so that he had nothing left for his own physical heart.

In Christian Science, I was taught Mary Baker Eddy's version of the Lord's Prayer, in which she substitutes or enriches the line "For Thine is the Kingdom, and the power and the glory forever" with her interpretation as "For God is infinite, all-power, all Life, Truth, Love, over all and All." The words have changed a bit since I attended Sunday school. We would say God is omnipotent and omniscient. For years, I looked back and forth from the evening news to this line and ask, "Where is God and the Life, Truth, and Love in the world's events?" My naive self concluded Life, Truth, and Love may not always be equal to the human definition. Perhaps our definition is limited to always meaning "goodness." Perhaps, I concluded, God was in the darkness too, with the lower vibrating energies and emotions, namely fear and anger. For if God is everywhere and everything, much like Elvis in the song "Elvis is Everywhere," then God must also include suffering and darker human moments. I've seen this theory of mine supported in other beliefs and writings, most recently Paul Selig's book *Beyond the Known: Realization*.

If the Divine (my preferred term) is everywhere and in everything, then it must have been present in America prior to 1865. The Divine was certainly present in Mr. Douglass. It could be concluded that the Divine was present during Mr. Douglass' childhood experiences. It could even be concluded that Mr. Douglass' experiences were necessary for him to become who he became. The long-term perspective shows that, as a result of his harsh experiences, humans were freed. I understand that seeing the Divine in current world events is difficult, I do (I really do). But again, the long-term perspective helps ease that difficulty. I may not understand the reason for humans' suffering, but I have faith that the Divine is there, somewhere.

CHAPTER 4

Claude Monet

The Historical Claude Monet
An absolute personal favorite of mine, Claude Monet, is the quintessential artist archetype. Born on November 14, 1840, in Paris, Claude Monet created amazing paintings of light. He is known for his series of haystacks, cathedrals, and water lilies that catch the ever-changing light. It is believed he would have multiple canvases set up in a row and move through them as the light changed. Claude Monet died of lung cancer on December 5, 1926, at his home in Giverny, France.

The Sensitive Claude Monet
Claude Monet was by all accounts an angry man, as supported in Ross King's biography titled *Mad Enchantment: Claude Monet and the Painting of the Water Lilies*. King writes often of Monet's anger, summing it up nicely with the phrase "dreadful fits of temper."[1] Monet would even get angry at the rainy weather, which kept him from painting outside.[2] His friends believed this temperament stemmed from Monet's search for perfection. If it wasn't for his goal of perfection—this "necessary condition" of suffering, striving, and torture—we wouldn't have so many masterpieces of beauty and light.[3]

Monet often reported his "suffering" to his friends. At the start of each canvas, he would have such "great hopes of producing a masterpiece." However, Monet said, "Nothing comes out that way," a common feeling among many striving artists in any medium. "I am unhappy," he said, "very unhappy."[4]

His creations make it evident that Monet loved gardening and nature, being one of the first artists to paint outside, en plein air. He also loved animals. He kept his dining room windows open so the sparrows could fly in and eat the birdseed he left for them. Monet fed chickens by hand, allowing the chickens to roam free even among his gardens. However, he drew the line at cats and

33

dogs, believing they would harm his gardens, a hint that he loved nature first and animals second.[5]

A "man of few words," Monet kept his end of conversations very short. He only replied yes or no, if replying at all, and kept his thoughts to himself. Not a fan of conversation, deep or otherwise, he is quoted as saying, "I have nothing interesting to say," pointing to both his humility and lack of interest in society.[6]

Monet was also known to enjoy reading, specifically reading aloud in the evenings. He read anything he could get his hands on—the classics as well as the works of his contemporaries, both fiction and non-fiction.[7]

It is also important to note that Monet chose to live far from the madding crowd in Giverny, France. Today, it is over an hour's drive from Paris, while the commute was even longer and more arduous in his day. His home and gardens are well-known and visited by many. Monet created a safe haven for himself, a protective space surrounded by beauty and plenty of opportunities for creation, far from people, critics, and society.[8]

The Historical Impact of Monet's Sensitivity

Whatever Monet's goal was, it is clear his paintings create a sense of calm and were termed "the Great Anti-Depressant" by Sotheby's. It is also clear Monet was aware of the soothing effect his creations had on others, describing his work as a "peaceful meditation."[9] His work is still enjoyed by world tours, studied, and copied (at least artists are attempting to copy it). I attended an exhibit of his in January 2020. The morning before my visit, I was contemplating Monet. I remembered that it was his painting that led me to choose college, which led to a career and a life. Funny when I think of it. I was 18 and trying to decide on a college for my major, art history. I had visited Washington, DC, and the Museum of Art years earlier. I was stunned by a painting; it pulled me across the room. With each step, I saw something different in the painting—more details, different colors. Eventually, I was close enough to read the placard—"Morning Mist" by Monet. My mouth was still agape, my body tingled, and my mind reeled. When I had a choice of where to live and be educated, I chose to be near that painting.

While the details of my relationship with Monet may be unique, the feeling or effect is not. Monet's work creates calming environments and gorgeous vistas that are still unique. No one has managed to capture the complexity of the atmosphere and light. No one. He is considered one of the greatest artists and the father of Impressionism, all because he loved the simple act of being and painting outdoors, trying to capture "the light."

My Opinions of Claude Monet and his Sensitivity

While it is certainly clear Monet was searching for perfection in his work and throughout his life, it is also clear he felt he never attained it, always trying to capture natural beauty and its divinity. Monet's work attempts, and in my opinion quite miraculously, to encapsulate a moment, a natural and common occurrence of the combination of earth, fire, and air. By that, I mean, the landscape, light, and air. Looking at the metaphysical meanings of those elements, we find something interesting. In the metaphysical world, the earth represents the physical body, while fire represents the mental body and air the spiritual body. In other words, Monet tried to create an image of the body, mind, and spirit. Monet always attempted to capture the ephemeral light, a combination of fire and air, or the mental and the spiritual. Working outside with many canvases to capture a moving living being, he wanted to describe the Divine on canvas. A worthy cause indeed, but if he was unaware of his true goal, it would've been impossible for him to be satisfied had he achieved it or to find comfort and acceptance in the attempts, thus the angry temperament. Just as an unaware HSP believes something is wrong with them because they are exhausted after grocery shopping, he believed he fell short of his goal because he was not aware of his true self and therefore his true work. However, I think we can all agree that his attempts are more than successful; they are Divine in themselves. And in my humble opinion, he succeeded, especially when you illuminate his canvasses and notice his paintings change and deepen.

Monet's temperamental anger was, of course, part of his Sensitivity and stemmed from his feeling of not being good enough, a classic issue with HSPs. When we consider what he was doing—capturing the Divine on canvas—we can give him a little slack. HSPs often feel less than others or not good enough; we always strive for perfection.

What we as humans do not realize is that we are already perfect. Even when something can be improved upon, it is still perfect in its imperfection. The Japanese call it Wabi Sabi, the Buddhists call it Samsara, and Mary Poppins says it's "practically perfect in every way." To return to our previous statement regarding the Divine and its constant presence, another word for the Divine is the Creative Force, or the Creator. If something is created, be it dinner or a tree, it is Divine, the Divine is present. Therefore, Claude's paintings are divine in their very being.

If you've been privileged enough to see Monet's original canvases, you will feel a sense of peace and calm—and yes, even the Divine. When I was 19, I was most fortunate to view his Waterlilies, installed at the Tuileries in Paris (they now hang at the Musée D'Orsay), a room with four huge canvases depicting the four seasons of Monet's Pond. I sat there for hours, soaking up the colors, the light and the darkness, the quiet and the peace. An experience such as this can teach a Sensitive the impact of being surrounded by natural beauty and encourage one to seek nature.

Monet's coping mechanisms consisted of leaving the city and finding nature, escaping from the maddening energy of Paris, and embracing gardening and the landscape of his home, Giverny. Epitomizing his humility and love of nature, both common HSP traits, he said, "I am only good at two things: gardening and painting." Being surrounded by the beauty of nature was Monet's solace, a practice many turn to more and more these days. Spend any time in front of his pieces, and you'll want to get into nature too.

Another possible coping mechanism for Monet was his painting itself. He would escape the stress of the physical world by running away into his paintings. Not giving up, always having hope his current work would be his masterpiece, and always having the courage, passion, and drive to strive for perfection in painting the Divine. Monet painted well into his later years, even when his eyesight began to falter, which was a source of great frustration for him. You can see his frustration in his later paintings, which have more darkness and less detail. This points to a possible compulsion, perhaps even an addiction. One might say it was like his religion, his spiritual practice.

CHAPTER 5

Dr. Reverend Martin Luther King, Jr.

The Historical Dr. Martin Luther King, Jr.
Approximately 111 years after the birth of Frederick Douglass, Dr. Reverend Martin Luther King, Jr. was born in Atlanta, Georgia, on January 15, 1929, into a home and family that were "quite ordinary."[1] We all know his name; some of us even get a day off or can save on a mattress thanks to him. We know his "I Have a Dream" speech, or at least parts of it.

Dr. King was a preacher and an activist. He was a leader of the Civil Rights Movement during the 1960s. He was killed on April 4, 1968, aged 39, in Memphis, Tennessee.

The Sensitive Dr. King
In his book, *The Autobiography of Martin Luther King, Jr.* (edited by Clayborne Carson), Dr. King writes about his early years as full of love and security. He reports that "my home situation was very congenial,"[2] his childhood home was filled with "lovely relationships" everywhere and an environment where his basic needs were always met.[3] This loving, stable, and secure environment formed Dr. King's belief in a "God of love" and a "basically friendly" universe.[4] He writes of his father as a man who would never fight or argue and who was smart with money.[5] Oh, that all beings should have such a positive formative environment!

Like Douglass, Dr. King used his mind and imagination to create a world of equality and justice. Dr. King remembered his daily bus ride to school and his response to being forced to the back of the bus. Even though his body sat in the back of the bus, "I left my mind up on the front seat. And I said to myself, 'One of these days, I'm going to put my body up there where my mind is.'"[6]

Many metaphysical authors refer to the Mind as being the power behind the ability for manifestation, such as Rhonda Byrne in her book (and movie) *The*

Secret, which teaches us how to use the mind to manifest. With both Frederick Douglass and Dr. King, we see their ability to use their minds as a first line of defense and manifest their future. In both men, we see them intuitively putting *The Secret* to good use.

Dr. King grew up "deeply conscious" of the "varieties of injustice" in his society.[7] At the age of 14, on April 7, 1944 (in the midst of World War II), Dr. King won an "oratorical contest" with words of wisdom far beyond his years. "So as we gird ourselves to defend democracy from foreign attack, let us see to it that increasingly at home we give fair play and free opportunity for all people."[8] Do those words sound like a 14-year-old to you? It sounds more like an "Old Soul" or Sensitive to me.

Like most HSPs, Dr. King writes humbly of his extraordinary intelligence. We see such an example of both abilities in his writing about how he was one of the "top students" in his high school and how he glossed over the details of skipping two grades and entering Morehouse College at the age of 15, writing only that he was a "pretty young fellow" at college.[9]

At Morehouse College, Dr. King began to use his intelligence and desire for knowledge to form strong opinions about inequality and injustice. He wrote, "Noncooperation with evil is as much a moral obligation as is cooperation with good."[10] A voracious reader and seeker of truth, Dr. King was highly influenced by Henry David Thoreau's *Civil Disobedience* and other social philosophers.[11] Education led Dr. King to his righteous conviction, and his calling developed. "Evil must be resisted," and "no moral man can patiently adjust to injustice."[12] Dr. King states, "I always had a deep urge to serve humanity."[13]

After reading Karl Marx and Friedrich Engels' *The Communist Manifesto*, Dr. King concluded his belief in a "creative personal power in this universe who is the ground and essence of all reality." This quote speaks directly to Dr. King's ability to integrate others' beliefs into his own belief system, picking what resonated with him and making them his own. Many people throw the baby out with the bathwater, dismissing an entire philosophy because they disagree with part of it. History shows us that following your heart AND mind can lead to great things, such as Dr. Kings' success as a peaceful and impactful leader. "History," he wrote, is ultimately "guided by spirit, not matter."[14] Today, Dr. King still teaches us the importance of finding and embracing our whole selves by following Spirit and trusting where we are led or pulled rather than what nifty toys our neighbors have.

Dr. King confesses that outbursts of emotion, even in the "Negro religion," were uncomfortable for him. Dr. King wrote that he didn't understand and was even "embarrassed" by "the shouting and stomping." He often said that if people "had as much religion in their hearts" as they did in their "legs and feet, we could change the world."[15]

Dr. King always felt called to the ministry. However, at Morehouse College, he began to question the fundamentalism of his Sunday school teachings and what he was learning in college, reporting his difficulty merging "many of the facts of science" and religion.[16]

The Historical Impact of Dr. King's Sensitivity

Like Frederick Douglass, it was Dr. King's sensitive heart and his connection to the church that gave him the strength to right the wrongs of society. I am both grateful for Dr. King's convictions and his work but saddened that the work was needed and is still unfinished today. Hopefully, humans will eventually and quickly evolve into truly sensitive, heart-based beings.

Dr. King grew up in a stable and soft place, perfect for an "orchid" of his caliber. One can easily draw a line between his secure childhood and his strength of conviction and perseverance in his adult life and all his accomplishments. We know Dr. Martin Luther King Jr. precisely because of his Sensitivity.

My Opinion of Dr. King's Sensitivity

Ah, Dr. King. One need only look at a photo of the Reverend to feel his Sensitivity, his loving energy, and his quest to make the world better for everyone. His eyes are soft and welcoming, and they sparkle with a secret that seems to tickle him. He knows, as his smiling eyes tell us, and his heart and words implore us, that we will be alright, but things need to change.

The Civil Rights leader grew up in a modest home filled with love and support, the perfect environment for him to blossom. Dr. King is a prime example of when a Sensitive is in its perfect environment, or comfort zone, in the early formative years. Like Saint Hildegard, an Orchid can grow and make a beautiful impact. Dr. King writes of his early years as a child in his autobiography. He states how he never wanted for anything and always felt loved and secure. He believed this was the basis of who he became; he always felt he could accomplish anything because he felt loved and safe. The early years of any human are key to their emotional and mental stability, but even more so for Sensitives. If we experience a rocky start, those bumps can continue to ripple throughout our later years, translating into larger hurdles if not dealt with and processed. Dr. King's early life shows Sensitives the importance of an emotionally safe childhood.

Dr. King's autobiography also alludes to a possible coping mechanism he employed, that of mental strength and visualization, what some would term "manifesting." When he was a boy riding the bus to school, he was sent to the back of the bus. His response was to think, "My body may be in the back of the bus, but my mind is in the front." He seemed to always have patience and hope that one day things would change. He believed his situation was only temporary. This belief in a bright future may have been his solace and his method for dealing with the present.

When we read Dr. King's sermon, "A Tough Mind and a Tender Heart," we hear his theory for strong and loving Sensitives. He spoke of our need for balance between the head and the heart. He calls for us to be tough-minded ("astute and discerning") and tender-hearted, asking us to combine the "toughness of the serpent and the tenderness of the dove."[17] This is the perfect goal for Sensitives, who are heart-based beings with the desire to rush in and help, fix other people's problems, and remove their pain. This may sometimes be a mistake. What we perceive as help, others may construe as pity or a lack of trust. What we perceive as suffering or struggle may be part of their agreed-upon life lesson. (We speak more about life lessons in Part III, Chapter 25, when we discuss soul curricula.) So having a discerning mind by understanding and having faith that everyone is given exactly what they can handle ("God never sends us more than we can handle"—Mother Theresa) is a helpful reminder when your soft heart wants to take over.

Dr. King's energy was soft but strong, magnetic, and charismatic. People wanted to be near him, to hear him, and to see him. Yes, his cause was just, and his words lovingly called people to action. But there was more to his "celebrity." I have watched many documentaries about Dr. King, and every time I do, I feel his warmth, his love, and his energy. This is the loving energy many Sensitives carry, or, put another way, the level at which we vibrate. It is why strangers will tell you things—they feel safe around you. It is why narcissists love us; they feel we will validate them (and manipulate us). It is why so many people want to be near you or react to you.

The documentary, *King: A Filmed Record . . . Montgomery to Memphis*, focuses on the last few months of Dr. King's life. I noticed many similarities between the lives of Dr. King and Jesus. I can only imagine that the energy between the two was also very similar. People want to be near or touched by that high level of love. Conscious or otherwise, people feel separated from the higher vibrating energy, namely love, and they miss it. When they feel that loving energy, simply put, they want more and clamor to get it, similar to the throngs of teenagers the Beatles drew when they "invaded America."

Dr. King shows us what can happen when we are loving and thus vulnerable. Society has long hailed the strong, silent type, wanted us to keep our emotions in check, and been shocked and uncomfortable with emotional outbursts. Consider 1880s New York high society, when everyone "who was anyone" was proper and acted conventionally, calmly, and rationally, not aware of emotions (or at least not showing them), similar to a society of Stepford Wives. If emotions got the best of someone, most likely a Sensitive, prompting an outburst, they were shunned, carted off, and locked away somewhere far away. Individual emotional outbursts reminded society of their own emotions: grief, sadness, and frustration. It reminded them how close their emotions were to the surface and how easily those emotions could get the better of them. And maybe they felt a little jealous of the outburst. The collective soul of society may have said, "Oh, how nice it would be to recognize and release all this tension."

Yes, the fear of showing emotions equated to being vulnerable and weak, but Dr. King shows us the value and importance of being loving and emotional, a.k.a. sensitive, and how it can move mountains. He shows us that loving words are not weak but highly impactful. We still hear his loving words in his speeches, and we feel the impact of his work with the passing of the Civil Rights Bill.

Recently, when contemplating Dr. King, I was struck by this simple equation: Loving strength + Pure thoughts = True Power. We felt Dr. King's love; we heard his pure thoughts in his speeches, which in turn created a pure power for his cause and his followers. Many Sensitives shy away from power; we are happy just being in the shadows, supporting others. This may be due to the fact that we misunderstand power. Humans have long defined power as being in control. The phrase "most powerful man on Earth" connotes (at least in my mind) the 1960s Batman TV show. When Batman finally kicks the snot out of the villain, the screen is filled with POW, BOP, and BAM! Yes, POWer, and even pOWer, has a feeling of causing pain to others, at least to Sensitives. And so we shy away from it. But what if power—real power, true power—was completely different? What if True Power was loving and pure? Then would sensitives embrace power?

Consider the power of the Colorado River and the Grand Canyon. For millennia, the Colorado River has flowed, meandered, followed the lay of the land, and slowly worn away the rocks, creating the Grand Canyon. The river doesn't control the rocks and doesn't cause them pain. The water simply does what it does, and the rocks do what they do. And millennia later, voila, the Grand Canyon. Now that's strength!

The speeches of Dr. King were well thought out and written. Many photos depicted him writing his speeches or sermons. Much thought went into his speeches—pure and honest thought. Naturally, his speeches reflected his invigorating thoughts, inciting humans to do and be better. A divine goal indeed and a purely loving thought.

Dr. King exemplifies loving strength and pure thoughts, thus creating True power. True power is not telling people how to live, think, or be. True Power is loving yourself and others. True Power is believing in a peaceful outcome. True Power is . . . well, let's face it, I don't really know what True Power is, but I know what it isn't. The closest example I've seen of True Power occurred in my front yard. One day I saw two adult female elk and one granddaddy male elk. He was magnificent. And he was calm, unlike my dog, who barked like crazy at the elk. My dog turned inside out, trying to get the elk off our land, who was not phased. He looked up from his grassy lunch at my dog and just stood there. Again, calm and beautiful as can be. Until . . . the elk took one step, just one step; it wasn't even a big step, but a baby half step, toward my dog's direction and stood still. That little step was enough to quiet my dog down. My dog calmly came inside and laid down while the elk and his harem continued their lunch. Now that's power, my friends. The elk didn't get rattled because he knew my dog was no real threat. The elk simply moved just enough to let my dog know everything was okay.

Humans have come to equate leadership with power, power with control, and control with fear. Dr. King shows us that loving leadership requires strength, confidence, and sensitivity. He is the epitome of catching more bees with honey than vinegar. He didn't storm the castle with an army. He simply stated what was wrong and what needed to change, and then proved his point. Now, it is true that many of his followers had to be trained not to respond to the hate that was thrust upon them. It is a natural response to defend yourself. But Dr. King wanted to show the world the hatred behind the unfair situations and highlight the peace and goodness of the oppressed. True Power.

True Power is stepping into your own innate strength and confidence, being who you are, who you might be, and feeling free to be your sensitive self. Dr. King taught us that loving strength, when combined with Pure thoughts and thus pure actions, creates True Power.

SECTION 2 - INVENTORS AND INNOVATORS

Now that you have learned more about the character trait by meeting a few classic Historical Sensitives, let's look into the lives of other Sensitives who expand the HSP mold, namely Inventors and Innovators. One of the greatest things I love about Sensitives is the natural ability to think out of the box. Our thinking process is different than non-HSPs, and therefore lends itself beautifully to be integral when developing new ideas, technologies, or products.

CHAPTER 6

Florence Nightingale

Most people may be more familiar with the Nightingale Complex than they are with the woman it's named after. You may know Florence Nightingale as "The Lady of the Lamp" from her work during the Crimean War. Some consider her a saint; others think she was a hard-hearted boss. But it's in the details of her life we will see if she was an HSP, even possibly an empath.

The Historical Florence Nightingale
Florence Nightingale was born on May 12, 1820. She worked as a nurse in the Crimean War, from 1854-1856, where she earned the title Lady of the Lamp, for her tireless nursing of wounded soldiers. During which, and for the rest of her life, Florence Nightingale insisted, proved, and fought for cleaner hospitals, established nursing schools, and vastly improved the reputation of nurses. She is considered to be the founder of modern nursing. She died on August 13, 1910, in London at the age of 90.

The Sensitive Florence Nightingale
Gillian Gill in her biography, *Nightingales: The Extraordinary Upbringing and Curious Life of Miss Florence Nightingale*, writes of Miss Nightingale as a "delightful little girl," funny, energetic, "curious and sensitive,"[1] "an intelligent

and sensitive little girl."² At Nightingale's core, she required the "need for solitude" and sympathy, or "total empathetic support."³

Author Gill further describes Florence as "an alien creature" who was an "oddly intimidating woman" and even when experiencing great physical pain and illness to the point of being "unable to bear the mere whiff of a close family member" she continued to fight for her cause.⁴

Young Nightingale was "shy, awkward" and "dreaded the prospect of coming out" to society.⁵ Her "love of solitude," her "daydreaming,"⁶ and her love of animals⁷ all point to her being a Sensitive and an empath.

"Dreaming" was a "key aspect" of Florence Nightingale.⁸ She was unable to control her dreaming, causing her to come "close to a nervous breakdown in 1850."⁹ This described "dreaming" sounds more like an ecstatic meditative state, similar to Saint Hildegard's experience, frequently experienced by HSPs/empaths. In these sometimes hour-long states of "absorbed reverie," Nightingale would be "so absorbed in some imagined adventure" that she was completely unaware of her surroundings.¹⁰

On February 7, 1837, the stressed 17-year-old Nightingale experienced a spiritual moment when "God spoke to her and called her to His service."¹¹ There is little evidence of this event, merely a single "private note" written thirty years later.¹² Apparently, she told no one. (Sound familiar? Similar to Saint Hildegard, perhaps?) This event seems to have been highly emotional for Nightingale, since her family was Catholic and mysticism was unknown in her household, she kept the experience to herself.¹³

The Historical Impact of Florence Nightingale's Sensitivity

After her spiritual moment, Florence Nightingale was torn between her belief that "God had personally chosen her" and what she would do with this knowledge, namely, how she would serve. (Again, remind you of anyone?) We now know she radically changed nursing from what was then little more than prostitution to the honorable position it is today. She fought for cleaner hospitals and more (or any) sanitation practices, all from the confines of her bed.¹⁴

My Opinion of Florence Nightingale and her Sensitivity

Florence Nightingale was first and foremost a Caregiver, as well as a Sensitive and a warrior for change. Considered a rebel among British society, she balked at her typical role in society as a woman and fought for better sanitation practices in hospitals and improved training for nurses. Like many of our historical sensitives, she saw room for improvement and made things better, bringing deaths in hospitals down from 69% to 18%. Florence was often considered a hard woman, a driven woman, in fact, she considered herself a "man of business" with no time for dilly-dallying. She was on a mission.

Considering her time and place, Nightingale was rather open-minded. With Louis Pasteur, born two years after Nightingale, patenting his pasteurization process in 1862 and continuing his work inventing vaccines in 1877, her world was only beginning to learn about bacteria and microbiology. Many chose not to believe Pasteur's work or the presence of invisible beings running around killing humans, dismissing him as crazy. But with Nightingale's interest in science combined with her visual mind, she studied and proved sanitation practices thereby improving and saving lives. Being open to new possibilities and solutions paved the way for Florence to become who we know her to be.

Being open-minded is a hallmark of being Sensitive. It is what makes us curious. It is why we have difficulty making decisions. We are often considering the other side of issues and causes. Sometimes it can drive us crazy. A client of mine confessed, "I am envious of people who are more closed-minded than I, at least they can make a decision." Yes, being open-minded may keep us from deciding between chicken or fish at a wedding, but it also keeps us open and available to new ideas, like Florence Nightingale. Our open-mindedness allows us to see the world differently, and, like Nightingale, develop new solutions.

I also believe Florence worked so hard for better sanitation practices upon her return from the Crimean War because she felt guilty for the soldiers she didn't save. I believe that while she did what was best at the time with the information she had, she felt could've done better especially in light of the new information after the war. For some HSPs, a lack of knowledge is no excuse for incorrect behavior. "I should've known better," we tell ourselves, forgiving all others but never forgiving ourselves. Out of her possible guilt came a professional nursing school, which is now part of Kings College in London, and sanitation reform.

My belief that Florence acted out of a feeling of guilt is further supported when we consider Sensitives tend to take on blame or responsibility for things they couldn't possibly be responsible for. Sensitives feel the weight of the world and take responsibility for everything from a broken plate to world atrocities. "I'm sorry," we say, "I left that plate too close to the edge." I'm sorry, we think, I didn't pray harder or earlier when a mass trauma event occurs. We can very easily feel guilt and blame for things and rarely do we release those low vibrating energies, creating a weight and a feeling of exhaustion or lethargy causing us to spiral down emotionally.

PART II : THE HISTORICAL SENSITIVE PERSONS

The classic archetype of the HSP is the geek or nerd. We are different, we think different, we believe different. For some we are seen as weak and can be targets for bullying. Recently, in the last twenty years or so, we have seen a rise in school shootings. With Sensitives comprising 20% of the population, it is easy to extrapolate the statistics to conclude 20% of those school shooters were Sensitives. I believe the percentage is even higher. Many of those troubled young Sensitives were reportedly bullied and picked on to the point where they believed the only thing to do was make a huge scene and grab a gun. Can you see the pattern? A young Sensitive is their own authentic self. A non-HSP sees them as different and therefore weak. The non-HSP takes advantage of the Sensitive by pushing them around, bending the Sensitive to their will. This cycle is very similar to Sensitives and narcissists for the same reasons. Now the Sensitive is beaten down into despair and chaos. The Sensitive comes to believe they need to take their power back (and I agree) and they grab a gun (I do not agree). This is the dark side of taking blame and responsibility and a meager attempt at controlling their world and their chaos.

Like Nurse Nightingale, Sensitives need to feel loved—remember Hildegard and the Orchid environment. They need to feel wanted and like they have a purpose; they need to feel they matter. But making the evening news about death tolls is not the way to go about it. The way Miss Nightingale used her feeling of chaos and lack of control is a healthier way to go about it. She used her feelings of shame for the higher good. If Nightingale felt guilt, she used that energy and her guilt to change the conditions and make the experiences for others better.

There is an ancient Islamic prayer I learned from one of Gregg Braden's audiobooks. I have changed the words slightly, but the sentiment remains the same.

Bless the Suffering.
Bless the Inflictors.
Bless the Witnesses.

I go to this prayer/affirmation when I see or feel great suffering in the current events. But I really came to understand the power of this mantra when a school shooting occurred mere blocks from my home. As I drove past and helicopters and police cars arrived on the scene, I realized that the person in the school that caused all this frenzy must have been in such a dark and fearful place; they must have been so far away from love to think this action was needed. And so I asked: bless the Suffering, bless the inflictors, bless the witnesses. I also realized we humans can be all three (the Suffering, the Inflictors, and the Witnesses) simultaneously. We can witness our own suffering and the steps we took to inflict that suffering. While I believe Nightingale was not aware of this specific prayer, I believe she lived this prayer. She witnessed the Crimean War. She saw the suffering. She learned of the partial cause (i.e. the Inflictor), that of the bacteria. She knew her God-given mission was to improve the situation. And so, from her bed for over thirty years, she fought, hoping to cleanse herself by cleansing hospitals.

It is even possible that Nightingale was intuitive about the existence of bacteria and its effects. She and her 38 nurses arrived in Turkey on November 4, 1854. The first thing they did was clean—clean the hospital, clean their residence. Approximately 9 years before Mr. Pasteur made his discovery of microbes, Nightingale was cleaning, possibly inherently, intuitively knowing it needed to be done. Many Sensitives KNOW without knowing why. It is what makes us Sensitives, our sensitivity to subtleties in our environment, our claircognizance. We may not know why we cross the road when we do or how we know where those lost keys are, we just know.

Florence Nightingale is less known for her statistical and graphical mind. She was the first female member of the Royal Statistical Society in 1859 and is considered a pioneer of information graphics. These two interests take a very specific and rare mind, one that uses both hemispheres of the brain, the analytical left and the creative right. Luckily, this ability is seen often in Sensitives. Many of us are able to cross brain hemispheres, making connections and combinations in new and fascinating ways allowing and supporting us to do great and impactful things.

CHAPTER 7

George Washington Carver

Do you like peanuts or peanut butter or peanut butter cups? You can thank Professor George Washington Carver. Ok, he didn't invent peanut butter cups or even technically peanut butter, but he did bring peanut farming to the south, re-engineered agriculture, and developed over 325 peanut-based products for a wide variety of uses. The National Park Service titled him "the most prominent black scientist of the early 20th century."[1]

The Historical George Washington Carver

George Washington Carver was born circa 1864 as an enslaved man on the Carver farm in Diamond Grove, Missouri. He earned his bachelor's and master's degrees at the Iowa State University. He was a professor at Tuskegee University. In 1921, he testified before Congress about the merits of farming peanuts. He died on January 5, 1943, in Tuskegee, Alabama at the age of 78 as a result of injuries sustained from falling down the stairs.

The Sensitive George Washington Carver

From a very early age, Professor Carver loved nature but according to Gene Barretta's book *The Secret Garden of George Washington Carver*, he kept it a secret. Mr. Barretta writes, "No one saw how the child cared for his flowers and how much he loved them."[2]

Professor Carver was "weak" and "small for his age . . . [with] a high-pitched voice," perhaps due to his many childhood ailments namely whooping cough and pneumonia.[3] Being "a sickly child" benefited the Professor, as being unable to work allowed him more time to explore.[4] This exploration really paid off for the young Carver. By the time he was 12, neighbors and friends called him "The Plant Doctor" and consulted on plants and their care. Professor Carver believed "the garden was a true gift from God, whom he called the Great Creator."[5]

It is clear that Professor Carver was an HSP. He loved nature, retreating daily into the woods his entire life, just one of many ways Sensitivity can present itself and a great technique for cleansing and grounding. We have already seen a few historical sensitives and will meet more who used nature as a release, a comfort, and a possible coping mechanism.

Like Saint Hildegard and her many talents, Professor Carver was more than just a scientist, he was also an inspiring teacher, a talented musician, and a gifted painter who became "a symbol of African American success and interracial harmony."[6] Like Mr. Douglass, Professor Carver's "soul thirsted for an education."[7] Self-taught in his early years by experimenting with flowers, Professor Carver went on to receive a bachelor's degree in agriculture from Iowa State College in 1894, being the first black man to "study, graduate, and teach" at what was then named Iowa Agricultural College.[8]

He received his master's degree in 1896 making him "the only African American in the United States with advance training in scientific agriculture."[9] He loved school and learning so much that he went on to teach at the Tuskegee Institute in 1896.[10]

Professor Carver's "genuine love of humanity" was widely returned.[11] Professor Carver came to be loved by his students and area farmers, teaching them better and more earth-friendly farming techniques. From his early years, Professor Carver had a "deep desire to share what he knew."[12] His love of humanity only grew with age, and this love and respect was returned as seen in the amount of letters he received. Later in his life while at the Tuskegee Institute, he received piles and piles of letters asking his advice on a myriad of subjects. Routinely, he read the letters at night, then retired to bed. In the morning, he would have clarity and write his responses. I believe his responses were more intuitively derived from his dreams than from his knowledge.

But thinking he was just an egghead, nerd, or scientist would be a mistake. Professor Carver was interested in anything regarding plants, even drawing and painting them. And it was actually his artistic ability that got him into college. In 1893, one of Professor Carver's paintings was exhibited and won an honorable mention at the Chicago World's Fair, a fact which made Professor Carver very proud.[13]

The Historical Impact of Professor Carver's Sensitivity

With warm, loving energy and a sweet smile from this heart-based human, Professor Carver "had a knack for interesting his audience on his research."[14] He loved the earth, learning, and humanity so much, his enthusiasm and loving energy was contagious. In the PBS documentary *George Washington Carver: An Uncommon Life*, he is quoted saying "I love all humans."[15] And in 1921 he addressed Congress on the "values of the peanut."[16] His education and enthusiasm led him to his unique way of seeing the world saying, "When you can do the common things in life in an uncommon way, you will command the attention of the world."[17] A very Sensitive and true viewpoint, indeed.

The humble and amazing Professor Carver is quoted to say "I am not a finisher . . . I am a blazer of trails" allowing others to continue what he began along the "various trails of truth."[18] Professor Carver wanted all beings to live well and be happy. While he believed he was part of the solution, he realized he was not the only solution. His wisdom and humility reflect his sensitivity. But he knew that the solution was much bigger than himself; he was happy to just get the ball rolling.

Professor Carver changed agriculture. He offered new techniques and ideas about how and what to farm. Not only did he revolutionize farming, but he gave us all peanut butter, now a main staple in many people's diets. From kids' peanut butter and jelly sandwiches to Elvis' favorite peanut butter and banana to the television show *Friends*' character Joey's favorite peanut butter fingers, peanuts and peanut butter are used for quick energy or as a main protein source. And we can all send a big hug of thanks to Professor Carver.

My Opinion of Professor Washington Carver

When I look at the photos of Mr. Washington Carver I just smile and tears of amazing joy and gratitude well up in my eyes. That immediate response tells me I am witnessing love, kindness, and compassion—the embodiment of the Sensitive. He feels like the best grandpa or Santa, you just want to crawl up in his lap, get a great big hug, and thank him for being his loving authentic self.

It is said that when Professor Carver first arrived in the Deep South of Alabama, he immediately knew the cotton crops were draining the earth of nutrients. You could see it, he said, the land was dry and non-fertile. He knew this to be fact, cotton was hard on the earth. He seemed almost surprised no one else knew it. By looking at this incident with an eye for the Sensitive, it makes all the sense in the world.

This incident shows further the intuitive claircognizant nature of us Sensitives. We know. Another example of this clear knowing is my mother. She is excellent with plants. After being her daughter for over a half-century, she finally, just recently told me she can hear the plants. She can hear them tell her where the plant wants to be, in the sunshine, in the corner. "Can't everyone do that?" She asked. "No, mama, they can't. You are special, you are sensitive," I responded, beaming with love and excitement for her budding awareness. Not everyone can see energy and auras, hear plants, or whatever you do so naturally that you think it's common. Not everyone has such vivid dreams they remember the details. Not everyone wakes up with a new song, painting, or story in their head. You are unique in that way. You are sensitive, you are intuitive.

Professor Carver was very privileged to find his purpose very early in life, that of understanding and learning about plants. He wanted to know everything he could about plants. He studied every aspect—chemistry, biology, and painting plants to capture their beauty and better understand them. Not everyone is so fortunate to find their calling in life so early, but Professor Carver shows us the importance of following your heart and maintaining that childhood innocence. He embodied the adage that when you do what you love you never work a day in your life.

Because Sensitives are energetic sponges it is easy for us to get caught up in other people's dreams and desires. For example, when I lived in Baltimore, my then-husband wanted to create a barbecue brewpub. We spent every free moment barbecuing in the summer and brewing beer in the winter. Once we drove eight hours just to have dinner at a barbecue brewpub in Charlotte, North Carolina, only to turn right around the next morning and drive home. We worked on a business plan; he worked on the fun stuff, namely the menu, design, and graphics and I worked on the meat of the plan, the costs and statistics. It wasn't until years later I realized . . . I had no interest in operating a brewpub. I was only interested because he was interested. I was helping him with his dream, but it wasn't mine. I had "caught" his contagious energy. While some may consider this a waste of my time and a diversion from my life path, I consider it a life lesson well learned. Like Professor Carver, stay in your own energy, and stay true to you.

Professor Carver was always his authentic self, focused on what made him happy, what felt good to him and on his path. You've probably heard the phrase, "Go with the Flow." Well, Professor Carver was in the flow of happiness with his study of plants. Abraham-Hicks would say Professor Carver was always in the flow, pointed downstream or in the vortex. Professor Carver reveals what being in the flow looks like—achieving amazing things by always being loving and kind.

CHAPTER 8

Nikola Tesla

Sure, we know the name Tesla today. Who hasn't seen those spiffy super-quiet electric cars? In fact, when I mention Tesla to friends, they assume I am speaking of Elon Musk and his car. But Tesla is much more than just a cool car. The man on which the car is based, Nikola Tesla, was an inventor. Heck, Tesla was more than an inventor, he was a Game-Changer, only he was born 100 years too early. The world wasn't ready for his ideas; they were too radical, too wild. But now . . . with more and more people interested in living off the grid and lighter on the planet, Tesla is the Man!

The Historical Nikola Tesla

Nikola Tesla was born "in the midst of a violent thunderstorm" at exactly "the stroke of midnight" on July 10th of 1856 in Smiljan Croatia or so writes Richard Munson in his biography *Tesla: Inventor of the Modern*.[1] In June 1884, Tesla emigrated to the United States where there were more work opportunities for him. He worked for Edison and developed our modern design of alternating current, the AC in AC/DC (electricity, not the band). He died in New York City January 3, 1943, of a coronary thrombosis, a blood clot in the heart. He is also known for his "thought experiments," marrying a pigeon, and his poor business skills.

The Sensitive Tesla

With an "impressive and extensive education," Tesla had an eidetic memory. Tesla spoke eight languages and could recite entire books from memory.[2] "Usually shy,"[3] Tesla "sought solitude" in nature throughout his life to "envision" his "nature-inspired designs. "The "sensitive young boy" observed nature "carefully" and with "such close attention" often leading to "profound insights."[4]

Capable of "performing calculations in his mind" Tesla's "greatest youthful joy" came from his cat. Tesla remembered fondly the "'magnificent Mack—the finest of all cats in the world,'"[5] pointing to his great love of animals, yet another sign of sensitivity.

Throughout Tesla's life, especially during his childhood, he experienced life-threatening illnesses. Often at death's door, his parents strongly suggested he not come home after his college graduation. Tesla came home anyway and contracted a severe case of cholera, the exact reason his parents wanted him to stay away. Tesla became so ill, that he drifted in and out of consciousness and was in bed for nine months. Tesla was beyond the doctors' help and only got healthy once he had made up his mind, demonstrating the power of his and the Sensitive's mind.[6]

Tesla is also known for being quite quirky or eccentric, and with 20/20 hindsight we can now understand him better as an HSP. His "wondrous and inventive mind was haunted by the obsessive" to the point where Tesla writes "the sight of a pearl [earring] would almost give me a fit."[7] Known to count his steps, Tesla "[made] sure they were divisible by three."[8] Obsessive Compulsive much?

Eventually, Tesla developed "episodes of seeing things with strobing intensity." His episodes became so "confusing," that Tesla couldn't tell if what he saw was "real or not." Tesla came to call his hearing and seeing abilities "extraordinary."[9]

The Historical Impact of Tesla's Sensitivity

During his lifetime, Tesla developed great advances for humanity, many of which are only being appreciated and further developed today. He wanted electricity to be free and available to all, but Edison, a businessman with an eye for profit, obviously won that fight, thus establishing our world of utility companies. Tesla laid the groundwork for our understanding of electricity, and much of his work is still used and hasn't been updated since, thus the need for upgrading the American national grid.

We are only just beginning to revisit and delve into his ideas. Tesla's historical impact is yet to be completely realized but no doubt will be great.

My Opinions of Tesla and How They Relate to Being an HSP

Ah, Tesla, that crazy brilliant guy. Have you ever met a genius? I mean an actual over 140 IQ level genius? I have known a few. And all of them were Sensitives.

PART II : THE HISTORICAL SENSITIVE PERSONS

Two were so "flighty" with their head in other places, thinking of other things, that they bumped into things all the time. They were so booksmart that they literally couldn't tie their own shoes, opting for Velcro. One genius friend was an anesthesiologist and the other worked in a think tank for a major car company, dreaming up new concept cars. Brilliant, brilliant people, but you'd never know to look or talk to them.

Another of my Sensitive genius friends would think so fast that he literally couldn't speak straight. His mind was always two sentences ahead of his speech. Once he calmed down and took a nice deep breath, mind and mouth melded and he could express himself well. That's how I imagine Tesla, goofy, quirky, and brilliant. Brilliant before his time.

So brilliant, was Tesla in fact, he couldn't possibly consider underhanded business tactics or being cheated. Yes, the little sweetheart was swindled, or rather contractually outwitted and he died penniless. Tesla was so focused on the good his inventions and ideas could have on humanity, that the thought of loopholes in contracts or being cheated was never in his realm of possibility. Living during a time of inventions, electricity, railroads, and all sort of new gadgets, how could the public not be interested in his life-changing ideas? Tesla was quite childlike and naive when it came to business or management. Innocent and unaware of the dog-eat-dog world, he was easily fooled by his competitors more than once.

Like Tesla, Sensitives have a trusting nature. We can be easily manipulated and taken advantage of. Tesla teaches us to beware and read the fine print (and understand what you are agreeing to); not everyone is as conscientious and kind as we are.

If, like Tesla, we Sensitives believe in something we can get very excited and focused. We put our whole selves into it sometimes to the exclusion of everything else. Mr. Tesla was known to be so focused on his work, working twenty hours a day, he often worked himself sick. Working all hours into the night, excited about the possibilities, sleep and shyness be damned.

For instance, I was working retail in a women's clothing store. I loved the clothes; they were so soft and cozy I loved working there. I would often work more hours than scheduled, taking on extra shifts so a co-worker could have some time off. They had one skirt I absolutely loved, I'd wear it to work as often as I dared. I would show it to anyone who was interested, which was nearly everyone who walked in the door. "You wanna see a soft beautiful skirt that's sized large? Come this way. You could have size 2 hanging in your closet AND it'll fit," I'd say. Needless to say, I sold the heck out of that skirt, if the softness and fit didn't get them, the small size did. My enthusiasm for the skirt translated easily to other shoppers. Of course, it was a great skirt. Like Tesla, Sensitives can easily get carried away with excitement, become extremely focused, and seem even more than a little crazy or manic. When Tesla's body was discovered in his New York hotel room, they also found boxes and boxes of his work. His mind never stopped working, focused entirely on his ideas.

During Tesla's school years and through his early twenties, he worked twenty hours a day. A little later in life, around his late twenties and early thirties, Tesla adopted a healthier regimen. He exercised in the morning, both walking and swimming, and even allowed himself a full hour for breakfast.[10] This practice of Tesla's is an important example of self-care, of living a balanced life.

Yes. Sensitives can get a little crazy and a little overwhelmed at times. We need our Me Time, our down time, our alone and recharging time. We can often feel overwhelmed, feeling like our world will end, like we just can't handle anything anymore. We can feel crazy, literally, uptight, and nervous. Consider Tesla's hallucinations and his not being able to know what was real. When, or if, you feel like Tesla, a little (or a lot) manic, it's time to slow down, it's time for self-care. Slow your breath and calm yourself. Seek professional help if you feel that's right for you. After all, it's quite possible Freud and Jung were both Sensitives themselves and 80% of mental health patients are Sensitives.[11] Therefore, seeking and asking for help may be just what is called for. Other times, merely talking to a friend may help move our anxious energy out and create a calming shift within us.

Keep in mind Sensitives can feel like Drama Queens, feeling as if we have an insurmountable number of things to work on when in reality, when looked at with a calm rational perspective, things are completely manageable. Since we sometimes feel like being a drama queen, making a fuss is the only way we can be cared for (rather than caring for everyone else). But your struggle is real within you, even if others do not understand, and you need to take care of you—the whole you. My strongest suggestion in this type of situation is to find someone who will believe you and care for you, a likeminded friend or professional who understands and will listen (See the section on self-care in Part III for further suggestions and techniques.)

> **SECTION 3 - LEADERS**
>
> Now that you are more familiar with the characteristics of HSP and their potential archetypes and have learned a bit more about potential HSPs in history, it is time to turn to people who were possibly HSP but not in typical HSP forms, in this case, leaders of countries.

CHAPTER 9

Abraham Lincoln

Practically everyone knows of Abraham Lincoln as the "Great Emancipator." We also know President Lincoln as "Honest Abe," an undisputed and common HSP quality. We learn in elementary school how he freed enslaved Americans. We see photos of him looking strong and proud in his stovepipe hat. But did you know that his beliefs on abolition changed over his lifetime? Did you know that while he thought slaves and all humans should be free, he still considered the white man to be superior?[1] To me, President Lincoln's growth over his life is one of the most fascinating things about him, especially when you consider he may have been an HSP, and possibly an empath. But don't take my word for it, let's look at what historians have to say, and there are many of them to choose from.

The Historical Abraham Lincoln

Abraham Lincoln was born in Kentucky on February 12, 1809. He was primarily a self-taught lawyer. He was the 16th President of the United States of America serving 1861-1865 during the American Civil War. Did you know Abraham Lincoln won the presidential election of 1860 with just under 40% of the votes? There were four candidates in that election, two of whom ran as Democrats thereby splitting the vote. Lincoln won both the popular and electoral votes with nearly all the northern states. Incidentally, Frederick Douglass endorsed Lincoln in the 1860 election, believing Lincoln was the most anti-slavery and least-objectionable candidate on the ballot.

In his second year as President, Lincoln wrote the Emancipation Proclamation, the 13th Amendment to the American Constitution. He announced the Proclamation on September 22, 1862, which took effect on January 1, 1863, and the last people were informed and freed on June 19, 1865, in Texas. President Lincoln was assassinated by John Wilkes Boothe on April 15, 1865, a mere six days after General Lee surrendered to General Grant at Appomattox, thus ending the Civil War.

The Sensitive Lincoln

When looking to prove President Lincoln's sensitivity, one only needs to read the index of the book *Lincoln's Ethics* written by Thomas L. Carson. Mr. Carson's index of President Lincoln's character reads like a textbook for HSP; "benevolence, kindness, careless appearance, generosity, honesty, honorable ambition, indifference to money, lack of social graces, love of learning, melancholy, mercy, nonconformity, independence of mind, permissive parent, prankster, strong moral convictions, reverence of the law,"[2] to list just a telling few.

Some of these characteristics may seem to fit the HSP character trait perfectly while others may cause you to cock your head a little. "Careless appearance, lack of social graces, permissive parent" you may ask what do these have to do with HSP?

A careless appearance, nonconformity, and indifference to money go hand in hand with the Sensitive and suggests humility, or a small ego, and an interest in the deeper meaning of life and therefore a disinterest in the "finer things in life," which many HSPs experience. The "careless appearance" of President Lincoln also suggests he focused on higher interests and therefore no time, interest, or energy for the more material and bothersome things such as clothes.[3]

President Lincoln's "lack of social graces" continues to support the idea of his higher interests it also points to his potential awkwardness in social settings and/or his disinterest in them, accepting social events only when necessary, something to be dragged to rather than something to look forward to, like all those awful office parties you must attend. The President's lack of social graces also points to an HSP characteristic of not wanting to be around people. Oh, we love people, in the abstract or one-on-one, but in large groups, in social settings, we do not.[4]

Carson's description of President Lincoln as a permissive parent is also quite telling of his HSP-ness. HSPs typically are very accepting and allowing, enablers to our core. Since we tend to see the good in all things, we easily give others a break, especially to those we love (but rarely to ourselves). As a "permissive parent," now known as an Enabler, President Lincoln was merely very accepting of his children and everything they did because he loved them so much all he saw was the goodness within them.[5]

For two more HSP qualities of President Lincoln, we turn to Michael Burlingame's book *The Inner World of Abraham Lincoln*. Burlingame writes of President Lincoln's struggle with depression and even suicide, both, sadly, common HSP traits.[6]

We all have experienced loss in our lives, as Rocket from the movie *Guardians of the Galaxy* says, "We all have dead people." And President Lincoln was no exception. But as HSPs do, he felt his losses very deeply which typically spiraled down to depression and occasionally suicidal thoughts. Burlingame, author of many books about Lincoln, devotes an entire chapter to the President's lifetime battle with depression, describing his "intense melancholy" as one of Lincoln's key personality traits.[7]

It is perfectly understandable for a 9-year-old boy to grieve when his mother dies, such as Mr. Lincoln experienced, when his first girlfriend died, or when two of his sons died (Eddie, age 3, and Willie, age 11).[8] Grief is common to being human. But, as Burlingame suggests, to "suffer emotional agony" throughout an entire lifetime is quite another thing entirely.[9]

Being such a sensitive soul, President Lincoln openly wept when he heard of the first death of the Civil War and wrote many letters personally to parents of fallen soldiers. Mr. Lincoln is reported to have said Hell "has no terror for me" when speaking after the first Bull Run Battle, pointing to the private living hell that was his life.[10]

Mr. Lincoln was suicidal at times, most decidedly after the death of his first girlfriend, Ann Rutledge. Burlingame writes Mr. Lincoln's response to hearing of her death was "somewhat temporarily deranged" causing his friends to keep watch for his safety. Mr. Lincoln was someone who truly felt emotions deeply and completely though he rarely processed those emotions.[11]

The Historical Impact of Lincoln's Sensitivity

Whew! The impact of Lincoln's sensitivity has been studied and written about for nearly 160 years. He is considered an American hero. It is only now, with the interest in telling history from many sides, that the whole and true Mr. Lincoln is being discovered and discussed. We are learning more about President Lincoln, warts and all. While humans still have more work toward equality, President Lincoln's Emancipation Proclamation was a huge leap forward. And it was all due to his ability to keep his heart and mind open, like a Sensitive.

My Opinions of Lincoln

Everything about Mr. Lincoln screams Sensitive to me. In fact, he was the historical figure that gave me the initial idea of Historical Sensitive Persons. Being an HSP, I was fascinated to learn why a Sensitive, such as President Lincoln, would go into public life. He was working as a lawyer, a rather successful one in Illinois—why go into politics? It seems he was always interested in politics and the nation's issues even as a young boy. Lincoln disagreed with the policies and beliefs of the current president of his time, Andrew Jackson, who wanted the government to stay out of the economy. Lincoln believed that the government should do whatever it needed to help its citizens, including influencing the economy. He felt strongly something needed to be done, so Lincoln ran for Congress.

Have you ever been worried about the state of the world or the direction of your country? Has a cause or some injustice stirred you to action? I have. When I was in high school, admittedly one of the most difficult times for me, a friend committed suicide. We had been friends since elementary school. His death was devastating to me, especially because he had asked me to spend time with him that fateful weekend. Oh, if I only had . . . As a result, I began training to counsel teens. I thank my dear friend for helping put me on my path of helping others. Like Lincoln, I saw a need that I wanted to make better.

With Florence Nightingale, we mentioned how Sensitives are open-minded and therefore willing to listen to opposing sides and change our minds. Sometimes, this leads to changing our beliefs. Like Nightingale, Lincoln too was open-minded and changed his mind and his beliefs. Interestingly enough, he seemed to walk a fine line when it came to slavery. He was against slavery; on March 3, 1837, he made his first public declaration on the subject saying slavery was "founded on both injustice and bad policy." But it seems he also recognized its economic importance and therefore only called for slavery to stop spreading to new states and territories.

He was not an abolitionist, someone who wished to abolish slavery altogether. We also know he was against black voting rights or serving on juries, considering them unworthy of such positions. To me, this stance seems a bit wishy-washy and very political. One can almost feel his struggle. He knows slavery is wrong, it goes against his religious upbringing and beliefs. But he also knows the South is economically dependent on slavery. And remember, he believed the government should be involved in the economy. What to do, what to do. His response was to continue to walk the very thin line by stating slavery should not continue to spread but remain contained in the existing states.

Lincoln's open-mindedness came into play while he was president. Always believed slavery was a moral injustice, but at the beginning of his presidency, Lincoln had no plan to change the status quo. He even considered shipping black people out of the country, believing white and black people could not peacefully live in the same country. He is remembered as saying the Civil War was not about slavery but about keeping the country together. Over time as the war and his presidential term progressed, Lincoln learned, partly from Frederick Douglass, and settled on the moral side of the issue, rather than the economic side and eventually wrote and passed the 13th Amendment.

Mr. Douglass noted the difference in Lincoln between their meeting in 1863 and a mere year later with Lincoln having a "deeper moral conviction against slavery."[12] This move toward a more equitable solution for Lincoln is not surprising to Sensitives. Lincoln did his homework, spoke to many people about the issue, and became more educated about slavery. By the way, can you imagine the meeting between Lincoln and Frederick Douglass? Two self-taught, highly regarded, successful Sensitives sitting together in deep ethical and philosophical discussion. Oh, to be a fly on that wall. One can even speculate, that Lincoln's ideas on white supremacy must have been greatly altered with his relationship with Mr. Douglass. In Frederick Douglass' published work *The Life and Times of Frederick Douglass, 1817-1882*, Lincoln is quoted as saying about Douglass "There is no man in the country whose opinion I value more."[13]

Lincoln's open-minded growth, from anti-slavery to abolitionist, over those four years was just enough of a shift to make all the difference in our world, demonstrating it doesn't take much to create a huge shift for Sensitives. Lincoln's shift teaches us how important and impactful our little shifts can be to us and our world. Depending on how sensitive you are a little shift may be all you need to create and send out ripples of kindness. The more sensitive you are the smaller the shift you may need. If you are feeling stuck, down, or depressed it's possible all that may be needed is a small change like rearranging your decorations, a new color pillow or sheets or even choosing to eat a salad. If you are not aware of your level of sensitivity, I recommend starting with a small change and working your way up, noticing your energy and emotions each time you make a change. Just a little rotation of your favorite tchotchke, (my grandmother called them "put-upons" because you put them upon your dresser or coffee table or shelf) is enough to shift the energy of your room, and you.

The "dark side" of being open-minded is the ability to be easily manipulated. Due to a Sensitive's open heart, mind, and energetic boundaries (all classic traits of the Sensitive), we can be easily manipulated and convinced into doing or agreeing to something we normally wouldn't. This is especially true when we are involved in some way with a narcissist-type personality, known in some circles as Energy Vampires. I've been in meetings where I volunteered for things I had no interest in doing. I've also agreed to romantic partners all kinds of things, from letting him drive my car when I knew he wasn't sober to allowing his three daughters to move in with us. What was I thinking? I wasn't. I was feeling, and not my energy. I was so wrapped up in his energy and wanting to please him and keep him happy, I lost my focus, my boundaries, and my 401k. Lesson learned.

I say this from a loving place, become familiar with yourself, your beliefs, and your energy. When you are aware of yourself and your energy you can better recognize and detect "alien" energy (that which is not yours). You can make clearer decisions and stand in your own power.

We thank President Lincoln for his sensitivity, his strong morals, and his open mind. For without him, this country would look very different.

CHAPTER 10

Harriet Tubman

Many more people know about Harriet Tubman now than I did in the 1980s when I went to school. I knew her name; I knew she was born into slavery, freed herself, was part of the Underground Railroad, and was known as Moses. Thanks to recent efforts to dig up the past and tell both sides of the story, Ms. Tubman and her efforts have moved to the forefront. All of my resources and the bulk of books published about her were published in the first decade of this century. Hooray!

The Historical Harriet Tubman

Harriet Tubman's birthdate is inexact, most sources report her date of birth sometime in March 1822, in Dorchester County, Maryland. Her name is recorded as Araminta Ross as an enslaved woman. At the approximate age of 27, she ran away from her enslaver, freed herself, and aligned with the Abolitionists in Philadelphia. The following year she returned to Maryland to lead other enslaved people to freedom. She returned 13 times, guiding 70 people to the North, to freedom.

But Ms. Tubman was much more than a guide (or conductor) on the Underground Railroad, which would be enough. During the American Civil War, she held many positions working for the Union Forces including cook, nurse, scout, teacher, and spy. John Brown, the abolitionist, described her as "a better officer than most" and "equally able to command an army as to lead fugitives from slavery" high praise indeed for her time.[1] In 1863, under Colonel James Montgomery, she became the first woman to lead an armed raid, resulting in the freedom of over 700 enslaved people.[2]

Ms. Harriet Tubman was also active in the women's suffrage movement as a speaker at both black and white suffrage conventions. In 1896, at the approximate age of 74, Ms. Tubman purchased 25 acres of land in Auburn, New York and established a home and hospital for African Americans in need, now known as the Harriet Tubman National Historical Park.³ Harriet Tubman died March 10, 1913, and is buried next to her brother.

The Sensitive Harriet Tubman

It is clear Ms. Tubman's entire life was dedicated to helping humans, whether it was through nursing, speaking, or guiding; I believe she was (and is) the epitome of a Freedom Fighter, Righteous Champion, and a Highly Sensitive Person. Harriet Tubman is often described in biographies as having a vivid memory, beginning with her first memory of "lying in a cradle."⁴ (How far back can you remember?)

She "saw things" and was a "true psychic." Author Beverly Lowry writes "The visions she described were sometimes nightmarish, dreamlike or prophetic. But the voices she heard . . . were pragmatic and specific. They told her what to do next, something like . . . Jeanne d'Arc."⁵ Ms. Tubman's contemporaries, believers, and skeptics alike verify "the indisputable presence of these extrasensory powers."⁶ The visions point to Ms. Tubman's clairvoyance while the voices suggest she was clairaudient. Ms. Tubman even describes dreams of "flying over fields and looking down upon them like a bird."⁷

Ms. Tubman was a "fix-it child" always looking for ways to "make things right from her earliest days."⁸ Lowry also writes of Ms. Tubman's "quick mind" and "sharp wit attuned to subtext and its messages."⁹ Ms. Tubman used her interest and abilities with language as a storyteller and a "sublime actress" to "dramatize, embroider, distract, and when necessary, deceive."

Ms. Tubman, while never learning to read or write, was highly intelligent and was able to read people and use the "white man's system" to her advantage. At one point she became her own agent, selling herself out to other enslavers, thus able to save some money for herself.

Harriet Tubman was understood and accepted to be a loner and unreliable in attending scheduled meetings. She also enjoyed being outside in the fields. She learned to navigate her freedom trips by the stars (she could always find the North Star) and the landscape.¹⁰

As a child, Ms. Tubman was described physically as "sickly" and a "weak young girl."¹¹ She grew into a mighty but diminutive 5 foot 2 inches with "awesome stamina,"¹² with a lithe athletic and strong body, of which she was proud. She would often perform "tricks" of strength to "prove how many pounds she can lift."¹³

All of these aspects, including the fact that she was more comfortable by herself and in nature, her dreams of flying, visions, and her intelligence point to her Sensitivity. These are established prior to her major life-changing head injury when she was a young girl around the age of 13. This near-fatal head injury impacted Ms. Tubman severely. With moments of narcolepsy and lethargy, she would fall into a "deep slumber" but would "presently rouse herself" and continue on with whatever she was doing. These episodes continued throughout her life, noted by one reporter who interviewed the then ninety-year-old Ms. Tubman. Researchers today surmise the head injury led to Tubman having Temporal Lobe Epilepsy (aka TLE).[14]

Understandably, after her head injury and survival, she experienced an "explosion of religious enthusiasm and vivid imagery." Ms. Tubman is remembered often to have broken out "unexpectedly into loud and excited religious praising."[15] While possible symptoms of her TLE, Ms. Tubman enjoyed a "deep and abiding spiritual foundation that remained with her throughout her life."[16]

Many of her sensitivities can be explained as a consequence of the life to which she was born rather than her being an HSP. Her fear and anxiety of being torn from her family, preferring to work in the fields away from the enslavers, her ability to find the North Star, and even her strong religious enthusiasm are all completely natural and common for a person of her time and situation. There is one account that I believe puts her firmly in the Highly Sensitive Person category. Her ability to forgive and understand the enslavers, to turn the other cheek so to speak. While weaving her story in later years, she tells her audience, "It was of no use to chastise" the cruel people because "they didn't know any better." Ms. Tubman said, "It's the way they were brought up." The children were taught and raised with a "whip in their hand."[17] While a true and loving statement, I believe it is high time we teach our children love and acceptance, honor and dignity.

To me, this shows Ms. Tubman's astounding ability for forgiveness, remarkable understanding and love for humanity. Similar to the Bible verse, "Forgive them; for they know not what they do," she separates the person from their actions; she sees the laws are wrong, but the people are not to blame. She fights vigorously against slavery but offers just as vigorous forgiveness for the enslavers. Simply amazing. Incredibly heart-based. Amazingly Sensitive.

The Impact of Harriet's Sensitivity on History

Harriet Tubman's legacy is currently enjoying a resurgence as we learn more and more about her every day. Her home in New York is now a Historical National Park. Many books have been published about her life. She is the focus of many documentaries and an Oscar-winning movie. Her life was all about serving humanity, and like "the fix-it child" she was, through her story of courage and unrelenting fight for freedom and equality, she continues to help humans.

Her sensitivities gave hope and comfort to many people of her time and continue to do so to this day. Her compassion and conviction for freedom for all humanity gave her the strength to return to Maryland again and again. Her courage and drive impressed many of her contemporaries, showing the true power and strength of people, regardless of their social standing. Like Hildegard de Bingen and Florence Nightingale, she was guided with a strong sense of duty, a mission to improve the world that carried her when times were tough.

Mrs. Harriet Tubman embodies the recently published book by Acharya Shunya *Roar Like a Goddess*. Shunya writes of righteous anger and fighting the wrongs of the world. Well, Ms. Tubman certainly roared and fought, her voice can still be heard today as a rallying cry against tyranny and inequality.

Harriet Tubman and her HSP-ness teach us how to be a good loving human, how to care for humans, and how to treat all humans with understanding and forgiveness. But she also shows us the importance of standing up and pointing out when an action or a law is unfair or unjust. Harriet Tubman teaches us the necessity of the righteous fight, of the freedom fighter. There are instances when fighting is necessary, especially in the face of inequality and injustice.

And it all started with a sensitive little "fix-it" girl wanting to "make things right."

My Opinions of Harriet Tubman and her Sensitivities

Humans come in all shapes and sizes. Humans are like ice cream. We all have the same main ingredients, but all kinds of different flavors. Non-Sensitives are like vanilla or chocolate ice cream, while average Sensitives are more like strawberry or mint chocolate chip ice cream, with a little extra. But Highly Sensitives are more like Ben and Jerry's ice cream, filled with all kinds of new and different ingredients, everything from nuts to raisins to waffle cones. Some of us are Rum Raisin, some bubble gum (my favorite as a child), some are like Rocky Road or Chubby Hubby. My point is we all are the same and we are all different. Some of us are clairvoyant. Some Sensitives can channel messages. And still others can see energy or hear messages. And others of us "just know." Some Sensitives, like Ms. Tubman, can read the lay of the land using nature to guide them to safety. Mrs. Harriet Tubman seems to have been clairvoyant and clairaudient. She used her meta-skills, or extra abilities to guide her and others to freedom, to the North.

I'd like to take a moment to share the symbolism of the North. In some northern hemisphere cultures North represents the Spiritual, a place of contemplation. To some Biblical scholars, the North represents the earth-bound Heavens, a celestial home, the direction of your personal hermitage. A place to consider your lessons learned and incorporate them. Prior to and during the American Civil War, the North meant freedom, a release from bondage, and a better and more equitable life. I find the correlation interesting.

Harriet Tubman is considered a Sensitive in my book primarily due to her incomparable ability to forgive. There are many quotes regarding forgiveness, from Tony Robbins to Gandhi to Shakespeare. You may have come across some of them. How forgiveness can help you. How forgiveness is more about you than the person you are forgiving. How forgiveness is not the same as forgetting. The Lord's Prayer speaks of forgiving your Trespassers and those who've trespassed you. (A fascinating aside, it is almost certain Harriet Tubman knew and prayed the Lord's Prayer. I find this a very interesting way to connect with her.) All these quotes and sayings are wonderful and helpful. But none, or few, mention forgiving yourself.

Sensitives are very good at forgiving. We can forgive at the drop of a hat. For those who deeply hurt us, with some processing and distance, we can forgive. But please, please, please remember to forgive yourself as well. Sensitives do not so readily forgive themselves. We forget ourselves in the process. We may easily understand the other party's viewpoint, put ourselves in their shoes, but we forget we need forgiveness too. We forget to dig a little deeper into our own intents, our own motivations. And we forget to forgive our own selves. You as much as anyone deserve forgiveness. Ms. Tubman was able to forgive her trespassers, amazing in its own right considering their horrible violations of her humanity, but she reminds us to include ourselves in the forgiveness process. Release all that guilt (and Sensitives can feel/pick up a lot of guilt) or whatever you may be harboring. From that quick interaction with a stranger, an important relationship, a friend, or a family member just let it all go but remember to include yourself in your forgiveness.

Harriet Tubman teaches us how impactful we can be when we embrace our extra abilities and use them for good. Where do you imagine the United States would be if Ms. Tubman had shirked her calling of supporting Abolition? What would history look like if she had allowed her head injury to stop her? It would have been completely understandable if she had just spent the rest of her life healing from her injury. But she used her injury, combined with her learned knowledge and her innate abilities, to become the person we love to learn about today. Embrace your rum raisin, rocky road, Chubby Hubby self and be proud!

CHAPTER 11

Ulysses S. Grant

President Grant may be best known for his tomb. Others, who know a bit more, may know him for his drinking and having something to do with the American Civil War. But as with most people, there is so much more to President Ulysses S. Grant.

The Historical President Ulysses S Grant
Born on April 27, 1822, in Point Pleasant, Ohio, Ulysses Grant was America's 18th President during the Reconstruction Era. He was commanding general of the U.S. Army under President Lincoln during the Civil War. General Lee surrendered to Ulysses Grant at Appomattox, ending the war. A lifelong abolitionist, Grant died of throat cancer on July 23, 1885, age 63 in Wilton, New York.

The Sensitive President Grant
President Grant was bullied in school for his name, Hiram Ulysses Grant. His initials, H.U.G, were considered rather unmanly, and therefore a target for bullies who called him "Useless Grant."[1] Over time Grant became "sensitive to public humiliation."[2] He even became the "steadfast protector" of underdogs, horses, and smaller boys, being "roused to fury" when he saw injustice.[3]

Many people have learned coping skills, most unconsciously, some even healthy; for HSPs it is a necessity. Drinking was President Grant's coping mechanism. President Grant is well known for his antics and parties in the White House, actions unbecoming of someone in his position. It is well documented that he was a third-generation alcoholic with both his father, Jesse Root Grant Jr., and grandfather, Jesse Sr., known as heavy drinkers.[4]

The truth is President Grant was more of a "solitary binge drinker," going months on end without a single drop. When President Grant became tired or stressed, usually when he was traveling, he imbibed for three or four months at a time.[5] President Grant used his drinking to "deal with his private sadness," the pain of his migraines,[6] and his depressive episodes[7] all of which are traditional Sensitive traits.

Contrary to what most people think they know, or assume, about President Grant, he hated war "with all my heart."[8] He was relieved when a battle was finished and couldn't stand the sight of blood.[9] Ever the strict Methodist, the young President Grant wouldn't even hunt for sport, choosing barefoot fishing, playing marbles, or swimming instead. Grant had an "aversion to taking any form of life."[10]

Ron Chernow in his book, *Grant,* describes President Grant's personality as "self-contained,"[11] awkward, and flustered especially "in large groups."[12] One of Grant's school friends described him as a "grown person," someone who acted older than their years.[13] Another of Grant's friends said he was "unusually sensitive to pain."[14]

In addition to Grant's drinking, another coping mechanism of his was his ability to control his emotions. Chernow describes Grant as "emotionally blocked" except with his wife and children when he "freely poured forth his bottled-up feelings."[15]

The Historical Impact of President Grant's Sensitivity

Many may consider Grant to be little more than an embarrassment to the Presidency. However, he was integral during the Reconstruction Era, signing the 15th Amendment giving black men the right to vote. March 18, 1869, a mere two weeks into his presidency, Grant signed an equal rights law thus allowing black people to hold a legislative position. In fact, during his presidency (1869-1877) there were 23 black men voted into the House and Senate. Some believe Grant's efforts during Reconstruction were very successful. So successful in fact that dissenting believers were very aggravated and pushed, and succeeded to an extent, to return to the old ways, the days before the Civil War and the 13th Amendment. But for those few years, life was on its way to becoming equal.

Being a lover of nature, President Grant established the first National Park, Yellowstone. He also established the Justice System and the forerunner of the National Weather Service. All of these were causes close to his heart, but no cause ran deeper to President Grant than equality for all men, a very sensitive and righteous cause indeed.

My Opinions of General/President Grant

Alcohol was clearly a coping mechanism for President Grant. While not a healthy or recommended technique, it is still a technique many unaware HSPs use. Many Sensitives will resort to drugs, alcohol, food or some other addiction as an escape mechanism. There are so many other healthy ways to "cope" with being a Sensitive. I actually prefer the term technique or tool instead of coping mechanism. The term coping mechanism implies there is something to work around or to get through. The term technique implies a way to empower yourself.

There are as many empowering techniques as humans on this planet. Finding a few techniques that work best for you may seem arduous and lengthy, but once you find The One (or a few) that benefits you it is worth the attempt and trials. Part III is filled with suggestions for you to try but here are some to get you started thinking about what type of technique would work best for you.

If you are a visual person, creating a visual of what healthy power looks like to you would be a good place to start. If that sounds too "woo-woo" to you, perhaps finding a photo of a beautiful scene or memory may assist you to relax. My mom has a photo of us when I was just a little thing that she likes to focus on when she's feeling blue or really tired. If you are an aural (sound) person you might prefer using music to shift your mood. Personally, I find classical music will calm and relax me, while some good ole classic R&B will get my boogie going every time. If you are more sensitive to smells, using essential oils or candles may do the trick. I know one Sensitive who baked bread because she loved the smell which reminded her of her grandmother. If you are sensitive to energies, perhaps try creating a safe place in your home, somewhere you can go to relax and release the day. Hopefully, you are beginning to get the idea. Use your strongest sense, whichever one that may be, to find comfort, relaxation and peace.

One healthy thing President Grant teaches about coping mechanisms or empowering techniques is his being alone. Relaxation techniques may be most effective when practiced by yourself, allowing you to really release everything else, all worries or issues. A time just for yourself, to be in your own space, your own energy.

We see President Grant's heart in the issues he tackled throughout his life. Increasing the legal abilities of the black community, national parks, and fighting for the little guy. President Grant may not have worn his heart on his sleeve, but he had a soft spot for the marginalized population. Even though he hated the sight of blood and fighting, like Harriet Tubman and many others, he put on his big boy pants and fought the righteous fight, a recurring theme with our Historical Sensitive Persons.

CHAPTER 12

Eleanor Roosevelt

Many of us know the name Eleanor Roosevelt. We may even remember her quote, "A woman is like a teabag, you never know how strong she is until she's in hot water." It seems like Mrs. Roosevelt was always strong; she cared for her husband through polio, campaigned with him (even, at times, in his place), and emotionally led the country through the Great Depression, WWII, and beyond. She is considered one of the greatest First Ladies, redefining the role forward. Mrs. Roosevelt is not remembered as beautiful or fashionable, she was loved worldwide for her warmth and depth of compassion.

The Historical Eleanor Roosevelt

Eleanor Roosevelt was born in New York, on October 11, 1884. She married Franklin Delano Roosevelt in 1905. As the wife of President Franklin Roosevelt, she was the First Lady of the US during the Great Depression and through World War II, 1933-1945. She was the first to chair the United Nations Commission on Human Rights. On November 7, 1962, aged 78, she died in New York City of aplastic anemia, tuberculosis, and heart failure.

The Sensitive Eleanor Roosevelt

To think Mrs. Roosevelt's childhood was bliss because she was born into a rich, famous and powerful family would be wrong. Her childhood was nearly Dickensian. The First Lady's parents were an unreliable alcoholic father and an emotionally closed-off mother, a skill she taught herself,[1] writes Blanche Wiesenthal Cook in her biography titled *Eleanor Roosevelt, Volume One The Early Years 1884-1933*. Eleanor eventually learned the same self-defense mechanism as her mother. Still, as a child, Eleanor could feel her mother's emotional wall and concluded she had done something wrong, that her mother didn't love her.[2] According to David Michaelis in his book simply titled, *Eleanor*,

Anna, Eleanor's mother, nicknamed her daughter "Granny."[3] It is clear that Eleanor was a disappointment to her mother; the nickname points to Eleanor's serious demeanor, her deep-seated feeling of responsibility, and an "Old Soul" from her earliest years. This feeling of responsibility is a common trait amongst Sensitives, as we often feel the weight and needs of humanity and, for some of us, a calling, to make things better. Remember Harriet Tubman. Sometimes this need to improve things is imparted on our families, some of us help our communities; Eleanor (and Harriet) helped raise humanity.

Eleanor's early life shows us the impact of a Sensitive's environment, how we Orchids can blossom when in our preferred environment. Eleanor's first fifteen years were filled with trauma and tragedy.

In the spring of 1887, at the age of 2 1/2 years old, she was involved in a shipwreck. This event, naturally, scared and scarred her, and resulted in her parents traveling to Europe a few days later without her. Most likely, this left Eleanor ashamed over her emotional outburst and abandonment, something she would learn to control in her later years.[4]

At the age of 6, in the winter of 1891, during one of her father's attempts to overcome his drinking, Eleanor "sensed her mother needed her" and for the first time in her young life Eleanor felt "useful and worthy." Continuing, she wrote this feeling of being useful was "perhaps the greatest joy I experienced."[5]

When Eleanor was 8, her mother died of diphtheria, the same disease that her older brother died of a mere six months later. Her father committed suicide a scant 15 months afterward.

Before Eleanor's 10th birthday, she had experienced trauma and tragedy of the deepest kind. This, quite understandably, sent her into a "vivid dream narrative,"[6] her form of escape, coping, and self-care. She spent her days reading wherever and whenever she could, devouring entire books in one day. This retreat into her dream world is an example of a Sensitive coping and may have been used as a form of detachment, a tool we will see again and again with our Historical Sensitives.

At the age of 14, Eleanor was plagued by anxieties trying to please people, possibly to ensure that nobody would desert her again, a sign of abandonment issues,[7] another common trait for Sensitives. Sensitives are born pleasers, turning ourselves inside out to keep others happy. Brendan Fraser's character in the 1999 movie *Blast from the Past* offers an interesting definition, saying being a good hostess, or gentlemanly, is a "way to show other people we care about them." When we apply this theory to Sensitives, we can see how easily it is for us to over-please and loose ourselves in pleasing others. For some, like Eleanor

Roosevelt, pleasing others can become a compulsion, a need, and a way to create a purpose and comfort for ourselves.

At the age of 15, young Miss Roosevelt was sent to England to attend Allenswood, a school for privileged young ladies established and run by Madame Marie Claire Souvestre. By all accounts, Eleanor's arrival at Allenswood was life-changing and is a perfect example of how a Sensitive can blossom when in their Orchid environment. "From her first school meal," Eleanor felt comfortable at Allenswood, standing her full height. Eleanor very quickly made friends and even displayed her mothering/leadership qualities by helping with homework and checking in on them. Eleanor loved Madame Souvestre's technique of teaching and encouraging her students to think for themselves and express their ideas. Her three years at Allenswood demonstrate the beginnings of the historical Eleanor Roosevelt.[8]

Eleanor's transition from the downtrodden quiet childhood Eleanor into a future First Lady Eleanor feels very fast, almost like a lightswitch has been turned on inside her. The speed at which Eleanor embraced her new environment at Allenswood and blossomed is amazing. In less than 24 hours, she was a different person. Similar to Hildegard, she finally felt safe enough to explore who she was and what she believed and to grow into her true self. Eleanor's flourishing experience at Allenswood demonstrates to us Sensitive Orchids our own possibilities when we are in an environment where we feel safe and valued.

Eventually, Eleanor learned to steel herself against physical issues like her mother, never allowing herself to give in to a multitude of challenges—anorexia, malaise, and chronic illness to name a few, even consciously rejecting suicide.[9] First Lady Roosevelt would however "take to her bed" when she experienced migraines throughout her early life, as well as "anguish and depression."[10] The migraines began to subside after the first ten years of her marriage, when "the life she so carefully knit together" began to manifest and "serve her."[11] When her emotions overcame her, she retreated into solitude, choosing long walks in the park[12] or even meditating and visualizing in an empty room.[13]

First Lady Roosevelt felt deeply for the suffering of others stating she hated to "see other people hurt."[14] The First Lady could easily put herself in other people's shoes, identifying with the "mistreated, misunderstood, or despised"[15] which only proved to strengthen her resolve to work harder.

The First Lady Roosevelt's compassion and empathy for such a demographic was well-received. Her vision of economic equality combined with her "magnetism of profound sincerity" made people believe in her.[16]

The Historical Impact of Eleanor Roosevelt's sensitivity

One of Mrs. Roosevelt's proudest accomplishments was chairing the United Nations Commission on Human Rights and the creation of the Bill of Human Rights. The First Lady always considered the next generation, the children. She was a teacher in New York before she married Franklin, teaching the underprivileged, where she later took Franklin and opened his eyes to the living conditions. While in the White House, Mrs. Roosevelt achieved much more than hold parties and redecorate, oh no, this woman worked and she worked hard. Many historians consider Mrs. Roosevelt to be the standard by which all other modern First Ladies are held, one of working for a cause and making a difference in the lives of their constituents, all Americans.

My Opinions on First Lady Roosevelt

Wow! What can I say about Mrs. Roosevelt? Besides that she was simply amazing, strong, and resolute in her position as a leader of a country, while she enjoyed and appreciated the simpler things in life. For example, her wedding dress was made of simple, probably heavy, satin with no fancy pearls or doodads. In fact, in her wedding photo (which is now available as a puzzle, by the way), the wallpaper behind her is more decorative than Mrs. Roosevelt herself. Even her casket was plain and unadorned. This is a theme throughout her life—simple, straightforward, and to the point. With a classic sense of design, she had very few "things" around her. When she lived in the White House, she created a room that was all hers and just for meditation, which she used often. This speaks to the importance of creating a space that is uniquely you, a place you love, and a place where you can relax. A place filled with the things you love, your sacred place.

One of Eleanor's greatest coping mechanisms was her ability to meditate. In 1930, when she was 46, yearning for an identity of her own and feeling overwhelmed and nervous, she found meditation to be very beneficial for her. After taking a class on "how to relax" she "prided herself" on being "the only one who really learned what [the teacher] was talking about."[17]

Author David Michaelis goes on to describe Mrs. Roosevelt's technique:

> "The method proved ideal for the kind of fatigue that would come over her in the middle of a day . . . All she needed was an unused room or office where she could stretch herself flat on the floor, feet uncrossed, hands relaxed at the sides, and let her mind go completely blank. Then, the trick was to imagine herself resting so heavily on the floor that she would 'get the feeling that [she was] going right

through the floor.' Ten minutes of this . . . restored energy more fully, she insisted, than a full hour in bed."[18]

There is a whole lot to unpack in Michaelis' little paragraph. This technique is very exciting to me in many ways. One: it offers a proven technique of meditation for us Sensitives to try and find relief. Two: I believe her repeated and routine use of meditation and the depth to which it helped her feel better, supports our search for Sensitives. Three: it describes one of Eleanor's coping mechanisms and self-care.

Sensitives often feel so tired, like Mrs. Roosevelt, we feel like we can't go on. In high school, I had what I called Dinosaur Days, those days when I was so tired I would imagine myself as a Dinosaur stuck in the tar pits of La Brea. I remember in the late 1990s telling a friend I just wanted to sleep for four years. I woke up tired, exhausted all day, and spent every waking hour looking forward to getting back to bed. I still experience days where I tell myself, we just need to complete this one task and then we can nap. The excess energy we unconsciously soak up can be very tiring and heavy, weighing us down and making it very difficult to do anything other than sleep. Mrs. Eleanor Roosevelt's meditation on becoming heavy is a great and quick technique to help us work with that sensation and get through our busy scheduled days, with no equipment or expense.

The very fact that Mrs. Roosevelt used this meditation lends credence to my theory she was a Sensitive. Her ability to perform the meditation so successfully shows her vivid imagination, common in Sensitives. Her need to perform the mediation due to her extreme tiredness is common in Sensitives. Her continued practice shows us the technique worked for her, and will possibly for us too. Her ease, and quickness, to perform the meditation shows her mental strength. It shows how Sensitives can use our minds for our good, our health, our self-care.

This led me to look for Mrs. Roosevelt's religious practices, a search I found to be surprisingly challenging. I scoured all the books on the First Lady of my local library, only to find one book with a brief nod to her beliefs. All the internet would tell me was that Eleanor was an Episcopalian who attended church regularly. All of this searching was very interesting to me, with paragraphs and paragraphs and pages and pages written about Eleanor and her achievements, but little to no mention of her religious beliefs. Until I found Dr. Harold Ivan Smith's quote "she was very public about her faith."[19] Then the dam broke and I found all kinds of references to her religion.

While Mrs. Roosevelt was a regular attendee of the Episcopalian church, it seems to me, she practiced more what we would call today spirituality. Her faith in goodness, kindness, and love held her up. She believed everyone had some good in them stating, "No one in the world is entirely bad or entirely good."[20] This belief of hers points to her Highly Sensitive belief in people and simultaneously to her ability to see multiple sides of an issue, a lack of duality, not either/or but rather shades of grey, a very common trait with Sensitives. Her specific religious beliefs may not have been specifically pointed out in all those biographies I searched through because everything she did was spiritual, for the highest good. With a strong trust in God and a deep "spiritual connection to the natural world,"[21] Eleanor was every bit working for the highest good, being spiritual every step of the way. This depth of spirituality, connection to nature and calling to improve humanity suggests First Lady Roosevelt may have been an empath.

CHAPTER 13

Princess Diana

Many of us remember the lovely Lady Diana. She was the living embodiment of a fairy tale to us—she was beautiful, she was kind. When we first "met" Diana, she was a kindergarten teacher just 19 years old who had captured the heart of a prince. We watched the engagement interview, the wedding, the birth of her two sons, the divorce, and her death. At one time she was known as the most photographed person in the world. Being of Welsh ancestry, I felt like she was my princess, and I enthusiastically watched her life unfold along with the rest of the world. I remember a friend of mine saying about a photograph of the Princess napping at an event, (a complete no-no in the royal world) "We forgive her because she was pregnant." Many girls my age, teenagers at the time, were entranced by her, her beauty, her story, (as we were told) and her unbelievable luck to have landed a prince. Of course, as her life continued we, and she, found out the life of a princess isn't exactly like the fairy tale books.

The Historical Princess Diana

Born July 1, 1961, The Honorable Diana Frances Spencer married Prince Charles and became Princess of Wales on July 29, 1981. She gave birth to the next king of England, William, on June 21, 1982, and Harry "the Spare Heir" on September 15, 1984. Her divorce was finalized on August 28, 1996, and she died in Paris, on August 31, 1997. The BBC reports the cause of her death as car accident. She was known as "The People's Princess."

Being a royal family member entailed, among other things, public appearances and charity work. In addition to her fashion choices, Diana was well known for her charitable work. She used her position and celebrity to shine light on subjects and situations that most people were afraid to talk about. In a time when AIDS and HIV were new and people were afraid of the disease, Diana opened the first AIDS unit in the United Kingdom. She was photographed talking and even holding hands with AIDS patients. At the time in April of 1987, the world thought of AIDS patients as modern lepers, kept hidden away and apart from society. The public did not know how the disease was transmitted. Once we learned the disease was transmitted via blood, we were still afraid of touching or being near those diagnosed. Seeing Diana visit and hold the hands of the ailing was profound. She, a princess, the next queen of England, spent time with modern lepers, and not only that—she touched them. She showed the world it was safe to be near AIDS patients, she brought the stigma of AIDS out into the light. The People's Princess even auctioned off some of her dresses with the proceeds designated to support AIDS patients.

She continued to use her celebrity after her divorce, bringing awareness to causes close to her heart. In January 1997, in a call to an international ban of landmines, Lady Diana famously walked through an active minefield in Angola. Her youngest son, Harry, repeated this courageous act 25 years later.

Other than Diana's marriage, her charity work and her haircuts, she is known for her tragic death. Diana died due to a car crash in a tunnel in Paris. Early reports of her accident (because yes, I watched them late into the night), mentioned the paparazzi, chasing her car into the fateful tunnel.

It seemed appropriate that the press was somehow involved in her death. From the very beginning, Diana's relationship with the media was complicated and made her very uncomfortable. Reporters were around her constantly, capturing every moment of her life right up until the end. We watched her funeral September 6, 1997, and bawled our eyes out when we saw her coffin topped with a letter from her sons simply addressed *Mummy*.

The Sensitive Princess Diana

Was Princess Diana a Highly Sensitive Person? Quite possibly. She was definitely an introvert, being repeatedly described as shy and kind. Her sensitivity becomes more apparent the more we look into her character. The National Geographic documentary *Diana: In Her Own Words*, published in 1998, offers us rare insight as the recordings of the interviews in 1991 capture her feelings and experiences directly from her.[1]

Diana remembered her childhood as an unhappy one. With her parents' constant arguing, her mother crying, and their eventual divorce when she was 7, one can easily conclude she felt unsafe. This is possibly where her low self-esteem, presented as humility, first began to grow. We see an example of her humility when she was 16 and met Charles. She remembered being "amazed" Prince Charles would show her any attention, asking herself "Why would anyone be interested in me?"

While her father, John Spencer, loved parties, Diana hated them, stating she always felt better alone. Often choosing to be by herself, Diana stated she wasn't interested in a "full diary" (the British term for calendar or datebook). "I kept myself to myself," Diana stated, which indicated an attempt to find comfort, a form of protection typical of an introverted HSP.

Prince Charles was her first boyfriend. Diana was never interested in boys, always keeping them away because she "couldn't handle it." Princess Diana often used the phrase, "It was too much," pointing to a sense of feeling overwhelmed, common among HSPs. She also kept herself "very tidy" feeling at the age of 13 she was destined to marry someone in the public eye—probably an ambassador of some sort, but not the "Top One," she joked. This feeling of clear-knowing or clairsentience points directly to her High Sensitivity. When combined with her preference to be alone and her humility, a conclusion can easily be drawn that she was in fact an HSP.

Contrary to the press coverage at the time, Diana had contact with the Royal family from an early age; she called Queen Elizabeth "Aunt Lilibet." She remembered being "shunted over to Sandringham" (the Queen's Norfolk home) for the holidays and she recalled the atmosphere at Sandringham being "most strange." She hated it and would "kick and fight" anyone who made her visit. The fact that to her, Sandringham felt "most strange" alludes to her ability to sense emotionally infused energy, another common trait with HSPs. The idea that she disliked the energy of a place so much that she, a British aristocrat typically known for being emotionally reserved, would throw a tantrum is telling of her sensitive nature. It also shows she was unaware of her abilities and had no techniques to deal with said abilities, other than pitching a fit, a common young Sensitive behavior.

In addition to clairsentience, Diana may also have been sensitive to smells, clairsalient. Her first memory as a child was a smell, the smell of her pram—her baby carriage. This again, to me, points to her sensitivity to smells, which we've already identified as a trait for HSPs.

It may have been Diana's empathy that garnered Charles' attention. She spoke several times of how the Prince must've felt. "He must've hated that," she said and told him empathetically, "You are lonely. You should be with someone who looks after you." "You don't need any aggravation." These memories point to Diana's level of consideration for Prince Charles, which may be natural in the presence of a Royal, but we see Diana's empathy and consideration for others repeatedly throughout her life.

In the footage of an early impromptu interview, Diana looked completely uncomfortable. She walked with her head down, excused herself when she bumped into a stranger, and was considerate of the cameraman's welfare. In early press photos, Diana repeatedly held her head down, uncomfortable with the attention, but considerate when responding and answering kindly. Diana stated she understood the press had a job to do—an extremely high level of compassion and empathy, considering how often she was hounded by the press.

We have already discussed the importance of overt support and care for Sensitives in our consideration of Saint Hildegard. We also see this desire to be unconditionally loved with Diana. It is clear Diana felt she needed more support—a clear theme throughout her life. She reported a lack of hugs during her childhood and a lack of support from the Royals later in her life. Diana reported that she felt she had no support in her childhood and absolutely no support from the Royal family at all.

Diana also admitted feeling very detached from everyone. While this can point to psychological issues, it certainly points to a defense technique for Sensitives. Detachment is a key technique in Buddhism. Once a person can step back from the emotionality of a situation and look objectively, that person can feel lighter and freer. Indeed, detachment from the physical realm is integral to enlightenment and is common for HSPs. Diana may have unconsciously detached from the physical world as a way to cope or function in such a physical and seemingly superficial world. We offer techniques to detaching in Chapter 22 – Mental Care.

Diana remembered when Charles proposed to her. In fact, she seemed to have a very strong vivid memory overall, able to recall dates and emotions, similar to that of Fredrick Douglass. When Charles proposed to Diana, she remembered hearing a voice inside telling her "You won't be queen, but you'll have a tough role." This event points to Princess Diana's possible clairaudience. While not as common as clairvoyant (clear seeing), clairaudient, meaning "clear hearing," is the ability to hear what is inaudible and is common in Intuitives. My interpretation of the event is that Diana heard a definite message with her extra-sensory hearing, giving her a peek into her future and offering her a choice.

Princess Diana also suffered from bulimia. She reports it was "a release of tension" for her. With just a mere off-hand comment about her body from Prince Charles, something clicked within Diana, and she began her battle with bulimia. This fact identifies two behaviors hinting of Diana's sensitivity. One; how deep and impactful words had on her, and two; while a physically unhealthy practice, a form of cleansing or releasing energy.

Highly Sensitive Persons are often easily devastated by the simplest, smallest of comments. We are often called shy or stuck up and typically viewed as different. Rejection is tantamount to death for us, and historically it was. When I think about it, I can better understand this debilitating fear we have of being shunned by our community.

Humans are social, pack animals. According to anthropologists, one of the reasons humans survived was because we were social and hunted in packs. Humans worked together to find and kill animals, encircling their prey and attacking together. When Europeans landed on the "New World," they needed to stick together for protection and safety, building forts and eventually cities. Humans used morality and commonly accepted behavior as a way to control the masses. But now, society is changing. Humans are smarter, and we are moving into an age more about the individual, so all that ancient programming can be discarded or transformed into something for our species' highest good. This ancient programming kicked into higher gear when Prince Charles made a careless comment about Princess Diana's weight. The comment affected her so deeply she lost 6 inches from her waist between her first wedding dress fitting and her last; she went from a 29" waist to 23.5" on her wedding day.

Princess Diana's bulimia (and her love of dancing and other athletics) may have been an attempt to release extraneous energy. Diana called it a release of tension, but the intention is the same. As a sensitive with no energetic boundaries, Diana would easily have soaked up energy from anywhere and everywhere. With all the attention she received, she may have felt all of it, all the love and admiration and all the cattiness and jealousy. All of it. With this amount of energy, a Sensitive needs to develop some techniques for release. Even Charles, on a certain level, was aware of this fact, as shown in his interview days before the wedding. He stated, "If you don't work out in your own mind some kind of method for existing and surviving this kind of thing, you will go mad."

In fact, the ability to release excess energy is the hallmark of a shaman: an empowered empath. In truth, every human has the ability to be a Highly Sensitive Person. What sets us apart is our natural capability, but it can be learned. I liken it to being an accountant. Anyone can be an accountant. For some it needs to be learned and practiced while for others it is so simple and easy. The hardest thing to learn for humans is releasing, letting go—whether it's memories, emotions, or last night's dinner. Sadly, in Diana's case, she binged and threw up as her chosen form of release. As a young adult in school, she was very active, swimming and ballet being her two favorite sports. Movement, in my opinion, is a very healthy and effective way to let go of excess energy an HSP may have soaked up. We discuss this further in Chapter 20 – Physical Care.

If you remember Diana, no doubt you remember the divorce and Camilla Parker Bowles' part in it. According to her recorded interviews, Diana was aware of Prince Charles' relationship with Camilla before the wedding, shattering Diana's fairy tale before it even began. This means Diana lived for 15 years with the knowledge that her husband had strong feelings for another woman; devastating for anyone, but unbearable for a Sensitive. Near the end of Diana's marriage, she confronted Camilla, an absolutely astounding thing for her to do. In her interview, Diana speaks of the night, the need to psyche herself up, the many times she backed down and didn't say anything. But one night she did. Diana walked up to Camilla and said, "I know." For Diana, this was a turning point. She stated it created "a shift, a tremendous shift" for her. She realized she didn't need the Royal family. Confronting her demons, so to speak, was very empowering for her. This is where we begin to see her change. She became more comfortable with herself and her role in the public eye. She walked through an active land mine field, literally, figuratively and emotionally.

While this episode makes for good drama, it is also a great lesson for us Sensitives. Traditionally, HSPs are shy, quiet wallflowers who run away from any sign of conflict or confrontation. We abhor it so much; we can make ourselves physically ill just thinking about it. And yes, Diana did, too. But she finally reached a point where she faced her fear, resulting in an amazing transformation. She went from a shy beautiful girl to an amazingly strong woman who could use her celebrity for good and highlight issues that were important and close to her heart.

Diana remembered "Emotionally, I was very screwed up, I thought." This sense of something being wrong with an HSP seems to be another common trait. The Nickerson Institute reports 80% of mental health patients are HSPs. Dr. Elaine Aron points out HSPs require the perfect environment for them to be well adjusted and thrive, just like orchids. As a result, mental issues can easily develop, especially in childhood, as well as a feeling of something being wrong with them. Many of my clients have reported a feeling of being an alien, or not fitting in even in their own family. While I absolutely understand and have compassion for this feeling, I want to point out that being different may be a good thing. As we have shown, being an HSP is a good thing. It may be a hard thing to be, but it is undeniably a good thing.

Lastly, I refer to Princess Diana's celebrity itself. From day one, we and the press were captivated by this lovely young woman. And it still has yet to fade, with the recent death of her former mother-in-law, Queen Elizabeth, there is a resurgence of Princess Diana. Documentaries are still available to anyone who wishes to remember or learn about The People's Princess. This clamoring to see and know the Princess points out her charm, her charisma, her energy—the very core of who she was.

PART II : THE HISTORICAL SENSITIVE PERSONS

How many times has a veritable stranger confessed something to you? I've heard "confidentially, I think I was a raccoon in a previous life," and other such non-sequitur comments or personal insights from complete strangers. Since everything is made of energy, we all give off an energy field. It seems the energy of Highly Sensitive Persons is very calming and attractive to others. While I have no data to support this theory, I believe Highly Sensitive Persons vibrate at a higher level than the majority of the population. On an unconscious level, with the majority buzzing around with no particular place to go, our energy is like a big comforting flower providing a sense of home, safety, and calm. Therefore, HSPs can easily attract attention, sometimes from too many or challenging people. Many of my clients have mentioned how their coworkers consider them to be the calmest person in the workplace. I can tell you from personal experience, when I was called the most grounded person in the company, I guffawed out loud. My mind constantly raced with tasks and my body always shook from nerves. How could I possibly be the most grounded of my coworkers? And if I was, holy smokes, what were my coworker's minds like? I shuddered at the thought. I have heard this type of interaction and reaction from many Sensitives. And it leads me to believe our level of vibration is calming or attractive to others.

When a Sensitive is in the public eye, that attraction can multiply and increase to levels of fervor. Think about all those young girls screaming and swooning for Elvis or the Beatles. Princess Diana experienced a similar situation. During her interview, the Princess remembered a conversation with Prince Charles. Charles spoke of how Camilla Parker Bowles was having a hard time with all the press outside her home, consisting of 2 reporters. Princess Diana looked out her window and saw 30 reporters. She said, "I never complained to Charles about the press, I didn't think it was my place." Yes, we and the press loved our Princess. We were drawn to her—couldn't get enough of her. Her energy was magnetic. She exuded love and compassion.

However, one thing Princess Diana never learned was to set boundaries. And that lack of boundaries was her downfall and possibly the inciting cause of her death.

The Historical Impact of Diana's Sensitivity

Princess Diana's sensitivity has and will have a lasting effect on our world first and foremost on her children, namely her son, William, the next King of England. William and Harry are very much like their mother; Harry possibly more so but the Princess's influences can be seen in both her sons. The idea of such a Sensitive on the throne is thrilling. While I am fairly sure Queen Elizabeth II was a Sensitive, as was her father and her son, now King Charles II, William is a possible double Highly Sensitive Person, receiving his Sensitivity from both sides of his family. With William carrying the compassion from his mother and the grounded energy of his grandmother to the throne, eventually, we will feel comfort and compassion again.

Princess Diana's sensitive legacy extends to the Royal family and what is allowed in a modern world, namely her divorce. Remember, Queen Elizabeth was alive in 1936 when the royals would not allow a King to marry a divorced woman. Now, a mere two generations later, the current King is divorced and remarried to a divorced woman. Hooray! The Royals are real people with struggles just like any human, proof money doesn't buy happiness. It must've been so challenging for Queen Elizabeth to know what the right thing to do was: the traditional path or the modern path. Princess Diana was so miserable as a Royal and quite emotionally vocal about her struggles that Queen Elizabeth had practically no choice but to order the divorce.

Princess Diana's sensitivity lives on most acutely in her son, Harry. He repeated his mother's walk through a live land mine field 25 years later. He stepped down from his royal duties to protect his wife Meghan, who was, like Harry's mother, not comfortable with the press and the racist comments. Because he is the spare heir, he can be more himself publicly. He does not carry all of the burdens of the monarchy's future on his shoulders so he can use his celebrity for causes as his mother once did.

SECTION 4: THE LESS THAN LOVING HISTORICAL SENSITIVE PERSONS

In an attempt to offer a balanced look at the Highly Sensitive Person character trait, I have scoured historical biographies to find possible HSPs who were not all love and light. Once people identify with the character trait, they find it difficult to understand how an HSP can be less than loving. It is important to remember that while the HSP trait leans more toward kindness and love, we are still humans and as such susceptible to human strengths and weaknesses.

As HSPs, we can be easily manipulated into doing things we wouldn't normally think of doing. My admittedly brief research has found a pattern of HSPs being seduced by power and using it for their personal gain; a cautionary tale to say the least. But let's delve into the darker side of history and HSPs. (If this isn't something you are comfortable with, please feel free to move on to the next section.)

I am hesitant to use simple terms like good or bad when referring to people and their actions or impact on history. This writing is not an attempt to condone or condemn; there is enough of that in our world. Again, we are simply looking at the person and their character or personality to see if they were Sensitive. Due to your possible sensitivity, this section will be short, glossing over the events and trauma these humans inflicted. I will be making my point and getting out.

CHAPTER 14

Niccolo Machiavelli

You may not be familiar with the actual man, Machiavelli. I certainly wasn't. I dismissed him immediately when in college I learned his most famous quote "The End justifies the means." To me, this 15th-century meme made me uncomfortable; it felt like carte blanche to do anything and everything to achieve one's goals. However, upon learning and reading more about the actual man, I discovered that he may have been a highly sensitive person and worthy of further investigation.

You may know Machiavelli best from his book, *The Prince*, or perhaps the personality trait named after his political viewpoints, Machiavellianism, a person who uses any means necessary to gain power (the underlying message of his famous quote). Machiavellianism is described as a "personality trait, someone who is cunning with the ability to manipulate."[1] This all sounds a bit cut-throat and devious for a sensitive, but let's examine who Machiavelli was.

The Historical Machiavelli

Niccolo Machiavelli was born on May 3, 1469, in Florence Italy, a time and place filled with many familiar names such as Medici, Savanarola, and Borgia. Niccolo's father, Bernardo Machiavelli, was a landowner but was not considered wealthy. His father was a bibliophile, a lover of books—the writings of the Greeks in particular. The printing press was invented around 1436, a mere thirty years before Niccolo was born, so books were new and expensive. Niccolo's father loved books so much that he brokered a deal with a publisher, earning his own copy of *Livy's History of Rome* by compiling the index, a task which took him 9 months to complete.[2]

Niccolo Machiavelli was a middle manager, an emissary, and a diplomat of the very early 16th-century, working for the Signoria, the governmental body of Florence. He was sent to places like Pisa and France to ask for potential financial or military support. Time and time again Machiavelli wrote to the Signoria stating that he did not have the authority, or power, needed for his situation and asked someone else, an ambassador, to be sent to negotiate more successfully. Machiavelli often felt out of his league and overwhelmed with his situation but, wanting the best for his city-state, he asked to be replaced by someone more adept. Repeatedly his requests and reports were not responded to or denied.

For the majority of his service as a Foreign Affairs Minister of the Florentine Republic, Florence was involved in a battle with Pisa. Pisa was an important port to the area and therefore to Florence. The question of who would control Pisa went back and forth for just over 100 years. The question was finally answered in 1509 when Florence defeated Pisa, with the help and command of Machiavelli.

While in office early in the 16th-century, Machiavelli developed the idea of a Florentine militia. His written recommendation on forming a military was drawn heavily from the writings of Livy and the ancient Roman army, although not stated outright. His concept was to no longer hire mercenaries to fight Florence's war, but to hire, pay, and train Florentine citizens to become a strong, loyal, and professional army. Machiavelli believed that militia men would fight harder due to a sense of patriotism and loyalty, thus winning the battle and the city. His recommendation was fully thought out, well-reasoned, and even included such details as the types of soldiers and bylaws.[3] One can almost feel Machiavelli's excitement about his idea, he finally had a solution. And it worked, he built his militia, and Pisa was overthrown and conquered by Florence.

Machiavelli was nearly 9 years old in 1478 when an assassination attempt was made on Lorenzo Medici. He was 29 when Savonarola was executed in 1498. In 1502, Machiavelli was 33 when he met Cesar Borgia (you may recognize his sister's name better, Lucrezia.) Some serious heavy hitters of history.

While Lorenzo Medici is known for his patronage of artists such as Botticelli, Da Vinci, and Michelangelo, and the flowering of the Italian Renaissance, he's also known for his misappropriation of state funds, a.k.a. embezzlement, a.k.a. stealing.

Savonarola was a Dominican monk who, through his prophecies and political activism, became ruler of Florence and eventually was publicly executed.

Cesar Borgia was named a Cardinal at the age of 18 by his father, the newly appointed pope, but resigned 5 years later for a career in the military. Doing very well for himself, he ruled over Milan and Naples but was unable to maintain his position due to, according to Machiavelli, his lack of support from the Papacy, Cesar's father. That must have been one uncomfortable dinner table.

With all these leaders and more swirling around Machiavelli, it's no wonder his writings have lived throughout the ages as handbooks for despots, tyrants, and dictators.

The Sensitive Machiavelli
Born amid the Italian Renaissance and a rebirth of Greek culture, Machiavelli loved learning, books, and history, especially the ancient Greek authors. He was known to retreat to his books for solace during challenging times.[4] Through his vast education, Machiavelli concluded people haven't changed since the Greeks. Machiavelli struggled with the same issues as the Ancient Greek authors. Therefore, he found guidance and comfort in their works.[5] When on diplomatic missions, he often used Ancient Greek philosophical points and paused to let the relevance to current situations settle in.[6]

The author, Erica Benner, in her work titled *Be Like the Fox: Machiavelli in His World*, offers an intriguing viewpoint that Machiavelli wrote ironically, even forward-thinking. Benner posits that Machiavelli wrote with the specific aim of causing the downfall of his readers, particularly rulers, essentially creating a how-to be overthrown (eventually) handbook.[7]

Machiavelli loved a "good conversation."[8] He was a prankster in his younger years. He loved creating a "sense of drama,"[9] and he was a student and observer of human behavior. He was a writer who reported on his observations. Machiavelli had the ability to step back from situations, talking with people of all walks of life to learn all sides of an issue, providing his bosses, the Signoria, with the most accurate reports and well-thought-out suggestions.

Machiavelli had a talent for communication, combining "boyish humility" with extreme knowledge and charm.[10] He was a good speaker, speaking "movingly" and using "the most suitable and affectionate words" to communicate his republic's plight.[11] With a talent for "deflating pretensions with only a delicate hint of malice,"[12] Machiavelli knew how much and when to reveal his feelings.[13] He knew what to say, when to say it, and how to say it. In one particular situation, Machiavelli slowed his speech down for Cardinal d'Amboise, giving the Cardinal time to absorb and conclude for himself.[14]

He was a "shrewd judge of men," reading through the facade and not manipulated by "nimble tongues" or "impressed by push-over victories."[15] He was a good and attentive listener, interviewing all sorts, from "gossip mongers" to men in the Florentine camp.[16] He had an amazing, possibly even eidetic, memory. When in attendance at a meeting between Bishop Soderini and Cesare Borgia, Machiavelli summoned "all his powers of concentration to store every word" in his mind so that he could write "an accurate record" back to the Signoria.[17]

All these abilities suggest that Machiavelli was likely a highly sensitive person with a strong intuition and an exceptional ability to read people—skills that would have been very useful for a diplomat.

The Historical Impact of Machiavelli's Sensitivity

Machiavelli is best known for writing the political philosophy *The Prince*. But he also wrote poems, comedies, and "carnival songs." He was an artist of the written word. *The Prince* and Machiavelli have become associated with ideas of treachery and deception, influencing many philosophers and earning a place in the "Hall of Fame" of philosophical thought.[18]

But I now believe time has been harsh to Signore Machiavelli. He was a staunch republican. Not in the modern sense of a political party, but rather, Machiavelli believed in a unified republic as the ideal form of government for the Italian peninsula. He believed in a people's government over the inherited monarchy or ruler. Benner presents a compelling argument, at least in my view, that Machiavelli's works are ironic or satirical and have been completely misunderstood since their original publication in 1532 and continue to be misunderstood even after nearly 500 years.

It may be time to re-read *The Prince* with a new viewpoint. While people's behavior may not have changed in 5,000 years, our viewpoints and beliefs (hopefully) have. And if they haven't, perhaps it's time they did. Machiavelli is perhaps the originator of the concept "question everything."

Machiavelli is known to some as the father of modern political science, based on his idea of ruling the world as it actually is instead of some silly fictitious utopia.[19] Forgive my sarcasm, but how's that workin' for ya? After nearly 500 years, we have governmental systems that are so intricate and intertwined with red tape that the unraveling of it seems nearly impossible. Improving one strand here squeezes and creates knots somewhere in the opposite direction.

We are at a crossroads, a time where people and their chosen leaders wish to bring about a more equal society and government. But, as I understand it, belief systems and traditions (the idea of how things have always been done) are getting in the way. Old thinking, like Machiavelli's writings, are holding back the evolution of society. A highly sensitive author wrote *The Prince* 490 years ago. It's time for highly sensitive inventors and thinkers to reimagine our governing bodies and the science of politics. I agree with Machiavelli; humans have not changed in 5,000 years, but perhaps it's time they do.

My Opinions of Machiavelli

When I think of Machiavelli as a highly sensitive person, I become even more amazed at his ability to merely observe and report. He lived during an extraordinary period in Italy, the Italian Renaissance, which was marked by both beauty and brutality. IF Machiavelli was an HSP, he was able to shield or protect himself from getting too involved, emotionally and energetically, and thus report and recommend accurately and intuitively. Today we, practitioners of energy, call this being in Observer Mode, a conscious form of detachment. I discuss the Observer Mode further in Part III, but I want to briefly mention it here because it is such an effective technique for Sensitives. It merits being highlighted and revisited repeatedly.

Observer Mode is when you emotionally remove yourself from the situation and look at it objectively. For instance, the year 2020. I think we can all agree that 2020 was a difficult and chaotic year, filled with highly charged emotional energy. But when I go into Observer Mode and calmly and rationally look at the events, I can understand the year better. Humans were forced to quarantine, either by themselves or in limited and constant company. Extroverts thrive on outside contact, enjoying being with others. Some might refer to them as "Vampires" because they draw energy and inspiration from other people. When an Extrovert is forced to be by themselves for an extended period of time, they energetically wither and go a little "crazy," which we observed. I often think sociologists will have a field day with studying the year 2020. As a Sensitive in Observer Mode, I found understanding, humor, and solace while living through 2020. Machiavelli was able to achieve the same technique, resulting in a removed, disinterested report of the events of his day.

I wonder what Machiavelli would feel about his work and how it's been received over time with his work being used as justification for cruelty and deceit. I honestly believe he would be shocked that 490 years later his work is still so popular and integral to both philosophy and politics. I'd like to believe Benner's topic sentence, Machiavelli wrote ironically. I believe, Machiavelli would chuckle and shake his head in dismay of how accurate and relevant his work was and still is. "They haven't fallen yet?" he would ask of the dictators. If he wrote a handbook on ruling with the intention of their eventual overthrow, how long is "eventually?" We have traded monarch for oligarch for autocrat. Not much has changed except the title. The desire for power still exists in some humans. Machiavelli would be both amazed and simultaneously not surprised.

Humans have changed since Machiavelli's day; some of us have evolved into more caring beings. Case in point, animal welfare. In just the last few decades there are stricter laws against animal abuse, animal rights organizations, and even spas where dogs can go to be pampered, definitely a move toward improvement in my book. Let's keep moving in the direction of more caring, more kindness, and more compassion. Let's move more into an Age of Sensitivity.

CHAPTER 15

Rasputin

Born Grigori Yefimovich Novykh on January 9, 1869, exactly one hundred years before me, Rasputin is known for his spooky eyes and influence over the last tsar of Russia, Nicholas II, and his wife, Alexandra. You may know Rasputin as the Mad Monk, despite his never taking holy orders or holding any official position in any religious organization. Many know the name Rasputin and the stories and mysteries that swirl around the end of the monarchy and the beginnings of communism in Russia. You may even be drawn to his time in history, it appears as another time of swirling energy and change. But, as Douglas Smith, author of *Rasputin: Faith, Power and the Twilight of the Romanovs* suggests, much of what we think of Rasputin may have developed after the fall of the Romanov dynasty and is therefore less than accurate.[1] One thing is certain, the name Rasputin is still alive and well and may be one of the most recognized figures of Russian history.[2]

The question of who Rasputin was is still hotly debated. In fact, Dr. Richard Spence states in The Great Courses class titled *The Real History of Secret Societies* (published as recently as 2019) that Rasputin was "clearly" a con man. But is anything clear when discussing Rasputin? Was he a man of God? Was he a charlatan? Could he really heal the Russian Prince Alexei? Or was it all just smoke and mirrors?

The Historical Rasputin

Little is actually known of Rasputin's childhood, right down to his name and date of birth. Due to Russia observing the Old Style calendar, many sources online write Rasputin was born on either January 21st or 22nd, while others state he was born on January 9 or 10th 1869 (I choose to use January 9th, because it is my birthday). The fact that little direct information about Rasputin and his first thirty years exists allows room for stories and legends to be created

PART II : THE HISTORICAL SENSITIVE PERSONS

and changed to fit the desired audience. Many stories portray young Grigori as a thief of horses, possibly leading to his nickname "Rasputin" which means "The Debauched One" in Russian. He was illiterate until adulthood, which was typical for his region and era, and was considered an "unruly youth."[3] A police report from 1909 describes the 20 year old Rasputin as a man of many "vices" including getting drunk and stealing before "disappearing and returning a changed man."[4] Rasputin would struggle and give into his vices his entire life, "frequently failing and giving way to sin," a fact Rasputin himself admitted.[5]

Rasputin's daughter, Maria writes in her book *Rasputin, The Man Behind the Myth* that his early years were filled with hard work on his father's farm, animal communication, and healing his father's horses. Maria never mentions her father's troubles with the law. She does go into depth with Rasputin's struggle with sex and its importance to his development. I do wonder, being a Puritan myself, if a daughter needed to know the size of her father's sexual member, but there it is.

Whatever the inciting reason (after having a vision from St Simeon or the Virgin Mary—Maria Rasputin writes that her father experienced a vision from "the Virgin of Kazan" the local name for the Virgin Mary[6] or to get out of hard work) at the age of 28 in 1897, Rasputin left his home in Russia, and his family of two young children and walked to Verkhouturye for religious study. He became a vegetarian, a wanderer, and a pilgrim and took on the mantle of a person experiencing a religious conversion. By 1905, he had a few followers, was introduced to the upper social circles of Moscow as a starets (Russian for holy man), and met Tsar Nicholas II and Tsarina Alexandra. According to Nicholas' own personal diary entries, Nicholas and Alexandra were quite taken by Rasputin immediately, seeing him repeatedly and as often as possible.

Rasputin's close relationship with the Tsar and Tsarina are stuff of legends. He is known to have healed many, including the hemophiliac Tsarevich Alexei, and to have had influence over the reigning monarchs. When rumors and allegations of Rasputin's nefarious and suspicious nature began to sweep newspapers and the upper crust, Alexandra did not listen or allow herself to be swayed from her opinion of him as a Holy Man. Alexandra believed Rasputin to be a miracle sent to save the monarchy, namely by healing her son. Rasputin's questionable acts stem from his touching and kissing women (his standard greeting for everyone, regardless of position) and by extension the allegations of sexual misconduct and even rape.

Rasputin influenced Tsar Nicholas, including his policy and political opinions. Maria Rasputin writes of her father convincing the Tsar against going to war. Rasputin was vehemently against the killing of anyone and talked Tsar Nicholas out of entering the Balkan War.[7] It was this influence over the Tsar that ultimately worried the aristocracy and members of the Duma, the Russian parliament.

One may easily conclude, in today's terms, that Rasputin was a sexual predator. He and his faithful followers always maintained the events that occurred between them were consensual and of a spiritual nature, pure and a way to get closer to God. Outsiders considered the events lurid, unnatural, and wrong. There were other holy men in the region with the same practices and allegations as Rasputin. Which neither clarifies, strengthens, or defends the practices. Adding to the muddling of Rasputin's story, Maria Rasputin writes that Rasputin maintained his marital vows until his wife permitted him to find comfort elsewhere after her emergency surgery, and even then remained faithful to one woman, Rasputin's long-time "servant" and lover Dunia Bekyeshova.[8] One tends to believe more a first-hand account, like Maria Rasputin, but given her close relationship, one does need to be wary of the author's bias.

The death of Rasputin on December 16, 1916 (December 29 in the new calendar and again varying sources state varying dates; some say December 17 and December 30 in the new calendar) is yet more stuff of legends, including a 2021 movie *The King's Man*. Legend says Rasputin was poisoned, shot dead, raised up, shot again. Then thrown in the freezing river. Even one of his murderers, Prince Yusupov, seems to have stretched or changed the story of Rasputin's death when Yusupov published his side of the story twice. Yusupov had fallen on hard times during the Russian Revolution and wrote of the murder for financial reasons.

One really must have a big belly laugh at the various and absurd portrayals of Rasputin's death. I have often imagined the scene complete with bumbling fools, like the Three Stooges, falling over each other thinking they have saved the monarchy, the country, and their own way of life, only to turn around and see Rasputin still alive, crawling up the stairs. The moment must've been beyond belief. It seems, the conspiracy to murder Rasputin included cyanide-laced cakes and wine but may have in fact been switched to aspirin at the last minute. He was shot twice in the chest. He appeared dead to his murderers. There was a human blood trail found in the snow, leading to the conclusion Rasputin stumbled outside. And he was found in the river frozen the next day with a point-blank bullet wound in the forehead. Maria Rasputin writes her father was shot in the head first, with four or five shots to the body, but ultimately died of drowning.[9]

The Sensitive Rasputin

When Rasputin is described by his contemporaries, his light blue-grey eyes or entrancing gaze is almost certainly included. What is also apparent about Rasputin is that he was either loved or hated; there doesn't seem to be an in-between with him. He was illiterate until his 30's, and he learned to read by reading the Bible. He had insomnia, a common experience for Sensitives. He was described as being clairvoyant and able to read people and see the future. And let's remember, his remarkable and, to some, inexplicable healing of Prince Alexei, an event which still denies a complete explanation to many. His daughter writes of many healings by Rasputin in his early years.

Rasputin's early wanderings and spiritual search feel genuine, at least to me. Rasputin "learned to read the Gospels, to contemplate their meaning, and to find God in all things."[10] "'I loved everyone indiscriminately,' he said. When bandits robbed him, he gave them everything he had saying 'it's not mine, it's God's.'"[11] These quotes describe to me a man who genuinely found peace and compassion and someone who wished to share his newfound viewpoint with as many as he could.

Rasputin's contemporaries described him as having a presence, one that was comforting and entrancing. "His eyes pierced you like needles."[12] He was comfortable in any social situation, from laypersons to the Russian court. In fact, it was this comfort or disregard for status or money, that seems to have been a point of contention with the upper crust of Russia. He is often described by witnesses as wearing peasant shirts, his hair and beard unkempt. The very idea that a peasant farmer would be comfortable and completely calm when meeting people of influence and country leaders is astonishing to both me now and those in attendance then. But it points to Rasputin's disinterest in society, money, or physical things and his confidence in his life's mission, one of loving all and eventually saving Russia.

His friendship with the Tsar and Tsarina inflated his head and ego. When returning from visiting the monarchs in St. Petersburg, Rasputin bragged of the gifts he received from Alexandra, specifically a silk shirt the Tsarina sewed herself (and was wearing at the time of his death) and an automobile. Rasputin's ego grew as the investigations and allegations grew, even becoming cocky with a sense of being untouchable (understandable given he was close friends with both God and the Tsar). At which time his spirituality either waned, was less important, or not reported. Maria writes no account of her father's ego growing or his spirituality waning. She reports that Rasputin lost his healing abilities while he was recovering from the first assassination attempt, a major knife wound to his stomach received on June 28, 1914, the day Archduke Ferdinand was killed, starting the First World War.[13]

The simple fact that Rasputin had a spiritual calling and healing ability is enough for me to consider him a Highly Sensitive Person, possibly empathic, especially given his clairvoyance, mystical future telling, and readings.

The level of controversy around Rasputin is a strong lesson to other Sensitives. Not everyone is ready to evolve, vibrate higher, and live harmoniously. We Sensitives may incur the wrath of fear-based humans. Some could even say, as I often do, that the reactions from others are more about them and their areas of weakness than they are about you. Much of Rasputin's experienced enmity stemmed from jealousy, from a former mentor Father Iliodor to his followers, even a spurned wannabe lover, and his eventual murderer Yusupov. According to Maria Rasputin, Rasputin remained his spiritual self, steadfast in what he believed was right and loving, while others around him wanted to corrupt him and use his abilities and relationship with the Tsar for their own good, rather than the Higher Good. When Rasputin remained steadfast in his beliefs, his followers turned against him. Rasputin's experiences only help to solidify my theory, that when you, as a Sensitive, feel attacked in some way, look to the attacker and follow their motives.

Yes, Russia was filled with discontent on every strata of life. Yes, there were "pot stirrers" to feed that discontent and fear. Yes, Rasputin was used as just one of many excuses for the people to overthrow the monarchy. And yes, Rasputin continued to be vilified after his death and after the Revolution. Sensitive Rasputin and his inexplicable abilities created awe and fear, but he was not the reason the monarchy was hated, but rather the last straw for the revolutionaries.

The Russian Revolution has been extensively researched and documented by experts, but it seems to me the heart of the issue was the Tsar's tone-deaf, detached, and untrained leadership, which bears the majority of responsibility for the Revolution. Maria Rasputin even agrees with me, writing the Tsar had "no guts."[14]

A Word about Tsarina Alexandra Federovna

Tsarina Alexandra, wife of the last Tsar Nicholas II, was born June 6, 1872, with the title Princess Alix of Hesse. She was the favorite granddaughter of Queen Victoria. Her mother, Princess Alice of the United Kingdom was Queen Victoria's third child and died of diphtheria when Alexandra was only 6 years old. This early and traumatic event seems to have had a huge effect on Alexandra, turning her from a happy child to a child of grief, seriousness, and great protection.

Several books describe Tsarina Alexandra's personality and easily confirm our question: The Tsarina Alexandra was a highly sensitive person. Many of her friends described the Tsarina as "shy," "terribly shy." Her shyness was often misunderstood as "haughtiness." For example, when Queen Victoria insisted Alexandra play the piano for an audience, Alexandra became nervous, her hands were clammy and described the incident as "one of the worst ordeals of my life."[15]

Candace Fleming, in her book *The Family Romanov,* describes Alexandra as shy, awkward, and having an extreme dislike for social events. Fleming includes detailed descriptions of the Tsarina's dresses, heavy brocades, dripping with diamonds.[16] My Sensitive Sleuth wonders if these heavily encrusted dresses were an unconscious form of energetic protection for the princess.

Fleming also writes of Tsarina Alexandra's personality as a child, noting her nickname was Sunny, a happy child always laughing. After her mother's death, Sunny became Cloudy overnight, "turned aloof, serious and withdrawn." The future Tsarina became "perpetually mistrustful" and "strangely empty of tenderness and . . . hostile," keeping "people at a distance."[17] A form of protection if ever I heard.

Tsarina Alexandra was a strongly devout person. She converted from Lutheranism to Russian Orthodox in order to marry Nicholas. She covered the walls of her bedroom with 700 religious icons. When her son, Tsarevich Alexei, was ill she covered his room and surrounded his bed with icons. When a challenging moment arose in her life, her response was to pray and pray harder. She came to accept all things mystic as an extension of the Russian Orthodox Church and therefore believed it all.[18]

The Tsar and Tsarina adored their children, protecting them from the world and choosing to play and spend time with the family instead of ruling a country. They were particularly protective of their young sickly son, Tsarevich Alexei, keeping his hemophilia secret as much as possible and the young man away from any potentially harmful activity.

One very telling characteristic of Tsarina Alexandra's sensitivity is her actions during World War I. Most of her life as a mother was spent worrying about her son's life to the point of illness (migraines and backaches) and seclusion, even from her daughters.[19] When she did participate in life outside her lilac-painted religious icon-filled bedroom, she usually sat down, resting. But when the world broke out in war in August 1914, she stood up, walked out of her protected sacred space, and converted one of her palaces into a hospital, where she and her two oldest daughters visited daily.[20] With the philosophy of "One must do what one can during times like these," Tsarina Alexandra was strong and solid, just like Eleanor Roosevelt during World War II. She found a purpose greater than herself and went to help however she could. This is a lesson every Highly Sensitive Person can learn from. When we are needed, we Sensitives are there, present, and ready to help.

I personally have experienced that feeling of certainty, usefulness. Usually, I'm flighty, skimming from task to task like a butterfly at the Botanic Gardens. Often flitting so quickly I've forgotten where I was flitting to. But a few times in my life I've known I was needed. And surprising myself (and everyone around me), I was grounded and sure of myself, knowing exactly what needed to be done and accomplishing the goal calmly and resolutely. I agree with First Lady Roosevelt; it really is a good feeling. I walked away realizing and understanding my sensitivities much more. I AM a butterfly, just hanging around until I am needed, then I am a rock. Huh . . . who knew? Tsarina Alexandra and First Lady Roosevelt, that's who.

The Historical Impact of Rasputin's Sensitivity

So how did Rasputin's sensitivity affect history? Rasputin's ability to heal (or at the very least, calm the suffering) seems to have become almost a footnote in the chapter of the Russian Revolution. What survives are outrageous stories of sex and murder. (Oh, we humans love our scandals and drama, don't we? And if that is what you are into, I suggest reading Maria Rasputin's book; it is filled with all kinds of drama.)

Rasputin's magnetism and energy attracted the upper echelon of Russian society. Those who were uncomfortable with him threw verbal daggers at him, which he seemed adept at dodging. But it was his friendship with Tsarina Alexandra that really caused a stir. Her faith in Rasputin always remained strong and unwavering, even if it was a little fear-based that her son would die if Rasputin couldn't help Alexei. Rasputin's sensitivity, combined with that of Tsarina Alexandra's, his desire to help save the empire, and her faith and desire to keep her son and future Tsar alive created such a deep and soul-binding energy that others became jealous and therefore nasty. Their relationship, along with Rasputin's very being, became another reason for the monarchy's downfall and the Revolution's outbreak, which reshaped the world and continues to have ramifications today.

Love him or hate him. Shaman or charlatan. Angel or Satan incarnate. Rasputin was a Sensitive.

CHAPTER 16

Joseph Stalin

Most of us know Stalin as the communist leader of Soviet Russia during the Second World War and his reign of fear. Stalin, to me, is a prime example of someone being both good and bad; it completely depends on your viewpoint. As an American, I was taught Stalin and communism were bad; Russians still hail him as a hero. Good or bad depends on your perspective. Again, my perspective and interest in Stalin is purely a Sensitive one, not one of judgment or blame.

The Historical Joseph Stalin

Joseph Stalin was born December 9, 1879, in Gori, Georgia, an area in southern Russia. His father was a shoemaker (Stalin worked in the shoe factory for a short time when he was a child), an alcoholic, and apparently abusive. His mother, determined her son would do well, worked every angle for her son's education, asking anyone, and possibly prostituting herself, for his scholarly sponsorship. In the summer of 1895 at the age of 16, he entered the seminary where he was a "bookworm" with "autodidact tendencies."[1] He completed a two-year mandatory parish school curriculum in a single year and continued on to the four-year curriculum. He was "the quintessential autodidact, never ceasing to read, no doubt as solace, but also because he remained determined to improve and advance himself."[2] (FYI, an autodidactic is someone who can teach themselves. I find it quite funny that I had to look that up, isn't it ironic?)

With his "sweet alto singing voice," Stalin enjoyed singing in the choir and even won prizes for his singing which was a source of pride for him.[3] He also enjoyed writing poetry, having a few published in the Iveria (a local newspaper).[4]

While in the seminary, he made friends with some revolutionary-thinking students. It is at this point he "becomes convinced that existing conditions are wrong and unjust" and "resolves to do the best" he can to "remedy them"[5] and begins his revolutionary path, similar to Harriet Tubman.

Whether from accident or genetics (or a combination of both), at the age of 6, his left arm and shoulder began to develop abnormally, a condition which remained throughout his life.[6] He also experienced the "litany of childhood diseases (measles, scarlet fever)"[7] and most notably smallpox, which left his face slightly pockmarked and open to ridicule and name-calling. Due to chronic sore throats and swelling (peritonsillar abscess), Stalin had a "softness of his voice; even after microphones were introduced, he could sometimes barely be heard."[8]

Stalin had a "reputation for self-centeredness,"[9] a "strong interest in the arts, especially the music world,"[10] and a strong work ethic fueled by an "unquestionably greater energy, indefatigable capacity for hard work . . . and above all his enormous particularistic organizational talent."[11]

Ruwan M. Jayatunge in *"Joseph Stalin - Psychopathology of a Dictator"* writes of Stalin's "inferiority complex" and his lack of sympathy as key to his pathology. Jayatunge writes of how in November 1907, at the age of 28, Stalin was inconsolable after his first wife's death: "Stalin was emotionally devastated." Stalin wanted to throw himself into her grave. He became "emotionally numbed and said to his friends 'my last warm feelings for humanity died.'" Stalin's numbness "becomes the central feature of his character."[12]

Stalin's Sensitivity Decoded

The question that is natural to ask, how can someone responsible for the "deliberate deaths of 6 million"[13] souls be a highly sensitive person? That's not very sensitive, you may have noted. In fact, it is downright horrendous. Yes, absolutely. The ending of 6 million lives is horrendous and hard to fathom. To us empaths such an event can hurt emotionally, spiritually, and even physically. But one can be an HSP and an inflictor of evil.

These admittedly handpicked qualities of Stalin point to his potential as an HSP. His love of the arts and music, his writing poetry, his insatiable endeavor to read, learn, and improve, along with his autodidactic ability all point to his sensitivity.

What I find fascinating about Stalin is his ability to shut off his emotions. After the death of his wife, he, apparently, became so overwhelmed with grief and guilt that he just turned his emotions off and detached to the utmost degree. Now, HSPS are known for their sensitivity to emotions. We can very easily be overwhelmed with emotions; it is a core characteristic, and processing our emotions is a key skill of being a Sensitive. Our emotions, and others', can drive us absolutely batty. We can be moved to tears easily by beauty (an

PART II : THE HISTORICAL SENSITIVE PERSONS

amazing sunset or the perfect song, even a Christmas commercial) and pain (the evening news).

But, I believe, it was Stalin's denial of his emotions that "turned" him dark. He was always ambitious and driven, yes. But his ambition, his initial mission or purpose, was that of a "freedom fighter" to make right the injustices of the world, make the world better, a more equal place for workers, not to kill 6 million souls. His ambition and drive turned angry and dangerous after he shielded himself, cut himself off, denied his emotions and who he was as a Sensitive. It was this denial of who he was and his abilities that made him the person history knows. It's a shame really, to think, he could've been one of the people who ushered in an era of equality for humanity. President Abraham Lincoln used his losses and grief to empathize and free the slaves. Stalin cut himself off from his emotions and killed millions. I guess the world and humans just weren't ready.

CHAPTER 17

Adolph Hitler

Adolph Hitler. Whew! That's a name that still packs a wallop after nearly 80 years. We all know what he did, and many have written about him and World War II. He is included ONLY to show the HSP character trait can be either light or dark. For this reason, we will keep our references and words to a minimum, purposely leaving out his own writings, as they are not reliable as fact and even today the darkness can be felt through the page.

The Sensitive Adolph Hitler

Adolph Hitler was born on April 20, 1889, in Austria. His teenaged friend, August Kubizek, wrote a book about his friendship with Adolph titled *The Young Hitler I Knew*.

Very little facts are known of Hitler's early childhood. Most historians gloss over Adolph's early life and describe him simply as a failed artist. Kubizek writes that their friendship was centered around art, both hoping and training to be artists in Linz and later in Vienna;[1] in fact, they met at the opera.[2] Adolph was interested in all forms of art, not only painting, (watercolors being his preferred medium) but also architecture,[3] and opera (he even composed one).[4]

With their friendship solely based on a mutual love of the arts and Kubizek's ability to smile and nod, Kubizek writes of a young man "passionately interested in everything,"[5] who made speeches even when Kubizek was the only audience member. "He just had to talk and needed someone who would listen."[6] In the introduction, written by Ian Kershaw, Kershaw posits the reason for their friendship was due to Kubizek's deference and willingness to listen to Hitler talk and talk and talk.[7]

Kubizek writes of a man who was intensely private with a short fuse and easily angered (similar to Monet), but Adolph was completely different when out walking in nature.[8] "The outdoors had an extraordinary effect on him,"

Kubizek writes. Adolph seemed to be a completely different person, feeling "at home" in nature. Adolph was relaxed, focused, and "collected" in the woods and hills of Linz. "He was never so collected and concentrated as when walking along the quiet paths." On sunny days, Kubizek writes, the "revivifying wind . . . drove" Adolph "into the woods and fields."[9]

This personality change seemed contradictory to Kubizek because while Adolph loved being outdoors, he couldn't live in the less populated country. "He needed people," Kubizek explains, he needed contradictory interests, he needed people's ambition, he needed their "intentions" and "desires," and he needed a "problem-laden atmosphere."[10] All these characteristics hint at Adolph being an extroverted Sensitive.

There is a legend among First Nation people, attributed to a few tribes, but this version comes from the Nanticoke Nation. The tale goes something like this, there are two wolves battling for domination within each of us. One wolf is good, filled with light and love and all things good. The other is filled with darkness, shame and pain. The question of which wolf wins is answered: "the The one you feed." Adolph Hitler is a prime example of what can happen when you feed the darkness exclusively.

The Buddhist tradition, as described by Tsultrim Allione in her book *Feeding Your Demons*, teaches, as the title would suggest, to feed both wolves, the light and the dark.[11] By giving your "Dark Side" space to be you actually banish or naturally quiet that Demon. I equate it to be similar to a two-year-old in the grocery store. Your two-year-old will repeatedly and incessantly repeat "Mommy, Mommy, Mommy" and if they do not receive a response, they will increase in volume, "MOMMY, MOMMY, MOMMY!" Until you finally, respond "What, baby?" At which time, the child quiets down and sweetly asks, "May I have a cookie?" "Yes, of course you may." And your child is happy, and you can continue shopping.

Many Sensitive (spiritually minded or otherwise) often tell me "Oh, this is awful to think" or "I shouldn't think bad thoughts" and they will ignore that "bad" thought/feeling and push it down, neglected and avoided. Humans believe that if we don't allow ourselves to think bad thoughts, they won't exist. But here's the rub, those thoughts do exist and will continue to grow and clamor for your attention like your two-year-old, until you acknowledge them. Resisting or denying your dark side (ie: starving the dark wolf) does not make it go away, it only makes it hungrier. Sensitives, and indeed all humans, need, at the very least, to acknowledge they have a "dark side," and at the very best, provide space for their dark side, let out those dark thoughts, and give them room to fly away. A very helpful technique for this is The Character Chat in Chapter 21.

My Opinion of the Sensitive Adolph Hitler

I have long suspected something "happened" in Hitler's youthful years. My research was very frustrating to me because I couldn't find any stories or evidence from his first 15 years. It doesn't take a genius to guess Hitler had some trauma/drama in those formative years. Finally, once I let go of searching, I came across Alice Miller's book *For Your Own Good: Hidden Cruelty in Child-Rearing and the Roots of Violence*. Robert Moore and Douglas Gillette further Miller's idea in their book, *The Magician Within: accessing the shaman in the male psyche*, referencing Miller by writing Adolph Hitler "was physically and emotionally brutalized by his father. His father never called him by name, used a dog whistle to summon him, locked him in closets for days for the merest infractions, and taught him that tender emotions were unacceptable to "real men."" Young Adolph admired his father's "strength"; at the same time, unconsciously, he hated him with an animal fury. From his father he learned too to hate and despise his "weak" mother, who was never able to stand up to her husband's brutality."[12] In her Preface to the British Edition, Alice Miller states "Hitler never had a single other human being in whom he could confide his true feelings; he was not only mistreated but also prevented from experiencing and expressing his pain; he didn't have any children who could have served as objects for abreacting his hatred; and finally, his lack of education did not allow him to ward off his hatred by intellectualizing it. Had a single one of these factors been different, perhaps he would never have become the arch-criminal he did."[13]

Finally, and sadly, some inkling of Hitler's youth. This information from Alice Miller hints at a small explanation for Hitler's unyielding devastation. "Adolph learned that gentleness, tenderness, and love had no power to help him. He learned to despise the human qualities that never came to his aid. Consequently, he repressed them whenever they appeared within himself."[14]

Hitler's reaction, that of being stiff and stern, to his abusive youth years, makes sense especially when considering his possible Sensitivity. Many of us Sensitives will make a vow, sometimes consciously out loud or otherwise, to never let "this" (traumatic event) happen again. I can remember being about age 12 when I felt I was "broken" and vowed I would never have kids because I didn't want to pass on this pain and mental anguish. Lo and behold about 40 years later, I am childless. I made that vow true. I can hear Hitler making a similar vow, whatever it may have been. With the memory and scars of his father so deep within him, keeping that vow would've been easy to do. I can visualize a young boy, shuddering and huddled in a dark scary closet vowing, "I will never let this happen to me again. I will never allow myself to be hurt again." In order to ensure his vow was kept, I can see him closing off any semblance of nurturing or caring for himself, building a huge stone-thick wall around his heart, and metaphorically picking up a weapon. I can feel the boy melting away and a really pissed-off fire-breathing dragon rise in its place.

I know it sounds crazy, but when I focus on that little boy, I feel sorry for Hitler. Without any skills, tools, and willingness to turn within and heal that small, scared boy, we can begin to understand how Hitler became Hitler. We get a Sensitive who only knows to fight and punish fueled by vengeance who directs his self-hatred upon others.

The Historical Impact of Adolph Hitler's Sensitivity

Again, the impact of this person is well known and documented, but we will attempt to highlight the positive long-term impacts. World War II was the first time humans began to feel like a cohesive global community, united against a common goal. The tragedies and traumas committed against humans roused the righteous fighters like never before. The war created a decided duality, forcing everyone to choose a side, Axis or Allies.

Today the world seems just as divided, with the Me Too Movement and the Black Lives Matter organization. I can draw a line from World War II to the Me Too Movement. With men going off to fight, women stepped into the workplace. Once the war was over and the men returned, many women kept their jobs, changing the workplace and society. Thus, the Working Woman began to gather strength and power. Enter the 1960s and feminism and by the 1970s and 80s, the Working Mother was commonplace. However, the behaviors of men had not evolved and thus today in the early 21st century, we see people setting clear boundaries due to the Me Too Movement. In my opinion, the Me Too Movement can be considered a result of the Second World War and Hitler. The effects of World War II and Hitler are still being worked out and evolving today.

The emotions of Germans between the wars were of desperation. Like the rest of Europe and America, Germany's economy was depressed. Germans were scared and angry, partly from the shock of losing the First World War. During the First World War, the German government disseminated false propaganda reporting only positive news. The factual news of Germany's loss sent disbelief throughout the population, including Hitler. Leaving citizens to ask questions like, "How did we lose, we were doing so well?" Enter a new false narrative, similar to the "Lost Cause" of the American South after the Civil War. The central theme, "We didn't lose the war, we were cheated out of the war, these guys lost the war for us. We will rise and be strong again." The Germans were angry and directed their energy, sadly, toward anyone different than the ultimate Germanic human.

Now, if Adolph was a Sensitive, an empath even, he was surrounded by all this anger and hatred. With no tools or techniques to release this energy, Adolph would have become filled and overwhelmed with the energy of his environment. Adolph didn't invent anti-semitism, it has sadly existed for centuries for various misguided reasons. He was in the middle of the swirling energy of hatred with no protection or cleansing. With the energy growing to astounding levels, he brought the anger and fear to a head and made it an undeniable force that had to finally be reckoned with.

An interesting side note, Adolph spent the bulk of the Second World War either underground in bunkers or outside of the city, outdoors. My Sensitive Sleuth again sees this as his attempt to release the energy of the majority and ground himself. It feels, to me, as if he wanted to stay away from the energy, the great whirlwind of hatred and anger that he unleashed. It is as if he knew the turmoil must occur for a better world to emerge, but he couldn't face it.

Today, there is more understanding and appreciation for being different—at least we are on the road toward it. The Second World War can be viewed as a huge lesson learned for humanity. With many sacrifices made for us to learn that lesson, let's hope it is finally and completely learned once and for all so humanity may evolve into a more accepting, equal, and loving society. To understand lessons learned and soul contracts, see the Sacred Contracts section in Part III.

CHAPTER 18

J. Edgar Hoover

Most people, if they recognize the name, know J. Edgar Hoover for his long-standing work developing the F.B.I. but he is more notoriously known for his files. He was known to have files on everyone in the public eye, including Eleanor Roosevelt and Martin Luther King. He is known to have had eyes and ears everywhere (talk about an invasion of privacy). You may be familiar with the movie *J. Edgar*, released in 2011 directed by Clint Eastwood and starring Leonardo di Caprio, which touches on Hoover's possible homosexuality. During Hoover's life and beyond, rumors about his cross-dressing and sexuality persisted. The question still swirls, unanswered, mainly because only Hoover knows the answer, and it's solely his business. Let's look at what we do know about Hoover.

The Historical J Edgar Hoover

John Edgar Hoover was born in Washington D.C. on New Year's Day, 1895. He lived his entire life in the District. As a young adult, he had a slender build, "slightly smaller than average,"[1] choosing education over sports. He had a stutter which he overcame by training himself to speak quickly, becoming the leader of the debate team. "He was smart, fit and well-trained." As class valedictorian and captain of his high school cadet corps, he led his school's group in Woodrow Wilson's inaugural parade in 1913.[2]

At the age of 18, Hoover worked in the Library of Congress and attended law school at George Washington University. He was impressed by the Library's organization and catalog system, a concept he would later use at the Bureau (and possibly his private files). As a Sensitive Capricorn who loves books and organization myself, I can completely understand his admiration for the Library.

After receiving his law degree in 1917, he began to work for the Justice Department. He was known to have a very strong work ethic, arriving to work early, staying late, working weekends, and volunteering for additional duties.[3] This work ethic combined with his "impeccable integrity,"[4] attention to detail, decision making, and "willingness to give orders"[5] caught the eye of Harland Fiske Stone, the then attorney general. In 1924, Hoover was named Assistant Director of the then-titled Bureau of Information.

Hoover cleaned up and straightened out the corrupt and poorly managed Bureau, established a dress code, job requirements (including no criminal history), and even physical standards for the Bureau's employees. Incidentally, Hoover did not allow women to be agents at that time, in fact, he didn't think much of women for most of his life. He served as the first director of the Federal Bureau of Investigation for 48 years (from the Teapot Dome scandal to Watergate). He became well known to the American public during the 1930s for his arrest of many catchy-named depression-era gangsters, like "Baby Face" Nelson, "Pretty Boy" Floyd, and "Machine Gun" Kelly.

But he's also known for his abuse of power. While not serving during World War I or any war, he loved the military, possibly more for its order, discipline, and organization than for the fighting. He ruled his bureau with an iron fist, and agents worked hard to avoid being verbally abused for the slightest infraction.

Hoover's files are the stuff of legend. He was rumored to have something on everyone, including the eight presidents he served, particularly Nixon. For example, when Hoover was nearing the mandatory retirement age of 70, it is rumored that Hoover forced President Johnson to sign an executive order allowing Hoover to remain in office indefinitely, which he did until his death in 1972.

Like Florence Nightingale, Hoover's strict discipline can be better understood when we consider his original Bureau of Information was rife with corruption and unprofessionalism. Agents were known to have received bribes to look the other way. Some agents had criminal records. Hoover was tasked with cleaning up the department as well as its reputation. He did this well. But it feels like he took his original task and ran with it to become the "most powerful man in America" through intimidation and blackmail. Anyone Hoover did not approve of, be it for their actions or beliefs, fell under his eye and scrutiny. Consider First Lady Eleanor Roosevelt. Hoover had her watched by his agents because, while living in Greenwich Village, she had bohemian friends who challenged traditional lifestyles and beliefs, and who held socialist views—both definite no-no's in Hoover's world.

PART II : THE HISTORICAL SENSITIVE PERSONS

The Sensitive Hoover

Hoover loved order, organization, and was known for his hard line and morals. He was a good student, earning "Excellent Plus" on his early report cards, "a star student from the start."[6] Anthony Summers, in his book titled *Official and Confidential: The Secret Life of J. Edgar Hoover*, writes of one account of Hoover as a "'high strung' child, 'sickly,' and excessively fearful, clinging to his mother whenever he could."[7]

Interestingly, as Assistant Director, Hoover found himself needing to make speeches that "terrified him."[8] I would've thought that leading the debate team, while arguing for the continuation of capital punishment and against votes for women, would have helped him overcome his stage fright. But apparently, like many HSPs, he was uncomfortable being in the spotlight. During the 1930s, with the headline-grabbing arrests, Hoover became well-known and nationally accepted. He learned to be more comfortable as a public figure, but still wanted the Bureau to be known more than him. However, by the 1960s, power may have gone to his head as he wielded his power of information easily and boldly.

J. Edgar Hoover had two big loves in his life, the Bureau and his dogs, Spee De Bozo, in particular. The Airedale was his constant companion at home. A photo of Spee De Bozo sat on Hoover's desk. Hoover even held a funeral for Spee De Bozo, which was "one of the saddest days" of his life.[9]

Hoover was a "brilliant chameleon."[10] Hoover could "conceal" his true beliefs and feelings when necessary. Hoover's aide, William Sullivan, said "he could be all things to all people . . . If a liberal came in, the liberal would leave thinking, 'My God, Hoover's a liberal.'"[11] The ability to be all things to all people is a strong characteristic for Highly Sensitives. It often leaves us wondering who we really are and what we really like. Do I like macaroni and cheese because I like macaroni and cheese or because my grandmother liked to make macaroni and cheese? This ability is an extension of being sensitive to the subtleties of our environment, a clairsentient. We can sense, or read, the room and become whatever the room needs to feel more comfortable.

William Sullivan is quoted regarding Mr. Hoover's ability to manipulate others. Similar to Harriet Tubman's acting and storytelling and Frederick Douglass' hustler's ability, Hoover "was a master con man." Mr. Sullivan says, "'One of the greatest con men the country has ever produced, and that takes intelligence of a certain kind, an astuteness, a shrewdness.'"[12] This ability can also be described as reading the person and being what that person needs, essentially a clairsentient chameleon.

According to Mr. Hoover's long-time secretary, Miss Helen Gandy, Hoover had his heart broken in 1918. The pain of the relationship rippled throughout his twenties, leaving Hoover with "no emotional connection with anyone except" his mother, Annie.[13] Similar to Stalin, Hoover's ability to keep people and emotions at bay was noted by a few of his contemporaries. Edgar's niece, Dorothy, is quoted as saying Hoover was "'inclined to push us all away.'" Another of Hoover's nieces, Margaret, said Hoover seemed to have a "'fear of becoming too personally involved with people.'" Furthermore, Hoover's aide, William Sullivan, is reported to have said Edgar "didn't have affection for one single solitary human being around him.'"[14] We have seen this capability before with Stalin and how he dealt with emotional pain. As highly sensitive people, we are prone to experiencing more emotions, deeper and stronger. The majority of emotions we feel are not entirely our own. If we are not aware of our ability to absorb the emotions surrounding us, we can be overwhelmed and potentially unable to function. When this happens, like Stalin and Hoover, we can shut off our ability to feel. It also seems this absolute emotional detachment may be when Sensitives become dangerous or dark, losing our sense of empathy and ruminating in our anger.

One of Edgar's high school classmates described him as "slim, dark and intense." Hoover's classmate continued, "he sat off by himself against the wall, and always had the answers. None of us got to know him very well."[15] This solitary lifestyle was a theme throughout Hoover's life. He chose to live with his mother until her death and then alone. The fact that Hoover was a loner also points to his possible sensitivity. Oftentimes, sensitives feel they don't belong, sometimes not even in their own family. If a sensitive lives around low vibrating emotions, namely anger, guilt, or shame, we can absorb those emotions and become depressed or lethargic. In order to cope, we wish and need to be alone.

Sensitives need alone time regularly. This Me Time allows us to release excess energy and recharge our batteries. When Sensitives are aware of their abilities, a common, and in my mind required, technique is to shed or release energies that are not their own. When a Sensitive is not aware of this ability, it can create serious havoc, both emotionally (as we've seen), physically, and in some cases, globally (i.e. Hitler).

Interesting side note, Dickerson Hoover, Edgar's father, described as "kindly and gentle," was known to have bouts of depression (termed melancholia at the time) and spent time in an institution for help.[16] Remember, the Highly Sensitive Person character trait is inherited.

J. Edgar Hoover was a religious man. He sang in the choir, was an altar boy, and taught in Sunday school. When in high school, he debated for capital punishment on the basis that the "Bible stands for Capital Punishment."[17] A lifelong churchgoer, he always kept a Bible on his desk. He took "religion very seriously indeed."[18] Hoover himself stated he could've walked one of two paths, one with the law or one with the church.[19] While we cannot trust the complete accuracy of his statement, it does show his strength of faith and could be a clue to Hoover's empathic abilities. Empaths are sometimes described as Sensitives with a spiritual component.

The Historical Impact of Hoover's Sensitivity

John Edgar Hoover lived during what is often referred to as the bloodiest century, the 20th-century. He lived in a city that was all about power and manipulation. He worked for and with eight American presidents, from Calvin Coolidge to Richard Nixon. He was the Director of the FBI during the Depression, World War II, the Cold War with Russia, the Korean War and the Vietnam War, the Cuban Missile Crisis, and the Civil Rights Movement, tumultuous times filled with fear. It was a time of controlling or being controlled, and J. Edgar Hoover appeared to have done both. Living with a controlling and religious mother for 43 years until her death, J. Edgar learned to control his emotions, mostly by pushing them down and not dealing with them.

Hoover controlled both his inner and global chaos with order and organization, a clear benefit for the FBI and possibly the nation. He established forensic techniques, such as a fingerprinting system and procedure, all of which are the basis of the Bureau today. He used his personal need for safety and security to develop the Federal Bureau of Investigation into a "premier national security organization with both law enforcement and intelligence responsibilities."[20]

His surveillance techniques opened the door to loosen Americans' right to privacy, a door that some believe opens wider and wider daily. His zeal for security, both personal and national, led to his critics accusing him of violating First Amendment constitutional rights. All of his accomplishments are a result of who he was, his strengths and his weaknesses, his Sensitivity.

Sensitives, more than most, feel fear. With Hoover in the center of power during a time of such fear, I can only imagine his ability to suppress his fear was a benefit to him, allowing him to function and perform his duties to the best of his ability. Hoover's inner control enabled him to push away the fear. Many Sensitives experience varying degrees of anxiety. In my opinion, this is a physical form of fear. For some Sensitives, this anxiety can be debilitating. Hoover seems to have been able to use his fear for the better, at least in his mind, by turning it outward onto others such as the country's criminals, making the country safer.

My Opinions of Hoover and his Sensitivity

Hoover was an intelligent man. A man of high and strict morals. A religious man. A man who spent time alone whenever possible. A man who loved dogs. A man who was overcome with emotions to such an extent, he learned to cut them off. A man who consciously crafted his reputation. A man who liked being in the shadows and out of the spotlight. A man who held himself, and all others, to strict discipline and control, to a level of perfection so high it was impossible to reach and therefore feared.

When we combine all these facts about Hoover, a picture begins to form, a picture of a Highly Sensitive Person, a man with extraordinary talents who wished deeply to make an impact on his country by making his Bureau respectable and professional (similar to Florence Nightingale). Hoover's ambition for perfection inevitably led to failure, as it was impossible to achieve or maintain. Esther Bergsma, in her book *The Brain of the Highly Sensitive Person; Why you shouldn't judge a fish by its ability to climb a tree*, writes that fear of failure is common in HSPs, presenting in reportedly 64% of adults and 60% of children. She also writes about how this fear of failure can present itself as perfectionism, also common in HSPs. "60% of HSPs worldwide" find it difficult to accept mistakes from themselves as well as others.[21]

I can completely relate to Hoover and his desire to be perfect and his fear of failure. I often catch myself holding my body very tight when I am doing something that requires delicacy or accuracy. It feels like I am a living game of Jenga—one wrong move and it's all over. I want whatever I'm doing to be right and supportive. Therefore, I will either wait until I have more information or clench my body while performing the perceived scary task. I wonder if Hoover clenched his muscles, too.

All of this leads me to conclude that J. Edgar Hoover was a Sensitive with a fear of failure, which drove his pursuit for perfection. When that perfection was not attained, Hoover lashed out as a form of release (fear and control). Not being a psychologist, it's fairly clear to me that J. Edgar Hoover had a deep unconscious hatred of himself. As a result, he turned that hatred onto others, like Adolph. Carl Jung is known to have said, "Everything that irritates us about others can lead us to an understanding of ourselves." Likewise, Marian Keyes succinctly stated, "The things we dislike most in others are the characteristics we like least in ourselves."[22] Greg Braden often writes about The Mirror, suggesting the outer world is a reflection of one's inner world. Hoover seems to have been the Poster Child for these philosophies. We can see his hatred for himself acted out against those who embrace his own rejected parts of himself. He felt different and did everything he could to be accepted by societal norms. Here were people who didn't care a flying fig about societal norms and lived their lives as they saw fit, not what society told them. We can see where Hoover would be both jealous and angered by their bravery to embrace their differences.

With this concept in mind, if Hoover had an unconscious and deep hatred of himself, he would have seen it everywhere, in his agents, in communists, in civil rights leaders. Everywhere. Reversing the theory like Greg Braden suggests, Hoover's outer world becomes a reflection of his inner world, revealing an image of his true self. Hoover saw imperfection everywhere and therefore felt imperfection within. Being unconscious of his own self-disgust, he naturally tried to control and improve the chaotic outer world. Thus, leading to a fear-wielding leader of the Bureau through intimidation, information, and becoming a powerful man in America.

His legendary files may have been a form of Hoover's attempt to control the chaos he felt within. Whether the files exist or not, the effect is the same. Nixon said "he's got files on everybody. Damn it!"[23] Hoover had control and used it to create what he thought was a better department, a better country, a better world.

If Hoover had turned inwards and worked through his feelings and perceived failings, rather than punishing and controlling the imperfection, he may have found peace and acceptance with himself and his creator. We wouldn't have had the 50s and 60s filled with tight eggshell walkers, trying desperately to stay within the lines of rules. It is possible that we may have seen an increase in individuals being, thinking, and contributing to society with a variety of new ideas and concepts, as we do now 50 years later. Hoover may not have had such a jovial relationship with President Eisenhower, which led to his carte blanche for wiretaps and bugs, resulting in the gradual dissolution of citizens' privacy and the First Amendment.[24]

Hoover lived in the center of swirling fear in Washington D.C. If he was an HSP, he would've been acutely aware of the Us versus Them energy. He would've wanted to do something about it, like how Harriet Tubman wanted to improve life for enslaved people. Being an unaware Sensitive, he responded with a tight fist, stepping on constitutional rights, rather than looking inward and dealing with his own feelings.

In this light, Hoover is a clear illustration of the importance of self-care for Sensitives. Hoover's lack of self-care, self-love, and self-acceptance resulted in self-hatred, which was transferred to anyone who was different from the norm. We can learn from Hoover what not to do as Sensitives. We see the depths and ramifications the lack of self-care has on a Sensitive and their world. We see how a self-hating Sensitive can lose their way and get lost in chaos and power, along with the ripples left in their wake. We may even be able to understand the punishing God of the Old Testament and how much it is still very much part of our current world. We understand how forcing others to live, think, and believe as we do can have dangerous and damaging repercussions.

CHAPTER 19

Historical Sensitives in Review

Let's take a moment to review these historical persons and see:

1. If they were in fact potentially highly sensitive persons and,
2. What archetypes they may have displayed and,
3. How this information may help HSPs today.

Hildegard de Bingen, Florence Nightingale, and Harriet Tubman

Saint Hildegard, Florence Nightingale, and Harriet Tubman can all easily be considered highly sensitive persons. All experienced visions, all kept them quiet, and all faithfully followed the messages they received. All experienced great physical challenges, but all persevered and continued to work through their pain to complete their calling. All of these women exemplify the Visionary and Champion/Leader archetype. Saint Hildegard guided more women to her new abbey, Nightingale led hospitals and doctors toward more sanitation practices, and Tubman led people to freedom.

All these women can teach us how faith in spirit can lead to great ripples of humanity. These women had such strong callings, that they felt they had little choice in their actions. Not everyone experiences this strong sense of purpose, but when we do . . . watch out world!

Claude Monet

I believe it is plain to see Claude Monet was both an Artist Archetype and an HSP. His love of the outdoors, animals, and reading and his strive for perfection make Claude Monet a quintessential HSP Artist. Even when he was frustrated with the end result of his creations, he still had hope, and he tried again and again to create perfection. As a crafter, I can personally understand Monet's feeling of hope at the beginning of a project and the despair upon its completion. Monet teaches us the practice of perseverance. Monet's love of color and light brings peace and calm to everyone and continues to do so throughout the ages. He demonstrates to us how our work, creating and following our hearts, can continue to heal others long after our bodies have expired.

Frederick Douglass and Dr. Martin Luther King, Jr.

Mr. Frederick Douglass and Dr. Martin Luther King, Jr, while unconventional as traditional artists, were masters of the word, which can easily be an extension of the Artist archetype. But these men used their Artist archetype for change.

We know Douglass' name because of his writings, primarily *Narrative of the Life of Frederick Douglass, an American Slave*. His words brought the real and harsh struggle of a people into the minds and hearts of his previously unaware contemporaries. But as we learned, Frederick Douglass achieved his fame because of his mental strength and ability to recall, analyze, and describe events he witnessed with such description as to project his readers into a world of vast extremes. With his vivid imagination, intelligence, and powerful mental strength, Frederick Douglass could certainly be considered an HSP, perhaps even an empath.

What is so amazing about Douglass is his strength of conviction and his accomplishments. If he was an HSP, how did he achieve such amazing accomplishments? It seems to me, it was his HSP-ness that gave him his conviction. His memory of his life as an enslaved man tormented him to the point of needing to make a change and break out of the typical shy HSP into a Champion of Rights. It was his love and compassion for all who experienced similar situations that kept him rebelling against the injustice of his world. At this point, it seems obvious to call Frederick Douglass a Freedom Fighter, a Rebel, and even a Knight worthy of emulation as both a human and an HSP.

Douglass' words influenced President Lincoln, thereby influencing the creation of the Emancipation Proclamation. Similarly, Dr. King's beliefs, expressed by his words, influenced President Johnson and the Civil Rights Act. These two great documents are definite Game-Changers to our society, laying the groundwork for our paths and continued endeavors for improvements today.

Dr. King's interest in education and the deeper philosophical questions combined with his spiritual calling all confirm his high sensitivity. To say Dr. Martin Luther King, Jr. was a religious figure seems belittling concerning all that he was and accomplished. But his accomplishments grew out of his core beliefs in spirit, love, and a loving universe. With his heart-based HSP-ness,

Dr. King was a Leader of a church, a people, an organization, and a movement. With his conviction of equality and peaceful civil disobedience, Dr. King was a Champion and a Game-Changer of history, and his words and work are felt and still needed in our lives today.

Both Frederick Douglass and Dr. King fought for equality and justice, as did President Abraham Lincoln and First Lady Eleanor Roosevelt, all of whom could be considered Leaders, Rebels, Champions, and/or Game-Changers.

George Washington Carver and Nikola Tesla

Because the HSP character trait closely aligns with the Artist archetype, HSPs are creative not only in physical forms like painting or writing but also in their ideas. When combined with our love of deep processing and thinking, this poises us beautifully to be Inventors, Innovators, or Rebels.

Given the evidence presented, Nikola Tesla and George Washington Carver can easily be considered HSPs. Tesla was quirky and brilliant; George Washington Carver was kind and brilliant. Both used their interest in nature and their intuition to innovate our lives. Both retreated into solitude to rest and recuperate. Both were highly sensitive. Both were Rebels and Innovators, and even Champions, attempting to improve our lives by loving and using the natural powers of the earth.

Presidents Abraham Lincoln and Ulysses S. Grant

Because HSPs are heart-based and feel emotions more deeply than others, this makes us great potential Champions. This sensitivity drives us to fight for the underdog, protect against injustice, and lead with love and peace. (Can you feel your superhero cape flapping in the breeze yet? Queue your personal superhero theme music.)

Presidents Lincoln and Grant, both Leaders, Champions, and Knights, led the United States with their hearts, more than their heads, showing us how love can truly lead the way. President Lincoln's sensitivity is undisputed, with his honesty and deep caring being his most endearing sensitive qualities. President Grant's hatred of violence and his binge drinking point to his HSP-ness.

Other than President Lincoln's deep desire and conviction to keep the country together and its ideals intact, I am not sure how he kept going. I've found no techniques he used for protection or regeneration of energy. It is quite possible that when one compares his photos taken at the beginning and end of his administration, he had no such techniques. But one thing is quite clear, with his goal of maintaining his country's ideals (that of liberty and justice for

ALL) completed, he quickly left this earth, yet another suggestion of his lack of protection.

President Grant's solitary binge drinking and presumed "disrespect" for the status quo shows his sensitivity and an HSP's need to protect and take care of oneself. Sure, there are healthier ways of self-care, but Grant shows us its importance.

Eleanor Roosevelt

First Lady Eleanor Roosevelt's need to occasionally retreat and meditate, along with her compassion for the underprivileged points directly to her sensitivity. With most of her work occurring after her position as First Lady, her archetypes were Champion, Leader, and Game-Changer. By becoming the first woman to serve in the United Nations, she was a role model for thinking, intelligent, and heart-based women.

First Lady Roosevelt had tremendous mental strength, like Frederick Douglass. And like Douglass, she used her mental powers for protection, guarding against weak thoughts and a weak body. She used her heart-based powers of compassion to feel for and fight diplomatically for the underprivileged with her heart-based words. Her regular practice of meditation teaches the need for HSPs to have time alone to recharge and release, demonstrating the potential benefits HSPs who adopt her techniques.

Adolph Hitler

Adolph Hitler was an Artist, a Perfectionist, and a Leader. A leader at a time when a country's citizens were afraid, struggling, and furiously blamed their struggles on other peoples, similar to some humans today. As an empath filled with that fear and hatred, Adolph used it to fulfill his narcissistic belief of his great destiny. But when I try and understand—not excuse—his actions and beliefs, I conclude, desperately holding on to any hope or reason, he was doing what he thought was right. It saddens many of us still today when we realize just how misguided his plan was, but perhaps he was trying to make the world and humans better.

An ancient Islamic prayer that I have modified a bit and use often is "Bless the Suffering, Bless the Inflictors, and Bless the Witnesses." I am often asked: How can I pray for the Inflictors to be blessed? After lengthy processing on my part, I've concluded that the Inflictors are actually in need of the most blessing. In their minds, they believe what they are doing is the right thing. And for their right thing to cause others suffering, they must be in a very dark place indeed, and therefore in need of help and blessing. Hitler offers us a chance to practice blessing the Inflictor.

The fact that Hitler was an artist of many mediums including, painting, architecture, and acting, like Saint Hildegard and George Washington Carver, suggests his HSP-ness. The fact that Hitler's personality changed when he was in the forest and fields suggest he was Sensitive and used his long walks to release and rejuvenate. The fact that he spent the majority of the war in bunkers is quite telling, perhaps he couldn't face what he had started and ran to the earth for protection, solace, and maybe forgiveness. The fact that Hitler needed people for inspiration suggests not only was he a highly sensitive person but an extrovert as well.

Yes, Hitler was an HSP. May he be a warning, a cautionary tale, and a lesson learned, to all HSPs to feed the Wolf of Light. He shows us, in reverse, the importance of releasing other people's energy, of grounding, of protection. He shows us that when HSPs become filled with other people's energy and practice no technique for releasing, dangerous things can happen.

Developing a Relationship with Historical Sensitives

So now that we have identified a few Historical Sensitives you may want to study your personal favorite historical person to see if they were Sensitive as well. If you find your favorite historical person is not sensitive, that's ok. You can still work with them; you can still explore and learn from them. If you feel compelled to do so and find yourself asking "What do I do with this knowledge?" My answer would be to develop a relationship with them. Then you might ask "How?"

My first suggestion would be to find a photograph of your favorite historical Sensitive, print it out, and hang it up somewhere, similar to working with your ancestors (see more about working with Ancestors in Chapter 24 – Spiritual Care section Animal and Ancestor Essence). Spend some time looking at the photo and notice the details. Say hello to the photo as you pass it by, begin a conversation, even perhaps ask for help with a situation, or ask, "What would you do?"

The next step I would recommend is learning even more about the historical figure, dig deeper. Discover more details about their personality. Become more and more familiar with your historical figure. Perhaps to the point where you would know how they would handle a situation or what they would do.

When you feel you have a connection, or to initiate a connection, I suggest meditating with the historical person. You can focus on the photo/image and sit comfortably, quietly, and relaxed. Perhaps call/think their name a few times (I repeat their name three times, but you use whatever feels good to you). Notice your body, how does it feel? More relaxed, cooler, hotter? Notice any sensations, twinges, pressures, smells, or emotions. Perhaps you just "sense" something, a knowing, that the energy of your historical person is with you. If you feel so inclined, introduce yourself, ask questions, and hold a conversation with them. You may be surprised at what you experience. Enjoy!

PART III

Being and Thriving as a Highly Sensitive Person

None of our Historical Sensitives are the epitome of healthy balanced life practices; perhaps that's how they became historic. Some, like Hildegard, Nightingale, and Tesla pushed themselves to the point of dis-ease, experiencing bouts or years of bed rest or multiple major illnesses. This level of pushing your limits is definitely NOT something I would recommend. It certainly seems Professor Carver, Harriet Tubman, and Eleanor Roosevelt lived more balanced lives. Many of them, such as Machiavelli, Douglass, Carver, and Grant had coping mechanisms, some were healthy such as reading, writing, and being in nature, while others were not so healthy, such as drinking to excess. There are lessons as much in what they did and did NOT do, so with everything take what feels right to you, and disregard those that don't.

Now that we have looked back to see how Historical Sensitives handled (or didn't handle) their sensitivities, it is time to look forward and offer some techniques for you to try and personalize to assist you in becoming a more empowered Sensitive.

One characteristic of a Highly Sensitive Person, as described by Dr. Aron, is "jumpy," while others describe us as Highly Reactive. Whether it's reading the room or looking out for danger an HSP's nervous system is always on alert, making us feel nervous or anxious. So as Sensitives, in my opinion, staying calm and relaxed physically is a high priority. Use whatever tools available (within the laws of the land, of course) with which you feel comfortable. It may take some experimenting and trial and error to find the right tools for you. Remember, just like Tesla, even "failure" is knowledge, you now know what doesn't work for you. I encourage you to continue to try to find ways to be relaxed and calm. Whether it's journaling or a spreadsheet or notes on your calendar, I also encourage you to keep track of what works and what doesn't. Food, aromas, textures, anything can become a trigger for you and your mind to relax.

The difference, I believe, between a highly sensitive person and an empath with impact, such as our historical Sensitives, is a matter of self-care. Self-care can be divided into five main categories: physical care, emotional care, mental care (otherwise known as positive mental attitudes), energetic care, (such as grounding and protecting or cleansing), and spiritual care. I will address each one of these in due course.

Please remember these are only suggestions. I am not a medical doctor or a nutritionist. I encourage you to find what works best for you, discovering what helps you feel better, stronger, and more empowered. The following is intended as a starting point, a springboard, for you to explore you, the real you, and nothing but you.

CHAPTER 20

Physical Care

Diet for the HSP

There are many ways a highly sensitive person may take care of themselves. With our Historical Sensitives, we have seen examples such as resting the body in Saint Hildegard, Florence Nightingale, and Eleanor Roosevelt. Harriet Tubman, one could conclude, took care of her body with her strong survival skills. Rasputin's technique for physical care was of a more intimate nature. While President Grant's habit for physical care of drinking is not recommended, it is still a technique, and widely used for unaware Sensitives. I'm willing to bet a high percentage of Alcoholics Anonymous participants are Sensitive.

President Lincoln is known to have enjoyed eating. It is thought he helped his wife cook dinner after a day filled with hard work,[1] a positive technique of physical care if ever I've heard of one. It is possible President Lincoln's physical body itself was his only "coping mechanism." He had a well-documented height of 6'4" and weight of 180 pounds (82kg) before his presidency, and it is presumed he weighed much less at the time of his death. This suggests a high metabolism rate, which could have been his body's innate nature of processing additional energy. All these techniques could also be considered coping mechanisms or ways to escape the heaviness of being human for Sensitives.

This brings me to ask—is self-care a coping mechanism? The American Psychological Association defines Coping Mechanism as:

"Any conscious or nonconscious adjustment or adaptation that decreases tension and anxiety in a stressful experience or situation. Modifying maladaptive coping mechanisms is often the focus of psychological interventions."[2]

Given that self-care, in my opinion, is used to bring about a calm and relaxed Sensitive, then yes, self-care can be considered a form of coping. It is a way to maneuver yourself through daily life into a more relaxed (and therefore empowered) Sensitive. Therefore, we can use the terms interchangeably, if you wish.

We'll begin with the tangible ways that relate to the physical self, beginning with the most obvious and impactful ways: food. While food may be the most impactful way to help you feel better, it can also come with some tricks and turns. You, like myself, may have spent the bulk of your life not thinking about what you put in your body. Personally, I have spent more than a few years eating McDonald's cheeseburgers, or whatever was available at the gas station, too busy or not really interested in food or aware of its effects on how I feel. My behavior created patterns and habits which I am still working to change and improve. So, if you can relate to this particular challenge, remember to be kind and patient with yourself. Changing your eating habits may take a little while to get used to, so give yourself a break if, or when, you stray from your new intentions. It's ok. Just notice your old ways are still part of you, and begin again.

Most highly sensitive persons are prone to being flighty, or not grounded. Consider Tesla and his ordeal with overstimulated senses or the wide array of projects by Hildegard de Bingen and Niccolo Machiavelli. With our nervous system always on high alert, being jumpy, or startling easily, I have found this to be a sign of not being grounded, or overstimulated, or even that some past trauma has been triggered. We'll deal with not being grounded first. And yes, honor any dietary restrictions you may have, but for now, consider placing weight loss goals on the back burner.

This may come as a shock or even a deal breaker for you Sensitives who are beginning your journey to a healthier path. Caffeine is considered a counter to calm Sensitive's nervous system. I know, I know, you can't live without your double mocha espresso. But you may have created a circular habit for yourself, needing more and more caffeine. I gently suggest you attempt switching to lower levels of caffeine, like tangerine tea for a little while. It may be difficult and possibly painful with headaches from caffeine withdrawal, but you may also eventually find your body feeling more relaxed and less jittery as you are able to make calm rational decisions. By the way, dark chocolate is a very nice substitute for coffee, especially when paired with the previously mentioned tangerine tea. Just a suggestion.

Foods can be quite grounding, in a good way. When you find yourself feeling jumpy or noticing you are flitting from subject to subject, or thought to thought, like a butterfly from flower to flower, find some calming, grounding foods. You know those days or moments, when you have endless errands or tasks in a limited space of time. Or when you meet a long-time friend and are so excited to share everything that you end up only telling them half of every story. Or when you spend your day going from helping one person to the next, with no time to help yourself. Those kinds of days.

When you have those days, consider President Lincoln's behavior and go to your comfort foods. Foods such as red meat, or black beans if you prefer. Carbohydrates, pastas, breads, and potatoes, all the things the Western doctors say should be eaten in moderation can be quite comforting, calming, and therefore grounding. A friend of mine happily says "I never met a potato I didn't like." Incidentally, Eleanor Roosevelt's favorite food was scrambled eggs and mashed potatoes while President Lincoln enjoyed venison, bacon, and biscuits—all good foods for grounding and calming down. If you choose to drink alcohol, dark beers in moderation, like stouts and porters may also help. Another friend of mine loves to have a steak and a pint of stout after a long day of intuitive readings. Spending the entire day in higher vibrating energy can be lovely and beautiful, but also physically exhausting. Mushrooms are also a great source of grounding and protein. Remember to treat your body with food. I have long felt food was so basic, boring, and human, I have forgotten to eat or felt I didn't need to eat. "I am a child of God, I am divine," I would say to myself, "I don't need to eat." Yes, you are a child of God and yes, you are divine, but you still need to eat.

A Word about Weight Loss

Many Sensitives struggle with their weight. Author Doreen Virtue in her book *Earth Angels* suggests one's physical weight is a form of energetic protection. My dear Aunt was always very heavy, needing to use a cane for added support by the time she was in her 40's. The bulk of her extra weight rested around her hips and thighs. This suggests to me that her root chakra (more on chakras coming up) was in need of strengthening, as was her sense of security, indicating she needed protection. The only way she knew how to protect herself was through added weight.

Doreen Virtue uses Elizabeth Taylor as an example of an Earth Angel, her term for HSPs. Elizabeth Taylor struggled with her weight and with love. But Taylor never gave up on love or food, always gaining and losing weight and getting divorced and remarried. Oprah is another possible example of a Sensitive who uses physical weight as energetic protection.

If you constantly struggle with weight issues and have tried all the diets without success, consider working on energetic protection or grounding. I'm betting, if you feel safe and are energetically grounded, the added weight will fall off naturally.

What are my Favorite Foods?

What are your go-to comfort foods? Consciously choosing to eat your personal comfort foods will go a long way to calming your nerves, body, and emotions. Again, my personal list may not be the healthiest according to dietitians, but right now we're not going for healthy or body conscious; we're going for calming, relaxing foods. Food that you love, food that perhaps has a comforting childhood memory. I'm convinced most of us love bread because the smell reminds of a perfect childhood memory (plus it's just plain wonderful). Perhaps chicken noodle soup was your childhood favorite. My comfort foods, both as a child and today, are mashed potatoes and macaroni and cheese. I think you get the picture by now. Take some time to think about your favorite comfort foods.

Why do I Love my Favorites?

If you've had issues with food, either generally or specifically, take some time to reflect on why certain childhood foods are so comforting. You might discover some interesting things about yourself. You may find those comfort foods come from outside yourself. For example, perhaps you love pizza because your mom loved ordering pizza since it was easier than cooking. Things like that.

Macaroni and cheese is one of my favorite comfort foods. I'll enjoy it whenever I'm run down. When I look at why I love mac and cheese I find it was the first food I could cook on my own. I'd make a blue box as an after-school snack. I felt so independent and adult. Now, when I open a blue box, I feel just like a kid again. Funny, eh?

Foods to Increase Dopamine

The Highly Sensitive Person's body works slightly different from non-HSPs. For example, dopamine. Although scientists have yet to figure out why, the body of an HSP responds differently to dopamine. Dopamine is a neurotransmitter in the brain's reward or pleasure center.[3] The usual response to material things just don't affect us that much. (Remember Presidents Lincoln, Grant, and Rasputin and their disregard for societal norms.) Having a great big tv or the newest phone means very little to us and is not as rewarding. Dopamine helps regulate the nervous system from overstimulation and exhaustion and creates a sense of reward for us. Foods high in tryptophan help create dopamine.

Turkey is the food most known for being high in tryptophan. So no need to keep up with the Jones, eat a turkey sandwich. President Lincoln was known to munch on a turkey leg a time or two, or three or four. Other foods that contain higher levels of tryptophan include cheese, peanuts, sunflower seeds, and eggs, according to the website Healthline.[4]

Intentional Eating

A moment must be spent to chat about intention and taking a moment for gratitude. Highly Sensitive Persons, as I may have mentioned, can be easily manipulated. While on the surface this may sound nefarious and definitively something to be aware of, I'd like to offer a different perspective. The ability to be manipulated can also suggest you can alter or change your habits easily. It may be likely that you are already doing some of the things suggested here. Being aware of your actions and adding your Intention may be all that you need to create a shift toward being a more empowered empath.

Taking a moment before eating and being aware and thankful for all the resources that went into that meal can be a powerful step to add to your daily routine. Before shoveling that sloppy joe in, take a moment, breathe, and consider the effort and energy that brought that sloppy joe to your plate. Take a moment to say thank you, not just at Thanksgiving as some Americans do, but every meal, and then take another moment to really feel your gratitude. Adding an intention, such as, "this food is for my highest good, it has everything my body requires to shine and accomplish what is needed of me today," (or something like that, you'll find your words), may be enough to shift and manipulate your energy.

In fact, adding intention to any action or emotion throughout the day can be incredibly powerful. Reiki Masters set intentions before beginning a session. You set your intentions all the time. Consider driving. More often than not you have a destination in mind when you get in your car and put it in drive. Your intention is your destination, where you want to end up. Adding the emotions of that goal, how you will feel when you get there, is the secret key to manifesting.

So, before your next meal take a beat, a breath, a moment to say thank you, feel thankful, and feel how good you WILL feel eating your meal and beyond.

Food to Feed your Chakras

My second favorite topic after HSPs is the chakras. I love learning about and playing with the chakras. And when my research combined the two with food? Wow! My heart chakra jumped for joy. You mean I can wear pretty, fun colors and eat dark chocolate and it helps me too? As an HSP, I need a reason to have fun. I can't go all willy-nilly, be frivolous, and only play. But if there is a higher reason or purpose, you bet I'm on board. So, with a little research I found that the color of foods can feed your chakras (even wearing colorful clothes helps). There are other authors who have much more information about chakras, Cyndi Dale for instance. Therefore, we will just touch on the basics here and suggest some foods to help build or balance your chakras. With President Lincoln's love of food, there are a few of his documented favorites to consider as his technique for physical care. Most likely on an unconscious level, President Lincoln ate what he liked, and what he craved may have been messages for his self-care.

Chakras, in case you aren't familiar, are little energy centers found throughout the body and beyond. Seriously, if you want to know more about chakras, (or start a life-long research project and love affair) check out Cyndi Dale's *Chakra Bible*.

There is much discussion about how many chakras a body has, some say 7, others say 72, and still others say 112. We will just touch on the Western version and work with the standard 7 and the traditional colors associated with them.

THE ROOT CHAKRA

Located at the base of the spine, the Root Chakra is where most people start because it is known for security and safety. I think of the root chakra as the foundation of a house. If your house is built on a rocky foundation, the rest of the house is shaky, unsteady, and full of cracks. Likewise, if your childhood resembled Alison Reynolds, "The Basket Case" in *The Breakfast Club*, you may have security or safety issues to address throughout your life. Working on the root chakra is a good place to start.

While our historical Sensitives George Washington Carver and Frederick Douglass were born into slavery they seem to have had different experiences in their childhood. Professor Carver was enslaved by people who hated slavery but were low on funds and needed labor. As a result, Carver was treated more gently and taught to read. Douglass was born to strict enslavers and witnessed and bore the full thrust of what that meant, even being sent to a slave breaker to learn to be more subservient. Given that the first seven years of life are critical to feeling safe and secure, which affects the root chakra, we can conclude that Douglass' root chakra was likely slammed shut from fear and acted in survival mode for much of his life. Carver may have had a more open root chakra from being allowed to play in his garden. We can also conclude that Frederick's compromised root chakra did not stop him from fighting for the abolishment of slavery. In fact, his closed root chakra may have been a huge part of who he was, creating his strong desire for his experiences to never be repeated, ever, again to anyone. We can surmise it was Frederick's compromised root chakra that encouraged him to become his driving force, wishing all humans to feel safe and secure, and thus served him and humanity well.

This is not always the case. For some Sensitives, a compromised or closed root chakra can paralyze us and prevent progress. Therefore, it is essential to work on healing it. The easiest way I know to work on the chakras is to wear and eat the colors of the chakras.

While everyone's chakra colors may differ, the traditional color of the root chakra is red. Eating red foods or root foods, such as beets and rutabaga, have been known to help feed and strengthen your base root chakra. Taking a hint from our Historical Sensitives, Mr. Lincoln's favorite food was a nice juicy red apple, either right off the tree or in a pie, it didn't matter to him. He also enjoyed a good piece of venison and bacon, both good for grounding and the root chakra. Tomatoes, apples, and cherries are all good root chakra foods. Adding in the intention of feeding your chakra will go a long way as well.

THE SACRAL CHAKRA

The sacral chakra is associated with creativity. With connections to the life-creating organs of the uterus and testes, the sacral chakra is typically associated with the color orange. Many historically highly sensitive persons were artistic, Claude Monet for example. The "artistic temperament" can easily be considered a synonym for the highly sensitive person. So the sacral chakra can be considered an important chakra for us.

When people think of creativity, or artistic abilities, they usually think of painting. But being artistic, or more accurately creative, can involve anything and everything. How you dress. How you cook. How you work. The truth is many historical sensitive persons were very creative. HSPs think differently, we see the world differently, we question the old ways and invent new ways. One of our favorite questions is "What IF . . . ?" It's pretty gosh darn exciting when you think about it. The only limit is our imagination, and HSPs have beaucoup imagination! (Remember, we are deep processors and think a lot.)

Even if your chakras differ from the traditional colors, using the typical color of the sacral chakra—orange—by eating orange-colored foods may help open a path to creativity for you. Foods such as oranges, of course, but also sweet potatoes, carrots, pumpkin, mangoes, or even Lincoln's favorite gingerbread cookies, may just be the trick to open up your sacral chakra and your mind to new creative ideas and endeavors.

Orange foods are known for their levels of vitamins A, C, and beta carotene. My grandmother always said, "eat a carrot, you'll improve your eyesight." Turns out, my grandmother and all the "old wives" were actually correct. Carrots and other orange foods contain beta carotene, a compound for the color, which has been shown to help the eyes and skin. Beta carotene has also been proven to "play a critical role in cell growth" in the kidneys, lungs, and heart.[5] When we look into the emotions connected with those organs (fear, grief, and anger, respectively) we find orange foods may help you be happy. Go figure, drinking orange juice really is fun!

THE SOLAR PLEXUS CHAKRA

This is a biggie for highly sensitive persons. The Solar Plexus Chakra is associated with the stomach and self-esteem or personal power. Given highly sensitive persons are typically shy, quiet, wallflowers, eating foods (or doing anything) to strengthen your solar plexus chakra is practically a necessity.

Like President Lincoln and Eleanor Roosevelt, Highly Sensitive Persons can be very humble. We tend to have low self-esteem and small egos. Some of us could use a little ego boost. With the solar plexus chakra associated with the color yellow, eating a banana may help you to feel empowered and good about yourself. Yellow foods, yellow clothes, yellow anything. And remember to add in a positive affirmation and intention such as, "I am enough" for extra umph.

In Michael Perlin's documentary *3 Magic Words*, a contributor stated eating a blend of oranges and pineapples will help you feel good about yourself. So, I gave it a try. And golly wouldn't you know it, my confidence and self-esteem increased. Eating yellow foods such as bananas, pineapples, lemons, yellow bell peppers, and squash may feed your solar plexus chakra and strengthen your self-esteem. President Lincoln enjoyed a good hearty corn cake, or cornbread as we call it today.

THE HEART CHAKRA

And now we come to the center of the body and the center of the highly sensitive person, the heart and the heart chakra. The heart chakra is about universal love for all beings. We see examples of an open heart chakra in Dr. King and George Washington Carver. Both held amazing love and hope for the human race. Professor Carver is quoted as saying "I love all humans." Dr. King had such love for all humans; he wanted us to be a better, kinder, and more compassionate species. One can easily conclude everything these gentlemen did was for the love and betterment of humanity.

This is the chakra which often has a great deal of trauma. All humans have some kind of loss and experience some form of a broken heart. As a highly sensitive person, we wear our hearts on our sleeves; we can feel emotional loss deeper than others. Therefore, healing that grief and heartache can be pivotal for an HSP.

You may have noticed the colors of the chakras are like a rainbow, with the root chakra starting with red and as we move up the body we move up in color. And you'd be right. The traditional color of the heart chakra is green. Some use pink as well but we'll focus on the rainbow colors and work with green. I find it fascinating the heart chakra is green just like a large part of the natural world—grass, leaves, and money. It has even been noted in the psychology of color to watch out for someone who hates green as they most likely have emotional and mental health issues. The color green is known to be comforting and soothing.

There is a plethora of green foods, especially vegetables. Kale, spinach, cucumbers, green onions, and cabbage (another of Mr. Lincoln's known favorites), just to name a few. In her article, "The 13 Healthiest Leafy Green Vegetables" Autumn Enloe states green leafy foods can help reduce the "risk of obesity, heart disease, high blood pressure, and mental decline."[6] Yes, eating your veggies can heal your heart, both physically and energetically.

THE THROAT CHAKRA

Working our way up the body and the rainbow, the next chakra is the throat with its color being blue. The throat chakra may be a bit blocked for highly sensitive persons since "speaking our truth," the core purpose of the throat chakra, may be scary for us. Highly sensitive persons tend to be more tight-lipped than others due to our keen understanding of just how much words can hurt. We can be easily devastated by words and as a result, we use our words carefully and cautiously if at all. How many times have you been involved in a discussion and ended up just nodding your head or pursing your lips?

We see examples of both a closed and an open throat chakra in Lady Diana and Frederick Douglass respectively. Lady Diana speaks repeatedly of how she didn't bother Charles because she felt it wasn't her place to complain. She speaks of how the monarchy and her husband provided her with little to no guidance or support. After looking deeper into her biographies, I have not found Lady Diana asking for support or guidance. This is a common trait with Sensitives. Reading, and providing for, other people's needs is one of our basic abilities. We do it so well that we do not realize we are unique in this ability. We think everyone can anticipate other's needs. Because of this, we don't speak up and ask for help for ourselves. Just like Lady Diana, we expect our needs to be met. Lady Diana offers us an example of the need to speak up, ask, request, and inquire.

Frederick Douglass shows us the positive impact of opening our throat chakras and how we can use our voices for good. His voice brought truth to a situation and uncovered the darkness through personal experiences, creating a tidal wave of support for change.

Eating blue foods such as blueberries, blue corn, or blue potatoes may help soothe the throat chakra and encourage you to speak from your heart. Blue foods are less available than green or yellow, but they still exist.

THE BROW CHAKRA

One of the key characteristics of the highly sensitive person is their ability to sense subtle energy. This can easily be understood as highly instinctive, intuitive, or clairsentient. The brow chakra is known as the center of intuition and therefore it can be concluded a highly sensitive person's brow chakra is more activated or open than that of non-HSPs. An interesting correlation I've noticed is purple, the color of the Brow chakra, is the favorite color of many HSPs.

The brow chakra's traditional color is indigo/purple and is located between your eyebrows. It has been referred to as the Third Eye.

Purple foods, such as Mr. Lincoln's favorite blackberry pie, eggplant, raspberries, grapes, and plums may help keep your intuition flowing and you being you.

THE CROWN CHAKRA

Ah, the crown chakra: the last main chakra located in the physical body. The chakra is known for connection, spirituality, and higher consciousness. Traditionally the color of the crown is violet, but many also use other colors, such as gold or white. White foods such as mushrooms, garlic, and ginger have been identified as supporting the crown. Since this chakra is known for spirituality, therefore foods with a history of spirituality like manna, milk, and honey may help support this chakra. But may I suggest spending some time with your own crown and feeding it foods that hold a special higher meaning to you.

Prayer before eating

Regardless of what you decide to eat, adding in a moment to say thanks before eating may go a long way toward bringing positive energy to you. Take a moment to think about where the food came from and consider how everything was provided for you from Mother Earth, our home.

When I was a young'un growing up in my grandparent's house, every night we had dinner together. Every night at the dinner table we held hands, bowed our heads, and said grace. This always ended up with us all squeezing hands as a sign grace was over and giggling about who started the squeeze.

Saying grace or praying before meals is a standard ritual for Christians. And more than a good idea for all humans, especially Sensitives. There are many forms of practicing thankfulness. I know one Sensitive who pulls out her singing bowls every dinner time. Oh, that does sound lovely.

The energy of gratitude is a powerful force. In the world of the Law of Attraction, feeling the energy and emotion of gratitude is the key to manifesting. The theory is that when you feel gratitude, more things to be grateful for are attracted to you. One can easily see commonalities between joy and gratitude. When one feels gratitude, or thankfulness, one feels joy for anything and everything.

For example, during the national American holiday, Thanksgiving, Americans spend much time, effort, and money on one meal. On the surface, this ritual may seem shallow and hollow until we consider that the meal and holiday, are merely a vehicle to create an environment of gathering, harvesting if you will. The turkey dinner is a reason to gather, around the table, around the television, around each other, around those whom we love and those we are thankful for being in our lives. This event of gathering and gratitude creates joy, laughter, and memories. We feel lighter, until the actual dinner, we feel a sense of calm and contentment; we feel peace. Now, in actuality, the preparation and perhaps the actual event may create some tension or stress, and opportunities to heal, but the core intention is gratitude, joy, and peace.

Dr. David R. Hawkins, MD, PhD, and author of *The Map of Consciousness Explained*, writes in his posthumously published book how emotions have vibrations. His book is the culmination of his life's work, that of identifying the frequencies of emotions and how experiencing those frequencies can assist you to feel healthier. Dr. Hawkins identified the frequency scale of emotions, finding love, joy, and peace to be among the highest vibrating emotions. He discovered the human body vibrates, with a few notable exceptions, at a frequency below 100 MHz, somewhere in the vicinity of 62-75 MHz, while the emotion of love vibrates at 500 MHz, joy at 540 MHz, and peace at 600 MHz.[7]

In Tansy Rodgers' article, "Practicing Daily Gratitude to Enhance Health," she writes of Bruce Tainio's work with vibration, stating "Gratitude vibrates at 540 MHz."[8] The exact same level of joy.

In "Can expressing Gratitude improve your mental, physical health?" Amanda Logan, nurse practitioner, writes the emotion of gratitude can "improve sleep, mood and immunity."[9] Gratitude can also decrease depression, anxiety, difficulties with chronic pain and risk of disease.

In the Greater Good Magazine, "Is Gratitude Good for your Health?" Summer Allen writes of gratitude's possible positive impact on the physical body.[10] "In one study, more grateful participants reported fewer health problems (such as headaches, gastrointestinal problems, respiratory infections, and sleep disturbances)." Please take note, that these health problems are common among HSPs. The article continues with another study, "they reported fewer physical symptoms (including headaches, dizziness, stomachaches, and runny noses)." Some studies have shown gratitude may impact a "whole slew of benefits—from fewer aches and pains to improved sleep to better cardiovascular health."

Therefore, taking a moment to be grateful before eating (or anytime, really), even if it's just the thought "Hello, Highest Good," can create a sense and an energy of joy. Even if the study findings, scientists, and gurus are wrong, still saying grace before a meal and being thankful as often as possible is certainly a good way to live. So before diving into those mountains of mashed potatoes, take a moment and consider where and how that potato, now on your plate all dripping with buttery goodness, originated. How was it planted? Who harvested it? How did it get to your store? Consider, just for a moment all the things that came together to make that mashed goodness and thank them.

Exercise or Movement

I don't know about you but I'm a fairly sedentary human. My movements are made up of going from one soft place to sit to another soft place to sit, similar to Saint Hildegard. I meditate (occasionally), I read (sometimes), and I drool in front of the television (a lot). I am not a mover and a shaker. I realize that there are healthier ways to live, and movement helps. Even just a gentle stretch or walk is a pleasant way to release extraneous energy. Our historical Sensitives most likely experienced similar situations and found ways to expel it. President Lincoln, when nervous before a speech, was known to have walked the streets, presumably to work his nervous energy out. President Grant hated fighting and killing and was always nervous before a battle. Feeling anxious and wide-awake, he walked around his camp and troops. When Rasputin felt an abundance of energy, he too walked (and walked and walked). Lady Diana enjoyed physical activity in the form of dancing, swimming, and playing tennis.

On those mornings when I've had too much coffee or I have something new to do, I can feel anxious or nervous, and it doesn't always feel comfortable. So, what do I do? I move. I shake my hands, wiggle my behind, stretch my neck and arms, and take a deep breath.

We are in a moment of time where yoga is quite fashionable and trendy. Growing up when Jazzercise was the hot exercise, I'm thrilled a more peaceful form of exercise is "hot." (Plus those headbands and leg warmers, yeesh!) Yoga is mindful movement, one connected with the breath. Traditionally yoga is much more than leggings and mats, it is a way of life with the physical exercise merely one part. But there are many other forms of exercise that are good for the body, mind, and the spirit.

Since one of a Sensitive's greatest strengths is the mind, we can easily daydream into far-off places. In fact, for some of us that is where we are most comfortable and our happiest. But as the saying goes, we are spiritual beings having a human experience. Being here, now, staying in our bodies in the present moment is one of the reasons we are here and needs to be practiced. Moving our physical bodies is a wonderful way to do that. After all, we must pay attention to where we are and where to put our foot down next.

Forest Bathing

Many of our Historical Sensitives practiced a form of Forest Bathing. Eleanor Roosevelt took long walks in her backyard or natural spaces in Washington DC. Tesla spent days on end in the hills of his youth. Even Hitler would feel lighter, better outside.

Forest Bathing is a Japanese term for "absorbing the forest atmosphere" and is all about spending time in nature. Kaiser Permanante writes, "The goal of forest bathing is to live in the present moment while immersing your senses in the sights and sounds of a natural setting."[11] The article goes on to explain the benefits of spending time in nature, such as lowering blood pressure, heart rate, and levels of cortisol, a natural hormone produced when the body is stressed.

On a warm summer day, the forest smells of pine trees and clean earth. I personally have found this to create a sense of peace, being closer to Divine beauty, and a sense that all is still well with the world and now science has discovered why. The health benefits of absorbing the forest atmosphere, its beauty, and natural calm can be summarized as natural aromatherapy. The more technical term, used in scientific research, is phytoncides, which are the natural essential oils from trees and have many beneficial medicinal properties. Phytoncides are chemicals which "encourage natural killer cell activity in the human body." Natural Killer cells (hang on, this really is a good thing) are "cancer-fighting proteins that literally seek and destroy tumor and virus-ridden cells." (See, I told you it was a good thing.) Beyond the cancer and virus-fighting, there are numerous other health benefits derived from forest bathing, including improved sleep, a calmer nervous system, lowered inflammation, and even reduced blood glucose levels.[12] Trees are a definite friend to humans and should be treated with respect and gratitude.

The evolution of the human has meant moving away from nature. We now have huge, highly populated areas with very little green space or nature within them. As a result, humans have also moved away from noticing the beauty and divinity of nature which was integral in the lives of our ancient ancestors. Our polytheist great-grandparents appreciated and made sacred many natural forms. With monotheism, we tend to look "up" and revere the heavens, as if peace and salvation are possible elsewhere. As a result, we seem, as a society, to have gotten away from treating our home planet with respect and divine love. The trend is turning back to balancing reverence for both Mother Earth and the heavens by going green and living with a smaller carbon footprint.

Many of us Sensitives hold nature deep in our hearts, seeing natural beauty as a reflection of divine beauty as Saint Hildegard did. She is quoted as saying, "The Word is living, being, spirit, all verdant greening, all creativity. This Word manifests itself in every creature."[13] Saint Hildegard points to the divinity in all living things, and as such we can move closer to the Divine when surrounded by nature. Forest bathing is a great first step in practicing the recognition and respect of beauty (The Divine) in all things. This awareness can then be translated back into the city, encouraging us to treat everyone with respect, as reflections of the Divine.

The practice of forest bathing is really quite simple. Go to a natural setting, even if it's a park in the city, and just Be. You can sit, you can walk, or you can just be in the forest. Soak in the aromas, and watch the sunlight and shadows play with each other. Feel the softness of the forest floor. Smile as the squirrels play and jump from branch to branch. One suggestion is to count your steps to really keep you in the moment. Another suggestion is to take photos of the beauty and search for three photo-worthy moments. (It won't take you long.) Forest bathing has a low impact on the body and can be done by anyone. There really is nothing like feeling the warmth of the sunshine on your face, the brisk morning air, and the soft breeze of the forest.

Earthing

Earthing is a technique similar to forest bathing but takes it one step further. Also known as grounding—a term we Sensitives often use—in this context, it refers to making direct contact with the Earth to absorb its "vast supply of electrons."[14] Scientific research shows direct contact with the electrons on the

Earth's surface can improve sleep and reduce physical pain. Most proponents of Earthing suggest walking barefoot but sitting, working, or sleeping outdoors offers benefits as well. Did you know when President Grant was just a little tyke, he preferred walking barefoot? We know Monet loved to garden; he loved getting his fingernails filled with Mother Earth. His gardens are still available to visit. Both activities are prime and common examples of Earthing, direct contact with our planet and her energy.

And how can we talk of tapping into the Earth's electrical current without mentioning our historical Sensitive Tesla? Tesla worked on using the Earth as an electrical current conductor and believed the Earth herself had an endless amount of electrical current, what others term ley lines. Earthing taps into that earthly current and provides subtle calm grounding energy. Similarly minded and predecessor of Tesla, Ralph Waldo Emerson writes of the rejuvenating powers of being in nature, returning to the innocence and wonder of childhood. Emerson writes, "Standing on the bare ground . . . the currents of the Universal Being circulate through me; I am part or parcel of God."[15] Not only does Emerson provide directions on how to ground by being aware and simply standing (ideally barefoot) but he also provides an amazing description of the feeling when one is grounded. A few years ago, I was walking a group of participants of an online group through a grounding exercise, during which I mentioned, "You may feel a tingling in the bottom of your feet." One participant replied, "The tingling is real!" This tingling feeling IS the Universal Being circulating through you, exactly as Emerson describes.

If you can't get outside, A. I'm very sorry, and B. there are a few companies who have developed technology to bring the benefits inside by tapping into the Earth's electrical conductivity. There are many products on the market available. I have used, and found calming benefits from, a grounding mat. The earthing products plug into the third (usually unused) hole of your electrical outlet. While some of us can't feel the current, or recognize it as such, everyone can experience the benefits. You don't need to feel the tingle to receive the grounding benefits. I usually use my earthing mat when I am traveling and have found it be quite relaxing and protective, and sometimes, I can't feel the grounding energy, the tingle, but I do feel calmer and therefore I know it is working.

Weighted Blankets

I do not like going to the dentist so much that I have often use the tiniest excuses to reschedule my dental appointments. But there is one thing I do enjoy about the dentist, that is the heavy cover when they take x-rays. Oh, it feels so nice and heavy, I can really feel my muscles relaxing in the chair. Tsarina Romanov may have enjoyed a similar relief when she donned those heavy jewel encrusted dresses.

Weighted blankets provide the same sensation. They come in varying sizes and weights and are available online. Studies have shown weighted blankets can help with anxiety, sleep disorders, and even assist with autism spectrum disorders. They can be a bit pricey, but there are a few available for a reasonable price. If you are a crafty sensitive, tutorials on how to make one are available online.

Tai Chi, Qi Gong

The ancient Chinese movement practices of Tai Chi and Qi Gong are wonderful low impact ways to move the body. Qi gong is actually recommended for energy workers as a form of mindful cleansing. HSPs are definitely energy workers of some kind, whether it be as actual energy workers such as Reiki or Quantum Touch healers, or simply by being a loving human listening and holding space for others. We Sensitives need a technique to cleanse our energy of others, and if you prefer a more formal technique, Qi Gong or Tai Chi are great choices to investigate and explore.

Support your Nervous System

As previously mentioned, one characteristic of a Highly Sensitive Person, as described by Dr. Aron, is "jumpy," while others describe us as Highly Reactive. In either case, HSP's nervous system is always on alert, which in turn can make us feel nervous or anxious. With this in mind, staying calm and relaxed physically is a high priority for Sensitives.

When we speak of the nervous system, most people think of the brain and the spine. The nervous system's job is to detect "environmental changes that impact the body."[16] The nervous system becomes taxed by anxiety and chronic stress and can easily switch into sympathetic or "Fight, Flight or Freeze" mode. Given the fact that Highly Sensitive People are highly aware of their environment and many experience stress or anxiety often and easily, it makes sense the nervous system could easily become overloaded and need support. Adding natural supplements to your daily routine may assist in easier and more relaxed days. As with many of my suggestions, checking with your physician may be a good idea before adding supplements.

The first time I encountered reiki, the reiki master said, "And remember, take your B's." B vitamin (and all of the B's, especially B-1, B-6, and B12) have shown to assist in supporting the nervous system. Lecithin has also been shown to help. I personally love magnesium, which is known to assist and support the nervous system. I have found using magnesium, taken either before or after a particularly high-energy day, to be very calming. If I'm mindful enough in the morning I can take magnesium, and my day tends to be smoother; I am calmer and more relaxed. Or if after a high-impact day, once I'm back home I can take the magnesium and "recover" quicker. There are many forms of magnesium, as well as other supplements for the nervous system on the market, such as magnesium citrate and magnesium glycinate, so researching or asking your physician may help. I use just Magnesium, and my mom uses Magnesium Citrate (and her sleep habits have improved markedly). As with many things, knowledge is power and can significantly boost your confidence in your decisions, creating a sense of empowerment.

Electrolytes

I have also found electrolytes to help speed up my recovery time. Like magnesium, which is an electrolyte, they help before, during, or after a particularly energy-draining day. I find it especially helpful when traveling or in a new environment. I even keep a few bottles of electrolyte drinks in my car, just in case I need to replenish when I'm "on the road."

So, what are electrolytes and why do they help Highly Sensitive Persons?

Electrolytes are minerals that, when mixed with water, help conduct electrical charges throughout the body. They assist with feeding and cleaning out your cells and support the healthy function of your nerves, brain, and heart.[17]

When our bodies get dehydrated, we can get headaches or migraines, a common discomfort of HSPs. Hildegard and Roosevelt, lifelong migraine sufferers, may have benefited from more electrolytes.

Anyone who has a history of headaches and migraines knows the best solution is lying down in a quiet dark place. When we have migraines, everything is too bright or too loud. Highly Sensitive Persons' brains work overtime already, processing incessantly. When you add dehydration to the mix, you get headaches and/or migraines. Proper hydration is a simple way to help your body function easier and feel better. On an energetic level, water helps move things through and out. Adding electrolyte drinks may help even further. Drinks like coconut water, watermelon water, and smoothies are naturally high in electrolytes. One client of mine makes her own electrolyte powder. The internet has many recipes available, most of which consist of potassium, sodium, magnesium, and salt. Again, research and experimentation may be required to find the right combination for you.

PART III : BEING AND THRIVING AS A HIGHLY SENSITIVE PERSON

Miscellaneous Ideas

WEARING HATS AND GLASSES
I find it fascinating how many Sensitives are already doing things unwittingly to help themselves. For example, wearing a hat and/or sunglasses has often been suggested for Sensitives since it helps create a level of energetic protection and detachment. Many of my clients come to me already wearing hats. Sure, hats are fun and keep us warm, but from my perspective, they are already intuitively protecting themselves.

CLASPED HANDS
Another subtle practice I often see Sensitives doing, which is recommended for energetic protection, is clasping their hands. Many sensitives will either keep their fists clenched or clasped when in a public situation, even if that situation is an enjoyable one. While, as an HSP Counselor, I don't specifically recommend clenched hands, I do recommend gently clasping them together. On an energetic level, this closes the circuit and protects you from taking on any more energy.

CROSSED ARMS
Similar to clasping the hands, I also recommend crossing your arms and placing your hands just below the rib cage. Try it and see how you feel. Some reiki masters and other energy workers will do this after a session with a client as a way to disconnect or stop the energy flow. The really nice thing for energy workers is that the energy may continue to flow and you will end up giving yourself a little good energy—always a good thing.

ATLAS HUG
And yet another easy thing to do is what I call the Atlas Hug. Many of my clients have reported a sense of feeling lighter and more comforted after giving themselves an Atlas Hug.

There is an acupressure point on your shoulders known as GB21 for those familiar with acupressure. For those not familiar, it's located right where the shoulder rotates upward. To find GB21, cross your arms, place your hands on your shoulders and lift up your arms until they are about level with the ground. Use your fingers to feel around for a particularly sensitive spot. If you are like me, sometimes every spot on my shoulders is sensitive, so just feel around you'll find the spot (or another one, it's all good).

I call GB21 the Atlas point because it is believed to be a "release valve" for collected energy. Many humans, especially HSPs, feel like we have the weight of the world on our shoulders, just like the Greek mythological character Atlas. Placing light—and I do mean light—pressure on this point works like a pressure cooker valve, releasing excess energy. I had one client report, after finding the point on one side, feeling lighter, but unbalanced. After they located the point on the other side, they reported feeling more balanced.

Once you locate GB21, take a nice deep inhale through the nose while raising your elbows. Remember, your arms are crossed, and your fingers are on your shoulders. When you exhale, drop your arms and let gravity do its job, letting your fingers apply a little more pressure to the Atlas point. Stay there just a moment and take stock of how you feel, noticing any shift or change in your body or mood. Ah! Doesn't that feel better?

Confetti Clearing Cannon

When my hands are not free to give myself an Atlas Hug, namely driving or in public, I will practice the Confetti Clearing Canon technique. This is a variation on the Atlas Hug, or just applying light pressure to the GB21 acupressure point, but occurs only in the mind.

I use this technique regularly when my neck or shoulders are tight or cramping. Here's how it works.

1. I visualize the GB21 pressure point as the end of a circus canon.
2. I visualize the canon setting off Roman candle fireworks and confetti. I've chosen the color of hot pink for my confetti and fireworks.
3. I imagine the confetti catches the wind and spreads out in my immediate vicinity, including the cars behind me. (I usually giggle and smile at the thought of the cars and drivers behind me driving through hot pink confetti and loving energy.)
4. I imagine the Roman candle flares up, up up, high into the sky.

Amazingly enough, my neck and shoulders feel better and more relaxed after releasing my tension to the world and above.

After practicing this visualization for a few years, I can now merely think "confetti clearing canon" and violà! My neck feels relaxed.

Anchoring Technique

One of my favorite techniques is an old standby, the Anchoring technique. This technique takes practice and repetition for it to really take effect, but I've had great success with it as have my clients. I love this technique simply because it is so easy to do and practically unnoticeable in public.

1. Move into a comfortable position and relax. Just allow your shoulders to drop, perhaps your eyes to close, and your hands to open naturally. Allow your breathing to deepen and lengthen, with each exhale allow your body to relax even further.
2. Notice how comfortable, relaxed, and safe you feel. Perhaps remember a time when you felt really safe. Maybe when you were a child, safe in a loved one's arms. Remember that moment, that feeling and let that moment and feeling wash over you.
3. Once you feel secure and safe, press two fingers together lightly. I usually use the thumb and middle fingers, but any combination that is comfortable for you will work.
4. With your fingers together, continue feeling safe and relaxed. Stay here for a few minutes.
5. When you are ready, open your eyes and wiggle your toes to gently return to the room.

That's it! You have just created a new neural pathway, a trigger for your body to feel safe and relaxed, an anchor for you to return to when needed.

Now, for this to become strong and really effective, repeat this exercise once a day for about three weeks. Once the trigger is nice and strong, begin to press your fingers together occasionally when you are in public. You'll be amazed at how that feeling of safety you established during meditation will wash over you even when you are out and about. Start with easy public moments and work your way up to challenging moments. Perhaps start with just sitting at your desk when working, then grocery shopping, then eventually perhaps when you are asking for a raise.

If you are not a tactile person, use your strongest sense (your hearing, smell, or vision) to bring back the effect. For example, if you are more visually inclined, pick an object that has meaning to you and program yourself to calm down when that object is seen. The same can be done with your other senses, such as a certain smell or fragrance. This technique can also work with colors, shapes, or sounds (your favorite song perhaps).

This technique gets stronger the more you practice in solitude and then in public. As I mentioned, it takes practice and that ugliest of words, discipline. But it can absolutely work.

Treat Yourself to Me Time

As a Sensitive, you spend all your time helping others, helping them to feel more comfortable. We can easily burn out, and if not cared for, we can become resentful of our loved ones for not caring for us as we care for them. Therefore, building in time for yourself is essential. HSPs need time to ourselves to recharge our batteries (and to release extraneous energy). However that looks for you, do it and do it regularly. Stalin would treat himself and recharge his batteries by reading. Monet also loved to read, often out loud in the evenings (a great time to treat yourself to Me Time).

Treating yourself, also known as self-care, is more like brushing our teeth rather than a regular teeth cleaning. Both are necessary, but one is done daily. So, schedule that massage, take those long lingering baths, and savor your food. It isn't selfish; it's required for you to continue your job.

The Importance of Sleep

Here is a fascinating tidbit of history for you. Sleep was incredibly important to Adolph Hitler; he routinely slept until 10 A.M. He loved, valued, and protected his sleep time so much that his staff were afraid to wake him, ever, including the morning of June 6th, 1944. His staff received word of the Allies invading Normandy reportedly at 4 A.M. No one wanted to wake Hitler up to inform him. No one made any moves to respond to the invasion including Rommel, who waited and waited. Everyone waited until Hitler woke up a full six hours after the first reports and didn't respond until 10 hours later. This resulted in the Allies' success that day, and soon after, the war. So, we can thank Hitler himself and his sleep patterns in part for the Allied victory.

Hildegard von Bingen understood the importance of sleep back in the early 12th century. She understood sleep provides time for the body to regenerate and encompasses both passive and active forms of healing. She also recognized that the amount of sleep needed varies from person to person.[18]

Sleep is essential to all Earthlings but very important for Highly Sensitive Persons. Many HSPs report having sleep issues, usually waking up sometime throughout the night. Sleep time is the time when our bodies can regenerate and heal. It is also a time for Highly Sensitive Persons to play or work in our dreams. A subset of Highly Sensitives is DreamWorkers. Many of us have vivid and really weird dreams. Some of us wake up with full operas, books, or some form of inspiration. Many of us have dreams of flying, just like Harriet Tubman. And at times, we wake up cranky, tired, and even achy. Whatever the reason (and there are many theories), how you feel when you wake up sets the tone for the new day. Discovering personalized techniques to work off the previous night's sleep is key to having a good day, and hopefully will translate into a good next night's sleep.

We have already touched on the idea of Highly Sensitive Persons having "attractive" energy which translates to being charming or charismatic. Pamala Oslie, in her book *Life Colors*, calls this having a Yellow life color. Oslie compares people with Yellow Life Colors to Labrador puppies. Everyone loves them, wants to be around them. And Yellows, like Labrador puppies want to please everyone. Seemingly, this is a good relationship, but we all know how much puppies sleep after a busy day. Oslie, curiously enough, also writes how Yellows wake up achy and tired. She recommends a nice gentle walk in the morning to shake off the night and get things moving. I've found this personally to be most helpful. There are many ways to get moving in the morning, a cup of tea, a gentle shower, a little stretching or yoga, or even some lively essential oils. Whatever works for you will be the most effective.

As previously mentioned, HSPs can have a dickens of a time achieving a good night's sleep. I have heard many suggestions from clients about what has worked for them. My favorite comment was, "The best sleeping pill I've found is listening to an audiobook." Love that! Some Sensitives have removed all electronic devices from their room. I've found this to be helpful for me, except when I wake up in the dark and have to walk to the other room to know what time it is. I've also found that listening to music or playing and cuddling with my furry companion goes a long way to shake off the night.

Pre-Bed Prayer

There is no shortage of sleep aids. A quick search on Google and you'll find a plethora of suggestions, many of which you may have tried. But I've found a pre-bed routine to be most effective, which includes setting the intention of sleeping deeply, waking up feeling refreshed, and ready to accomplish whatever the day brings.

This routine is similar to saying your prayers before bedtime. While I have no hard and fast facts, I have every faith Dr. King, Saint Hildegard, and Harriet Tubman said their prayers before bed. We do know all three historical Sensitives prayed regularly and it's easy to conclude that they prayed at the end of the day, likely giving thanks for their day. Adding a request, an expectation of deep and restful sleep may be an effective technique for a good night's sleep and thus a positive morning and productive day, allowing you to be more grateful at bedtime. (See the logic and cycle?)

As you are settling into your bed, take a moment to give gratitude for your day, your immediate night's sleep, and your wonderful next morning. I say a little poem before I close my eyes. I have found the mornings I wake up groggy and cranky are usually followed by a night I forgot to repeat my poem prayer. And so, I continue my pre-bed poem every night (until I forget again, and so it goes).

CHAPTER 21

Emotional Care

We have established that Highly Sensitive Persons are an emotional bunch. We are easily overstimulated and emotional. When we are overstimulated, those emotions tend to lean toward more of a cranky nature, such as anger, exhaustion, or fear. Sometimes these emotions can take over and surprise us. Consider Hoover, Stalin, and Hitler before and after they cut themselves off from their emotions. Monet expressed his frustrations by yelling and painting. We see in our Historical Sensitives a few doting parents, such as Lincoln, Grant, and Lady Diana. It is possible that their families were their coping mechanisms as an escape from their challenging work lives, wallowing in joy and familial love. Tesla loved animals, especially cats, and especially his cat, Max. Rasputin loved and considered everyone reflections of the Divine.

Being Aware of Your Emotions

Awareness of emotions is very helpful for Sensitives. Now, you may say "awareness of my emotions? I know what I'm feeling." If that's true, wonderful! But some of us are not aware of our emotions. I routinely ask myself, "What am I feeling now?" The answer often surprises me.

Taking a moment to recognize what you are feeling can go a long way for your emotional health. Stalin and Hoover were aware of their emotions, namely grief. When they both felt overwhelmed by their emotions, they simply stopped feeling and cut off their emotions. Thereafter, these historical Sensitives were created, and the events they are known for occurred. Stalin, Hitler, and Hoover (to a lesser extent) teach us the importance of emotional health and what NOT to do for the good of humanity.

Ask "Is It Mine?"

I was chatting with a client the other day. She relayed how someone mentioned the power of asking, "Is it mine?" My client chuckled and responded, "Laura is always saying that." Yes, I am, and yes, I do recommend asking the question "Is it mine?" often. To my mind, it is one of the most powerful tools in a Sensitive's tool belt. It is the first step toward an HSP's emotional and energetic health.

We can easily surmise Sensitives Lincoln and Hitler felt the full weight of their time and place, the American Civil War and the Second World War, and were filled with emotionally charged energy. We know President Lincoln was overcome with emotions when he heard of the first death of the Civil War. We know he died only a few short days after the war ended. We also know Hitler spent most of his war either in bunkers or in the mountains, far from the madding crowd. Both can be considered forms of release. I wonder, what our world would be like if Hitler had known about the "Is it Mine?" technique.

As an empath, I often feel emotions and have no idea where they came from. Asking the question "Is It Mine?" whooshes away anyone else's emotions, energy, and physical pain, allowing me to process my own.

It's easy. It's free. It's powerful. I highly recommend you give it a try.

Hot Bath/Shower

I cannot overstate the beauty of a hot bath or shower. Lady Diana would have heartily agreed. She understood the healing and releasing powers of water. She started each day swimming. Saint Hildegard recommended baths and saunas for skin issues. Rasputin purposely neglected bathing to increase his suffering, a goal we wish to avoid. When we add in the idea that Rasputin's lack of hygiene was a common complaint and added to the reasons for his murder, Rasputin teaches us what not to do.

When adding Epsom salts and the intention of cleansing extraneous energies, a hot bath or shower is pure magic. In the metaphysical world, water is thought to represent emotions. In the magical world, salt is known as an energetic cleanser and protector. So, put your hands together and you get a relaxing way to wash away excess emotions and energy while calming and protecting your own.

Compartmentalization

My mom loves boxes. Little boxes. We have literally boxes filled with boxes. We have so many boxes we don't use them. But mom loves them, so we keep them. Confidentially, I like boxes too because they are great for organizing, compartmenting, and keeping like things together.

Come to find out, my mom uses figurative boxes as well. When she feels an emotion but is not able to process it at that moment, she will put it in a box.

She decorates it with pretty wrapping paper and bows, making it attractive so that someday when she is ready, she will want to open the box and deal with her emotions. It's quite ingenious really.

Compartmentalizing emotions in this situation means directing your emotions to the appropriate target, thus helping to identify what you are feeling and who you are feeling it for. Case in point, you have a bad day at work; nothing went right. Your boss yelled at you. You spilled coffee. Your company's thingamabobs were sent to the wrong address. Just an icky day. But, now it's over and you must take care of your family and make dinner. "Oh, gracious will this day never end?" you think on your drive home. In the past you may have walked into your home all blustery and angry, yelling at your kids, your dog, and your coat rack. You yelled at anything except the person or thing you were really angry at. But now you have awareness. You realize you are not angry with your kids, your dog, or your coat rack. You compartmentalize. You direct your emotions to the appropriate place. You love your family, so you direct love to them. You are frustrated with your job, so you work with that. Identify why you're frustrated. Why does your job trigger such frustration? What energy, emotion, or memory does your job bring up? Ask this kind of processing, delving questions, when you can really give them the time and space they require.

Compartmentalizing your emotions can help you identify your deeper feelings so you can realize you're not mad at the dog. You're not mad at your partner. So, who are you mad at? And more importantly, why?

Boundaries

Many, many, MANY of my clients have asked about boundaries. I could write for days about all the times I've let my boundaries down, or my lack thereof, and the ramifications of doing so. But that may be counterproductive for you. We all know or have experienced what lowered or no boundaries feel like. Many times, I have volunteered for something which I had no business, or desire, doing all because I was swept up in the energy of the moment.

For assistance with healthy boundaries, we can turn to Machiavelli. He seemed to have had a tremendous ability to set and keep boundaries. Machiavelli considered the value of recognizing one's limits and working with and within them to be a virtue, a strength, and a necessity. I agree, especially for Sensitives. When we review our historical Sensitives, we see many of them not saying "no" in the traditional form. Rather, we see our Sensitives saying, "No more," and in that respect, we can consider them setting boundaries. But with regard to setting personal boundaries, we see very little.

Because Sensitives traditionally have lower self-esteem or confidence and have a great desire to please and be accepted, we often have little or no boundaries. We say yes to anything and everything, only to regret our words or the agreed task later. But boundaries are possible. Boundaries are necessary. Boundaries are good and even healthy for you. There are a few books out there about setting boundaries. I have read and recommend *Boundaries* by Henry Cloud and John Townsend. (Just FYI, it does have a Christian slant to it.) I do offer some energetic boundary/protection suggestions/exercises in Chapter 23 Energetic Care, but here are some suggestions for you to try for setting emotional boundaries.

Be Authentic - Allow, Process, Release

When we use our Sensitive Sleuther casting our eyes on authenticity, we see some of our historical Sensitives become the people we know because of their authenticity, for example, President Lincoln, Eleanor Roosevelt, Dr. King, and Lady Diana. These historical Sensitives put their heart into their life's work, were passionate about people, and publicly honest about who they were. We consistently find that people who are honest, authentic, and open about their vulnerability become known for their trustworthiness. Lincoln is known as Honest Abe. Eleanor Roosevelt was known for helping children and the marginalized. Dr. King is known for his passion for equality and justice. We loved Lady Diana because we saw her as vulnerable and a fresh face for the monarchy. We loved her even more when we found out just how much she struggled. While we haven't previously spoken of James Taylor, he is well-loved for his songs which are honest, human, and deeply vulnerable, and that is exactly why we love his work so much. History shows us the value (and payoff) of being ourselves to the world. Being honest and authentic is attractive to others.

Highly Sensitive Persons are typically so busy pleasing and caring for others that we often don't know what we want or need. Giving all our time and energy to others can often lead to burnout. We need time for ourselves, to recharge our batteries and give ourselves care. This means taking moments throughout the hours, days, and weeks for ourselves. What do YOU need? What do YOU want? What are YOU feeling? And then allowing yourself to be or give yourself that. If you are feeling angry, like Monet, allow yourself to be angry. If you are feeling joy, like George Washington Carver, be joy. If you are feeling quirky and shy, like Tesla, be quirky and shy. Be honest with yourself. Give yourself the time and attention you would give to everyone else.

A helpful phrase I use often is "Allow, Process, Release." Allow whatever you are feeling and give it space and time to exist to teach you whatever the lesson is. Oftentimes, it takes a while to identify what I'm feeling. Am I bored, lonely, tired? I just know it doesn't feel good so sometimes I move on to the next step, Process, for more information.

Give your allowed emotion time to Process the lesson, the memory, the trigger. This usually requires some quiet time for deep reflection and perhaps all day or in some cases weeks or years. This is when Being Authentic can be most tricky. Yes, this can feel very uncomfortable, but that's the point. Be what you are feeling and allow yourself to "feel your feels" even if those "feels" are yucky. You don't have to always be your charming perky self. You are processing, deeply processing, old wounds, old traumas. The more you allow yourself time and space to process the deeper the healing.

Avoiding this processing time just prolongs the pain, like putting a Band-Aid on a broken bone. Sure, your feelings may lift, and you can skip like a child again, but the wound will never fully heal. So, if you are feeling low, feel low until you feel better. Whatever you are feeling, be honest with yourself, and let yourself feel your authentic, true self.

Once the feeling has been processed let it go, release it. Learn the lesson and let it go. Releasing the past, the pain, the trauma can be challenging for us Sensitives. But this step is just as essential as Allowing and Processing, if not more so. Once you have processed and learned the lesson, there is no longer a need to hold on to that energy. Release it. Release the energy back into the wild to assist somewhere else, to teach someone else. (For ideas on how to release life lessons review the Suitcase technique in Chapter 25.)

"I'll get back to you on that"

One technique I wished I learned a long time ago is getting in the habit of saying, "Let me check on that. I'll get back to you." This simple phrase allows you time to check in with yourself and see if whatever is requested of you is something you do indeed want to do, something you can do, or something you are comfortable doing. A few times I have agreed to a project, only to find out during the project that it wasn't fun or rewarding. I end up being "schmer-y," frustrated, unhappy, and unable to do a good job. Responding to a request with, "I need to check my calendar" or some honest variation is perfectly acceptable to the requesting party and to yourself.

We can easily imagine Eleanor Roosevelt using a variation of this technique, giving her time to mull over negotiations. We know she took a little time to decide how she felt about President Kennedy. When Kennedy was running for office, he asked for Eleanor's backing. Eleanor had to consider the request. She asked herself if she liked the young man—could he do the job? Ultimately, she decided she would support Kennedy in his campaign and his administration, growing to like and admire him more and more.

After consulting your higher self or your intuition about whether you truly want to fulfill the request and receiving your answer, remember to close the circle by replying to the request. If your answer is no, you'd rather not fulfill the request, you are uniquely qualified to say no kindly and gently. (And you can say "No.")

Office Hours

A technique that has served me well over the years is what I call Office Hours. Taking on other people's challenges and toxicity can be exhausting, unbearable, and overwhelming. Setting mental and energetic working hours is a healthy way to set boundaries.

All businesses have business hours. Retail stores display their hours usually in their front windows. This is very helpful to customers; we know when we can shop and when we can't. The concept of business office hours is common practice. Why should it be any different for emotional and energetic work too? For example, "I am open to working with anyone between the hours of 10-4 Monday, Wednesday, and Friday. All other times are my own." At 4 pm, I envision turning over my Open sign to Closed. This technique can be considered an extension of carving Me Time into your day. If you have established office hours and defined closed hours, you can naturally have Me Time.

Observer Mode

We have already discussed feeling detached in the case of Princess Diana and how this can support a Sensitive. Princess Diana stated she felt detached or disconnected from her family. While this is a common feeling for Sensitives, a more accurate description may be feeling left out. Sensitives often feel like a sore thumb, sticking out and not fitting in because we are in fact different. Observer mode uses that feeling to your advantage.

Being an observer is different from detachment in that it is a way to step back from a situation or an emotion in order to review the situation from a calmer and wider perspective. We see the Observer Mode in Machiavelli's life. I consider Machiavelli to be the King of the Observer Mode. In one instance, he literally stepped back from a conversation between Cesare Borgia and Cardinal d'Amboise and memorized every word to accurately report back to his superiors. This is an excellent example of the Observer Mode in action.

To practice the Observer mode, sit quietly and review a situation, a personal or world event that is emotionally charged. When reviewing the situation, visualize yourself physically stepping back from the event toward a different point of view. I will actually bend slightly forward, as if I am stepping back from the event, and just watch the replay. This viewpoint allows me to view the event calmly, rationally, and realistically, without my personal emotions involved.

Alien Reporter

When world events become overwhelming, I suggest playing with the Observer Mode. A favorite variation of mine is pretending I am a reporter who needs to relay facts and insights to inform my readers. I have fun pretending I'm an alien reporter trying to explain human behavior. In short, I end up laughing my ever-loving head off at the crazy things humans do. How would Mr. Spock react or report this world event? He would calmly and rationally report facts and conclusions, perhaps even tilt his head curiously as if to say, "Them Humans be crazy."

Character Chat Meditation

For whatever reason, sometimes I can't shake or process an emotion. When this occurs, I will ask that emotion to step in front of me and chat. Similar to the Observer Mode, I exhale and visualize smoke which forms into a character or archetype. I give the character a moment to really develop. Then we chat, introduce ourselves, and I ask the character what it needs or wants.

I have done this a few times and am always surprised by the character. Sometimes I visualize a crooked old woman, while other times it's a circus performer Strong Man. Most recently, I saw Chet. I was having a day where I just couldn't move my emotions. I asked if it was mine. I asked what emotions I was feeling, recognized and acknowledged them, and gave them time and space to process, but the anger, resentment, and sadness persisted. So, I decided to try a Character Chat.

I asked my emotions to step outside. The funniest thing came to my imagination: fuzzy angry little monster named Chet. I imagined him spitting, growling, and snarling, similar to the yellow-green Tazmanian Devil from *Looney Tunes*. Honestly, it was hard to take Chet seriously. I imagined giving him a moment to stew and spit. When he calmed down, we had a chat. I asked him what he wanted. "Candy," he said. "Jellybeans," he said. He continued to list all sorts of sugary things. I realized he was being self-destructive. "You want to be self-destructive, here you go," I said and imagined handing him a ticking clock. I watched the clock count down. I watched him go "poof" and fade away with the breeze. And you know what? I felt better. I felt lighter. I had created a shift. By giving my emotions a shape, a character, a name, and a good laugh I had given my emotions time and space so they could process and move on.

Conscious Conversation

In my monthly support group, one of the most common questions is about communication. Sensitives avoid confrontation at all costs. Conversations can feel like confrontation, or can easily devolve into confrontation, so communication may not be a Sensitive's strong suit.

Communication is a huge topic, but I have two recommendations for Sensitives. My first recommendation is when in a heated discussion/argument, walk away. Excuse yourself, kindly, if possible, but leave the conversation. No progress can be made with anger. Return to the topic when both parties are calm and rational.

The most common question I hear about communication is dealing with a toxic person, usually at work. A toxic person is consistently cranky, always complaining, and never satisfied. A Sensitive will feel drained, tired, and exhausted after a brief connection with a toxic person. Toxic people are not necessarily bad people. Their energy just doesn't mesh with yours. If you cannot remove a toxic person from your life, i.e. a coworker, then I suggest a conscious conversation.

A conscious conversation is similar to a character chat, except the character you are chatting with is a specific person. For example, I had just started a new job, and I was very excited but very green, very new. I tried to make casual conversation with one of my coworkers, just getting to know them a little bit when I was met with a solid brick wall that only gave me short answers, burgeoning on rude. I got the hint and moved on. Later, when I was home, the memory of the interaction bugged me a bit, so I began my deep breathing, quieted my mind, and visualized my coworker. I imagined us sitting down calmly and having a nice chat. I imagined things I'd like to tell my coworker, such as, "We don't have to be best friends, but a peaceful working relationship would be nice," and so forth. Within the week our relationship was comfortable. Within the month other coworkers noticed the change.

If you have someone in your life whose energy does not feel comfortable, try talking to them in a meditative state. Picture them in your head and form the image to be nice and strong. Then calmly, and rationally speak your piece.

Laughter is the Best Medicine

I have recently been experiencing anger. This is new for me. In the past when I have recognized that I was angry, I would immediately become sad. These days when I'm angry, I stay angry. I consider this progress. The first time I experienced anger, I was working in a very nice little natural gift boutique. I was surrounded by lovely things, natural bamboo t-shirts, powerful rocks, and lots of encouraging artwork. I sat down and tried to focus on all the positive things around me when I realized I didn't want to be positive. I wanted to stay angry. I pouted and stomped like a two-year-old. It was so different for me, I talked to a friend about it. "I don't wanna be happy," I said, and I stomped and kicked. Immediately, I giggled and laughed. I felt better and lighter; I had moved the anger out and replaced it with laughter. I had honored my anger, gave it space, and released it with a comical physical action. Another time I was angry, my mom suggested hitting a pillow. The moment my hand hit the pillow, I remembered the scene in the 1999 movie *Analyze This* where Robert de Niro's character shot at a pillow, and I laughed and laughed. I felt better.

There is a growing number of studies to prove the adage that Laughter is the best medicine. Laughter increases oxygen intake, stimulates circulation, releases endorphins, and reduces cortisol. All of which is to say that laughter is great for a healthy body, mind, and spirit. From laughing until you cry to a slight chuckle, from a guffaw to a giggle, laughter is a wonderful way to shift your mood. So, the next time you are feeling moody or emotionally overwhelmed watch your favorite comic or sitcom.

Your Dictionary

I am a big believer in processing by identifying your experiences. For example, a few years ago I worked at a rock shop. A customer and her daughter came in and asked about stones. Since this is just about my favorite thing to do, I taught the little girl about stones. She picked her favorite and held it for a little while. I asked her how she felt.

"Like I'm going up an elevator," she reported.

"And, is that a good feeling?" I asked.

"Yes, I like that."

I regularly will ask a client if what they are experiencing is comfortable for them. Maybe the little girl didn't like elevators, I didn't know. We humans share common experiences like the first day of school, first dates, or job interviews, but each of us experiences them differently. For example, high school. My high school years were the toughest of my life. For my best friend, they were her best.

We had many shared experiences: football games, spring dances, and lunches. She thoroughly enjoyed our high school years. I, on the other hand, considered them complete torture.

The physic medium John Edwards explains in one of his episodes of *Crossing Over* how early in his career he needed to identify the meaning of what he was seeing. He reports needing to understand the meaning of a white rose. In effect, he was creating an agreement with the energy he was receiving.

Creating your own understanding with the energy can have a very empowering effect. However you receive messages, take a moment to notice how it feels to you. If it is an aroma, what does that aroma mean to you? What is your history with that aroma, if any?

Be easy with yourself

Sensitives can be very accepting of everyone, except themselves. We can be our toughest critics. My childhood curfew was always earlier than my mom would've set. My grades were never high enough. I never felt pretty enough, smart enough, or enough in general. This was due in large part to my being Sensitive. We rarely feel we are "enough." Since we are heart-based beings, we always want to make things better, including ourselves. What we miss is the fact that we are already more than enough. As Mary Poppins says, we are "practically perfect in every way." But we can also always do better.

After spending a lifetime of self-condescension, my mom told me one day, "Treat yourself like I would." Bingo, bango, bongo! I had a technique!

When you are getting down on yourself or in need of a rest, for whatever reason, try this little technique on for size. What would your mother (or your childhood primary care person) do for you? What would they say to you when you were beating yourself up? It was something along the lines of "You did your best," or "It'll be alright," or "Relax, you're being too hard on yourself." Phrases like this, or your own personal phrase, can do wonders for your nervous system, your mind, and your soul. When you were sick, what would your primary care person do for you? Would they tuck you into bed all nice and cozy? Would they bring you your favorite blanket and comfort food? Find those comfort zones and remain there, just for a little while, and let your body go limp as you relax.

One phrase that really gives me peace is, "If it could've been different, it would've." I first heard this phrase during a jewelry-making class. While creating amazing pieces of jewelry with the class, we chatted and got to know one another a bit. A piece wasn't turning out the way I had envisioned. A classmate said, "If it could've been different, it would have." Hearing her say those words was like a magic tonic for me. All the self-doubt about past decisions and actions was immediately forgiven. If I could've done things differently, I would've! My past actions were based on past knowledge, wisdom, and ability. I am a different person than I once was, so beating up my past self for not knowing better was silly and a waste of energy. If you find yourself returning to some old ancient event that gives you angst, let it go knowing that if it could have been different, it would have.

Now that you know things couldn't have been different you can rest easy also knowing you are always doing/being your best. This is a natural progression, or extension. If things could've been different, you are automatically forgiving yourself for any past issues. Similarly, knowing that you are always doing your best is a way to forgive yourself for any current issues. Follow my logic for a moment. If you understand past events occurred the best they could at the time, the same logic applies to any current (or future) events. Yes? So, in that light, you are always doing or being your best. Even on those days when you just "can't" anymore, those days when you are too tired to brush your teeth let alone keep any appointments, you are still doing your best. If staying in bed all day is all you can muster, that is your best that day. So, relax, and enjoy staying in bed, and know that you are always being and doing your best.

Sensitives Love Water

According to Judith Orloff in her book, *Thriving as an Empath*, Sensitives love water. Water is very soothing and healing and is associated with the emotional body. Sensitives can be very emotional. Sometimes, we can't control our emotions, no matter how hard we try. Taking a long hot bath or dipping your toe in a cool mountain stream or imagining you are beachside can be very helpful in shocking your body and soothing those hot emotions.

I have seen Sensitive persons completely change when they are near bodies of water. I knew a person who lived in the landlocked state of Colorado. When they were in Colorado, they were always angry, and nothing ever felt right to them. Everything was wrong and they loudly (and sometimes violently) let everyone know it. They were in and out of legal trouble. But when they were near the ocean, they were jovial, lighthearted, and everything was hunky dory. They were a different person to me. I was astounded to see the transformation.

Therefore, when you are feeling angry, hotheaded, or just plain *blah* try being near water or drinking water. It just might help; and hey, if it doesn't at least you are cleaner.

Sequoia Staircase Meditation

Living in the foothills of the Rocky Mountains, I am very blessed to be surrounded by trees. A common game I play with my mom is "See that tree?" and we laugh and laugh because all we see are trees. We are thinking of giving them names for clarification, but that would ruin the game. So, it just makes sense that my favorite mediation would include trees.

I have used and taught this mediation often, and I call it the Sequoia Staircase.

Begin by relaxing as before, in a comfy and safe place. Breathe deep and relax.

With each exhale allow gravity to take over and sink deeper and deeper into your chair.

Imagine you are in a wise ancient forest of Sequoia trees. These trees have been here for centuries and hold great knowledge and wisdom. Take a moment to really feel your imagination.

Begin to focus on one tree. Notice how huge this sequoia tree is, and how small you are in comparison.

Really look at the bark of your tree. A pattern in the bark appears, the shape of a door forms, then a door handle begins to appear. This is the tree's permission and invitation to go within the tree.

Step up to the tree, turn the door handle, and open the bark-encrusted door.

Walk through.

Inside you see a great round room, take a moment to look around.

To your right is a hat rack and table. Place all your hats on the hat rack, all your roles, all your responsibilities. They'll be there when you leave. Place everything you've been carrying, your backpack, your briefcase, your concerns, and your worries on the table.

Move to the center of the room. Notice two spiral staircases winding along the wall of the room. One staircase goes up, one goes down. You are welcome to use either staircase at any time. For now, move to the center of the room.

Notice how soft and cushy the floor is, and make yourself comfy by sitting or lying down.

Spend some time here soaking up the soft supportive sequoia floor. You may notice a tingling in your feet. This is the grounding energy of the earth. Allow it to spread throughout your body.

This is your safe space. It is yours to do what you wish. The more you return to this place the more you can explore and find many helpful tools, ideas, and guides. This is merely an introduction to your sequoia safe space.

When you are ready, begin to return to your physical room by wiggling your toes and fingers.

Honey Dripping Meditation

This is one of the first meditations I created. I have found it to be very relaxing. When I have had a crazy day, I practice this meditation immediately before falling asleep. I have found it works wonders for me to calm down and get a good night's sleep.

Move into a safe and cozy space where you can be alone and undisturbed for a while.

Take a few deep cleansing breaths, expanding the belly on your inhale and dropping your shoulders on your exhale.

Imagine that you are standing in your favorite place on earth, preferably somewhere natural and quiet.

Imagine a thick stream of honey is above you. It is an endless source of honey from a huge honey dipper in the sky.

Feel the honey as it hits the top of your head. Notice how relaxed your scalp feels. Feel the warmth of the honey on the crown of your head.

Allow gravity to pull the honey further down, allow it to relax your pores and soak in as deep as it needs to. Let the sticky honey pull out any old impurities (stress, pain, etc). Feel as the sweet honey fills the newly released parts with warmth and love (or exactly what you need).

Continue to feel the honey move down your body, to your eyelids, jaw, shoulders, and all the way down your spine to your hips, thighs, knees, and ankles.

Once the honey hits your feet, watch as the honey moves to the earth. Watch how all the stress, fear, and pain that it has pulled out of you makes wonderful, composted soil for the earth.

Witness how your released honey makes beautiful flowers, plants, and trees grow quickly and magnificently.

Scan your body. Do you still feel tense or pain anywhere? Move the honey to any remaining tense spots in your body. Allow the honey to pool in those spots, swirling and concentrating the healing honey in those areas.

When you are ready, slowly return to the room. Wiggle your toes. Shrug your shoulders. Stretch your arms. Open your eyes. Take a few deep breaths to become fully present and awake or take a nap as you see fit.

Forgiveness and Ho'Oponopono

Ho'Oponopono is a traditional Hawaiian form of family conflict resolution, similar to what some may call an Intervention. The process includes a spiritual component and family members confessing and taking responsibility for their actions. But most who are familiar with the practice today know Ho'Oponopono as a solitary personal prayer, derived from Joe Vitale's book *Zero Limits*. The prayer practiced today from Vitale's book is, "I love you. I am sorry. Please forgive me. Thank you."[1]

In the midst of my self-care, this prayer/practice came back to me and so I began to repeat the prayer. I found I was tripping over, "Please forgive me." So, I began to look at my feelings of forgiveness. Over the years, I have worked on forgiveness in a few ways. I've burned a forgiveness candle, a tall 7-day candle on which I wrote all whom I felt I needed to forgive. It was fascinating to watch the varying speeds the candle burned depending on the name written. I've processed my emotions by writing letters to past friends, family members, and partners. I've meditated on my relationships, turning the tables around to see their viewpoint. This has helped me better understand them, and, in turn, forgive them. I've visualized cutting energetic cords, disconnecting and releasing their energy with love. Each time, I was able to forgive them. Of course, I forgive them, for their sake and mine. But I realized I hadn't forgiven myself. I'd spent time, effort, and energy on forgiving others, but I'd forgotten to forgive myself.

Sensitives can hold onto shame, guilt, and regret until they become a large part of who we are. We already feel left out, like we don't belong anywhere, and when we add guilt, we can become laden down, heavy with energy and emotions, carrying our cross to bear. Our feelings of guilt become debilitating. We need to remember to forgive ourselves as well as others.

Forgiving oneself is perhaps the hardest part of the process for a Sensitive. I can get to a point of understanding another's motivations thereby leading to forgiveness. It can be tricky to obtain the same level of objectivity and understanding when forgiving oneself. The technique of Observer Mode (page 151) helps us to step back from our emotions and provide that objective viewpoint, thus giving us space to understand our own motivations, starting us down the path of forgiveness.

The Ho'Oponopono prayer includes, "Please forgive me." Here's where I get tripped up. In this phrase, I am asking for someone else to forgive me. I am, in essence, putting the responsibility of my healing onto someone else, thus giving my power away. Getting to a place where I am comfortable asking for forgiveness is a huge step.

CHAPTER 22

Mental Care

As we move up, the layers of being human, our next level is the mental layer. The mind is a Sensitive's strongest tool for protection, creating, or just playing. I call our world—the material world—the Linear World. The world of the mind—or mental layer—I call the Random World. Anything can happen in the Random World; anything can be created. Things don't have to make sense in the Random World like they do in the Linear World. In the Linear World, Tuesday always follows Monday, dinner precedes sleep, and roads always go in the same direction. In the Random World, anything is possible. There are no rules that need to be followed, no gravity to keep you attached, and no responsibilities or burdens. The Random World is pure energy, and energy can be molded and fiddled with to create whatever you wish. As such, there are a myriad of ways to care for your mental layer—your Random World. I present just a few ideas and examples to get your imagination going.

Many of our Historical Sensitives used visions and techniques as coping mechanisms, a form of mental care and mental health. We have a few Historical Sensitives with strong mental health practices, namely Saint Hildegard, Frederick Douglass, and Dr. King. Hildegard was certainly aware of the importance of staying positive, considering positive mental strength the key to a strong healthy body, writing often about mental defenses and a strong mental immune system.[1] We can also consider Tesla, President Lincoln, and First Lady Roosevelt to have had strong mental health practices. Since we have already discussed most of these figures, let's turn to Tesla and his mental care techniques.

While Tesla, the sweet brilliant little human that he was, known for his thought experiments, may not be the poster child for strong mental health, he offers some insights and techniques for strengthening our mental attitudes. With a possible IQ of 160, Tesla's mind was his greatest strength. He completed complicated calculations in his head by visualizing the math problem on a blackboard. He was able to recall the image of any book he had read. He envisioned models and their inner workings. Reportedly, he did not need blueprints; he could build his inventions directly from the visions in his mind. In fact, it sounds to me that he used his visions as a template for his creations. By that, I mean he visualized a particular piece of his motor, and then cut it out by tracing his mental image.

At one point in Tesla's life, he became acutely over-sensitized. At the age of 25, while working in Budapest in 1881, Tesla was "affected" and forced to his bed. Tesla's senses were always "extremely keen" but this time his sensitivities became unbearable and "nearly cost him his life."[2] His hearing became so acute; he could hear a watch ticking three rooms away. He put rubber pads under the legs of his bed to soften the vibrations from passing traffic outside. All his senses, even his body, were affected.

John O'Neill, author of *Prodigal Genius: The Life of Nikola Tesla*, writes of Tesla's experience as "thunderous pandemonium," an "internal explosion," and Tesla was "constantly wracked with twitches and tremors" and "a peculiar creepy sensation in his forehead." I have experienced this "creepy sensation" in the forehead and have noticed other Sensitives lightly scratching their brow when conversing about deeper subjects. I've come to understand this sensation as a sign of an active brow chakra (see the section about the brow chakra in Chapter 20 – Physical Care). I've come to smile knowingly when I notice a Sensitive do so. To me, it means the brow chakra, known for clarity and intuition, is open and the person is speaking from a more clear, honest, and intuitive place. During Tesla's experience, I believe his senses were so overstimulated that his physical body couldn't handle it. (To me this points to one reason why humans are so limited. We just can't handle the truth.) Over time, Tesla's body calmed down and he was able to return to his work. Incidentally, his huge breakthrough, developing the rotating magnetic field motor, would come mere months after this episode.[3]

When he became overwhelmed by his sensitivities, Tesla turned his attention to beautiful or peaceful images. He reports that this technique offered him moments of peace. When Tesla practiced breathing exercises, his body felt lighter (so light in fact, he thought he could fly, and repeatedly and unsuccessfully worked to develop the technique).[4]

Tesla also imagined traveling to places he'd never visited, mentally exploring new locations and filling in as much imagined detail as possible. He imagined loved ones to bring in the energy of love and consolation. Tesla used these techniques of visualization to fulfill his inventions. The mental powers of Tesla are the stuff of legends and show us the possibilities of the human mind, offering us techniques for visualizing solutions to problems.⁵

In the classic 1940 movie, *Lucky Partners*, starring Ginger Rogers and Ronald Colman, Rogers compares stubbing your toe to stubbing your mind. "Why should it be any different?" she asks. Many of us have been asking the same question ever since. It seems it takes approximately 80 years for humans to adapt to new ideas. Evolution is slow and gradual indeed.

In my lifetime, society has realized and finally embraced the importance of mental health. No longer is the word therapist whispered in dark corners. It has become socially acceptable, even trendy, to see a professional counselor for assistance. America even has a national mental health emergency phone number (#999). And thank heaven, it's about time. It's an excellent thing too, especially for Highly Sensitive Persons. We are no longer shunned by society, hidden away in dark and scary places such as dusty attics or dirty asylums, or labeled as "the nervous type" or "emotionally unstable."

As previously stated, approximately 80% of mental health patients are Highly Sensitive Persons. Given that we are often shy, feel things more deeply, and may seem a bit different or weird to others or even ourselves, it's no wonder we need some extra support. Moreover, we tend to process things more deeply and, like most people, are resistant to letting go. Of course, we need additional support. It's the world that's crazy, not us.

Now for the good news. A Highly Sensitive Person's mind is strong. Sometimes we think so much, our minds are so strong and busy that we can't sleep. We tend to think of deep processing as a negative thing, ruminating or worrying about things out of our control. But with practice, we can turn our busy minds to our advantage. We can use our minds for our own benefit, and in the case of many of our Historical Sensitives, the benefit of humanity.

We have seen in our historical sensitives how they used their "mental powers" to help them move out of a place of pain and into our history books, namely Dr. King and First Lady Roosevelt. These Sensitives used their minds to focus on what they wanted. Dr. King visualized being at the front of the bus and a world where people are accepted for their character. First Lady Roosevelt talked herself out of her depression. You are in admirable company when you practice positive mental health and visualization techniques.

Using our minds positively takes practice and discipline, but it can be done. This section offers some ideas as a starting place. These ideas are not intended as required steps or obligations but rather as a place to experiment and begin your journey to find and develop your own practice and tools.

Mental Care

Travel Like Tesla

We just learned how Tesla used his mind to calm himself down and relax. We saw how that relaxed state helped him with his work. Now, let's try it for ourselves.

1. Relax in a comfortable position. Allow your breathing to become deep, rhythmic, and calm (I bet you're already feeling better).
2. Imagine a place you've always wanted to visit. It could be here on Earth or somewhere else entirely. Maybe you've always wanted to travel to Cairo or to a place with beautiful turquoise water and soft sandy beaches. Perhaps it's Paris or the Great Wall of China. Or maybe somewhere completely new and different—maybe an imaginary place, another planet, or a location from Star Trek's holodeck or Doctor Who.
3. Let your imagination take you where you want to go.
4. Fill in some sensory details. What does the ground feel like? What does the air smell like? Do you feel warmth from a heat source or a soft cool breeze? Are there buildings or structures around? Is there a path of some kind? Follow the path and see what you find.
5. Spend as much time as you like exploring this place.
6. When you are ready, slowly return your attention to the room. Wiggle your toes and fingers. Gently move your shoulders, open your eyes, and stretch your body.

Welcome back! How does that feel? How does your body feel? Hopefully, rested and refreshed.

Hildegard's Visualization

In chapter 2 we discussed Saint Hildegard's vision of light. This is a visualization technique based on her writings about her visions.

1. Move into a comfortable position and let your breath relax and become naturally deep and rhythmic.
2. Visualize a bright light emanating from your heart.
3. Allow the light of your heart to rise and rise, up and up, higher and higher until it reaches the clouds.
4. See your heart-light mixing and melding with the light of the clouds, blending with other Earthlings' heart-light.
5. Let this cloud of heart light spread out until it covers the entire planet.

6. Watch as this heart-light cloud comes down and fills everyone and everything on the planet.
7. Let the cloud seep deeper into everything and watch as it lights up everything on our planet.
8. Stay here as long as you wish. When you are ready, slowly and gradually return to the room.

Eleanor Roosevelt's Meditation Practice

In *Eleanor*, David Michaelis recounts First Lady Roosevelt's meditative practice.[6] While we have already touched on this subject, I feel it is worth revisiting and attempting to update and incorporate her technique into an exercise you may want to explore.

1. Find a quiet space with no distractions.
2. Lie flat on the floor with your hands at your side and your legs uncrossed. You may prefer to sit in a comfy chair or lie down on a couch.
3. With relaxed deep breaths, allow your mind to turn completely blank. Let go of all your worries, tasks, and anything else weighing on your mind. If they creep back in, focus on your breath and return to a quiet blank mind.
4. Imagine yourself resting, relaxing, deeper and deeper.
5. Allow your body to rest heavily and deeply.
6. Feel your body's weight sinking deeper and deeper into the floor or whatever you are resting.
7. Stay here for a few minutes. Eleanor Roosevelt practiced this for 10 minutes at a time.
8. Slowly return to the room by wiggling your toes and fingers, opening your eyes, and stretching your arms and other body parts.

Volunteer

When First Lady Roosevelt was 18, having just completed her formal education, she served as a volunteer teacher for the Red Cross and the Navy Hospitals during World War I. Taking a cue from Eleanor Roosevelt, a lifelong volunteer, dedicating your time and energy to someone or a cause can be very beneficial for your emotional and mental health. It helps you get out of your head, forget about your troubles, and put your support and energy toward a worthwhile cause. It reminds you that there are others who need more help than you and helps you realize how blessed you are. So, the next time you are worried about something, ruminating and not progressing, find somewhere to volunteer, assist others, and get out of your head.

Watch Your Thoughts

This may seem like a funny thing to say. My grandfather, with his dry sense of humor, would've had a field day with that statement. He would say something like "Is there a cartoon bubble above my head?" (A fun technique you may want to try). However, being a watchdog of your thoughts is an ideal place to start taking care of your mental well-being. What do I mean? I mean pay attention to the thoughts in your head. Phrases such as, "I should've done that better," "I'm worthless," or "I'm not good enough," are very damaging to your self-esteem and completely untrue. On an energetic level, thoughts are energy, and like attracts like. Thus, self-defeating thoughts attract similar energy, feeding and increasing the self-hating monster. This creates a cycle where negative energy grows and perpetuates itself.

Again, we turn to First Lady Roosevelt for inspiration, as she did not permit self-defeating thoughts to rule her life or actions. She allowed negative or self-deprecating thoughts into her world only long enough to be recognized and shooed away or reversed into a positive belief, another technique well worth trying.

Similarly, we see strong mental practices in Saint Hildegard and Florence Nightingale. Both sensitive women persevered through their physical discomfort while remaining wholly dedicated to a higher power, a noble cause, and their greater mission. It must have taken a strong mental attitude to carry on, considering how physically uncomfortable they were. There's been many a day where I've said, "Not today," and crawled back into bed to rest—but not these ladies, oh no. When they did return to their beds, they continued to work, write, and in Saint Hildegard's case, draw.

So, watch your thoughts. It may take practice, but when a self-defeating thought scurries across your mind, slow it down, and process that thought. The next time you beat yourself up for something you did, take a moment. Ask questions such as, "Am I really not good enough?" "Am I truly worthless?" Author Byron Katie in her book, *A Mind At Home With Itself,* would suggest you ask, "Is that statement true? Is it REALLY true? Can I really believe that statement?" When you take a step back and look objectively at yourself, you'll find you have done admirable and worthwhile things (or the opposite of whatever your self-hating thought may be). Empirical evidence contradicts that thought. Be a detective and find it.

Allow me to tell you a brief story. One Thursday morning in March 2022, I woke up cranky. For no apparent reason, I was thinking snarly and judgmental thoughts such as "she should have thought of that" or "he should've known better." Once I noticed I was having these judgmental thoughts (and it took an hour or two), I realized those types of thoughts were not typical of me. I stepped outside and paced. Pacing soon became stomping, and the stomping evolved into crying. There I was stomping and crying like a two-year-old saying, "Meanies! Everyone stop being mean to each other!" I later found out that was the day Russia crossed Ukraine's borders.

I tell you this story as an example of how Sensitives can pick up energy from anywhere. I live nowhere near Europe or Asia. I do not watch the news (and haven't since 1999). I have very little direct contact with the city or the world. Still, the angry and fearful energy hit me like a ton of bricks. Since the emotional energy was so foreign to my character, I knew it wasn't mine.

I share this story to illustrate how your thoughts can either lead you or how you can lead your thoughts. Rhonda Byrne writes in *The Secret* about the power of your thoughts. She suggests your thoughts can manifest physically. So, if you don't know what you are thinking, how is your body feeling? If your body hurts or aches, it may be a signal that your thoughts may be detrimental to yourself.

I also tell you this story as an example of processing your emotions. Had I not given my emotions space to reveal themselves, I wouldn't have understood what was going on or been able to release them. I'm still amazed at how quickly those thoughts, emotions, and energy dissipated once I identified them.

And I tell you this story as an example of how powerful your thoughts can be. My experience started with a thought. It evolved into an emotion, which moved to an energy that I was then able to identify and release.

The Awareness Door Attendant

Awareness is one of the most powerful tools a Highly Sensitive Person can develop. When you are aware of something, you can take action, do something about it. When you have no idea, you can't. You just sit in a repetitive spinning cycle, getting nowhere.

Consider your mind to be similar to a metaphorical apartment building. A door attendant is the first line of defense for a building. They allow people to enter and leave a building. A seasoned door attendant can recognize who "belongs" in the building and who does not.

Placing a metaphorical attendant at the doorway of your mind can do a similar job, stopping detrimental thoughts from even entering your mind and assisting the helpful thoughts inside. Let your door attendant figuratively say, "Sorry but this building is closed." Give your mind a single entry point, easing your door attendant's workload. Give your attendant a name and a fun uniform. Play with it—this is your mind, and your thoughts make your mind's door attendant your own. Or if you prefer, use a different metaphor to play with. Maybe you prefer the concept of a bouncer—a big, strong figure with a stern attitude. Or perhaps your door attendant is more like a sweet gentle grandparent who lovingly guides self-defeating thoughts away. Whatever metaphor you use, or however you do it, be vigilant with your thoughts.

Just Like Me Mediation

There is a saying that people come into your life for a reason, a season, or a lifetime. There is one person who came into my life, I believe, to teach me this technique. We were briefly friends. We shared thoughts and exchanged ideas. I don't remember her name, how she came into my life, or how she left, but I am grateful for the technique she taught me. It has brought me great solace over the years.

She taught me a wonderful technique for increasing empathy called "Just Like Me." She explained that when you bump heads with someone, adopting the Just Like Me mindset can shift your energy to a more compassionate stance. This technique can also be used for world events, difficult relationships, physical pain or emotional strife, your anxiety, or anything else. I will use the example of a headache to demonstrate but again it can be applied in a myriad of ways.

When I am experiencing a headache, I will think "Just like me, this headache wants . . . attention. Just like me, this headache wants to be cared for. Just like me, this headache wants love. Just like me, this headache needs rest." And so on, going deeper and deeper into empathy for my headache.

The script may change for each individual or topic you work on. However, I've found this technique to help alleviate my pain as well as be enlightening for my mental and emotional self. It's actually pretty amazing.

Remove the Nots

One of the most challenging tasks I placed on myself was to remove the word Not from my speech. Initially, I found my words became quite verbose and clumsy as I tried to say something positive. Eventually, it became second nature, even in my thoughts. So much so that it took me a moment to decode someone else's words and phrases. Expressions like "You can't not do nothing" or "I'll never not want . . ." took me a moment to decipher and understand.

The concept of thinking positively was first illustrated to me in an animal energy class. The teacher explained that mental images are energy and are conveyed as such. When we work with an animal, we imagine our goal, what we want the animal to do, rather than what we don't want. For example, "Stay off the couch" conjures images (and therefore energy) of lying on the couch. When we say "stay on the floor" we imagine our dog comfortably lying in the sunshine on the floor, our goal. We become more aware of the importance of thinking and visualizing positively when we realize language, thoughts, and actions are just as much energy as the couch or anything tangible.

When we look to our historical Sensitives for guidance and examples, we find Monet, Lincoln, and Tubman as possible teachers. Monet was constantly striving to create his masterpiece, always unhappy with his final piece. We can look at this as if he thought his work was not good enough, and, in turn, that he was not good enough (a common concept with Sensitives). This NOT kept him working, pushing, and striving to be better. For some Sensitives like Monet, the NOTs do that. For others, the NOTs can be paralyzing, stopping us in our tracks. For some, just the fear of NOT can be debilitating, namely the fear of rejection or failure.

We can easily imagine Lincoln and Tubman not even considering the NOTs, thankfully. Lincoln was focused on keeping the country together. Not keeping the country together was not an option for him. (I'm so confused right now with all these Nots.) Put more positively, for Lincoln keeping the country together was the only option. Likewise, Harriet Tubman was focused on getting people to freedom; failure was NOT an option. I imagine failure was never on Tubman's radar. She kept returning to the South again and again, most likely filled with a sense of determination and righteousness—failure was inconceivable. No NOTs for Lincoln and Tubman. Indeed, we can posit many of our historical Sensitives were filled with conviction and purpose, the Nots never entering their imaginations.

Removing the Nots from our radar may take some practice deciphering and reversing our thoughts and words. The phrase "She's Not Wrong," while gaining laughs on your favorite sitcom, is actually negative. Funny, but negative. It is much easier and healthier to say, "She's correct," (albeit not as funny). I have faith that some sensitive screenwriter will come up with some clever positive phrase for us soon.

Another example is the phrase, "Don't forget." We say it all the time. "Don't forget to put the washing in the dryer. Don't forget to pick up eggs. Don't forget to eat." But what would happen if we said "Remember" instead? "Remember to put the washing in the dryer." "Remember to eat." It's a small but significant tweak to your language and intention. By saying or thinking "Remember" you are creating a to-do list for yourself. By thinking "Don't forget" you are setting yourself up to forget.

Remove can't, shouldn't, and won't from your thoughts and speech. Rephrase your words/thoughts into a more positive statement. "I'm positive I can't" doesn't count. Yes, it's funny, but we're not going for laughs, we're going for healthy mental practices. For example, "I can't afford that" may become "I choose to spend my money elsewhere." "I can't" becomes "I'd rather do something else." You can see how it can take more words to be positive, but it's worth it on an energetic level. By removing the NOTs from your thoughts and speech, you feel more empowered and judge yourself and others less, taking the first step to self-acceptance. Ta-dah!

Affirmations

You may think the word "affirmation" is reserved for people engaged in silly navel-gazing on mountain tops, and it used to be. Now affirmations are found everywhere. Consider your favorite meme or a company's tagline ("Feels good to pay less") as an affirmation. Who remembers the classic Saturday Night Live sketch, "And doggone it, people like me"? Yes, affirmations can be fun, healthy, and helpful as long as they are positive.

Affirmation is just a fancy word for repeating a positive phrase. Phrases such as, "I am worthy," "I am enough," and "I am divine," are examples of affirmations. You can even shorten your affirmation to one word, like "Love," or "Joy" and "Acceptance." I consider Dr. King's phrase, "I have a dream," to be an affirmation. He focused on what he wanted, his dreams, and his eventual positive outcome (one which we move closer toward each day). We can easily imagine our historical Sensitives removed the NOTs (Lincoln and Tubman specifically) and used positive affirmations to help them power through the tough times and accomplish their goals. Lincoln's affirmation may have been, "I will keep this country together." Harriet Tubman's affirmation may have been "I will get these people to safety." While Lincoln and Tubman may not have used affirmations the same way that we do today, the concept of remaining mentally positive was still present in their minds.

The idea behind affirmations is twofold. First, it keeps your mind focused on your affirmation, leaving little room for self-defeating thoughts. Second, it draws the energy of your affirmation closer to you. And who has two thumbs and wants more love, joy, and acceptance in their world? This girl!

Traditionally affirmations are done during meditation, but they can also be used at any time, anywhere. When you're walking, when you're chewing, when you're working out. Here's another story. Once upon a time not so long ago, I was in a relationship that had deteriorated into an unhealthy one. Each day, as I left my office, I took the stairs. Each step, I said the affirmation, "I am not afraid. I am not afraid. I am not afraid." I thought I was conjuring courage and banishing my fear, but energetically, I was attracting and increasing the energy of fear. If I had thought, "I am strong," or "I am safe," I would have attracted that energy, which is what I really wanted. When creating your affirmation, make it as positive as possible. Focus on your goal rather than your current obstacle.

Visualizations

If you are a visually-oriented person, like Dr. King, visualizations will be easy for you. However, if another sense—such as smelling or hearing—is stronger for you, visualizations may not be your bag. In any case, there are an unlimited number of guided meditations, i.e. visualizations, available out there. Visualizing is an effective way to use your mental powers for positive purposes. Athletes, particularly skiers and basketball players, use visualizations before competitions. Remember Dr. King and his ride to school? He imagined sitting at the front of the bus. He said to himself, my body may be in the back, but my mind is in the front of the bus. Visualization.

Here is a really fun way to turn your nagging worrying mind into a strong helpful mind.

SUPERHERO VISUALIZATION

While it is doubtful any of our historical Sensitives felt they were superheroes, history has shown they were. I can easily visualize Harriet Tubman and Eleanor Roosevelt wearing capes that majestically blow in the breeze. This visualization can be done either in a quiet place or, with practice anywhere at any time. This meditation is about you and imagining you as your most amazing self, the superhero you are. By all means, have fun with it!

1. Begin, as with all visualizations or meditations, with a few deep cleansing breaths and relax your body.
2. Visualize yourself in your secret superhero costume. Really have fun with it. The colors, the design, the cape blowing in the breeze.
3. Now add your "sidekicks," your guides, perhaps even some animals or ancestors. (After all, even Superman had a dog and a father.) Again,

have fun with it. Imagine them however they come to you. Your guides may appear translucent like a ghost, or fully present and dressed in current fashions, or even match your superhero costume. Perhaps your sidekick guides are a squad of cheerleaders or a throng of loving fans.

4. Now add your superhero theme song. Use a favorite song or make something up. Really feel the beat. Maybe some lyrics come to you, or perhaps a band surrounds you as they play.
5. Now visualize the standard "slow walk" scene used in nearly every superhero movie. Add some smoke and backlighting for dramatic effect, or whatever comes to mind.
6. Let your superhero movie play. Feel free to add anything that makes the scene uniquely yours—anything that evokes a sense of strength and power, whether it's an aroma or the texture of your costume.

Now, how do you feel now, huh? Pretty gosh darn empowered? There you go!

Obviously, you can play with your superhero. What is your superpower (besides boundless compassion and infinite love)? What is your superhero name? Play with the concept of being a superhero. Really become friends with your inner superhero, and maybe even let it come out to play occasionally.

HOT AIR BALLOON RELEASE VISUALIZATION

Humans in general, and HSPs in particular, have a hard time letting go of things. Sensitives will ruminate on an encounter, playing it over and over in our heads, coming to no conclusion and only increasing our regret. Allow me to offer a different technique, one of releasing. I really enjoy working with the metaphor of a hot air balloon when working with letting go or releasing.

Here's how it goes:

1. Get comfy, relax your body, quiet your mind, and focus on your breathing. You may want to add some white noise for your conscious mind to pay attention to.
2. Breathe deeply in, filling and raising your belly. Exhale gently and let all the tension in your body dissolve. Just continue breathing until it becomes natural and rhythmic.
3. Once your body is completely relaxed, imagine a hot air balloon. Make it any color and shape you wish, perhaps rainbow or the shape of a rubber duck, whatever image pops into your head.

4. While the balloon is inflating, take some time to fill your ballast bags—sandbags that hang from the side of the balloon. Fill your bags with anything you'd like to release, let go of. That old relationship, those words you said to a co-worker, that bite of chocolate cake you ate when you were on a diet. Place anything and everything you're holding onto that no longer serves you into the ballast bags.
5. Visualize your hot air balloon rising higher and higher in the sky.
6. When the balloon begins to slow down its ascent, drop one of your ballast bags. Watch as it falls to the ground and you rise higher. You can specify what you are releasing or just know you are letting go of something you no longer need.
7. Release another ballast bag, watch it disappear into the clouds below.
8. Notice if your physical body feels any different, and if so, where? Do you feel lighter? Does your chest breathe easier?
9. Release another bag. Notice your body.
10. Continue letting go of your ballast bags until you feel you've released enough for now and return to the room slowly.

One word of caution: I have used this technique with significant success. I released so much in one visualization that I was exhausted, feeling like little more than a puddle on the floor for weeks. When doing this technique, or any releasing technique, choose a day and time that will allow your body time to recover and release slowly in reasonable chunks. It is highly recommended that you release/heal ancient wounds at a gentle pace rather than releasing everything all at once. You'll get there with patience. Consider release techniques similar to cleaning out your closets for donation. If you donate everything, you'll be left with an empty house.

Variation

As I mentioned before, I've used the metaphor of a hot air balloon many times. Here is a variation you may find helpful. I tend to use this technique when I have a lot to release, for example a long-term relationship.

1. Begin as before, breathing deeply and calmly.
2. Imagine your hot air balloon inflating. Watch it flutter and grow.
3. Imagine your balloon is inflating with everything you wish to release. All the fights, all the things you did or didn't say, just turn them into hot air and fill your balloon.

4. Now let the balloon go, let it float into the setting sun.
5. With your physical exhale, visualize pushing the balloon farther and farther away from you and closer to the sunset. Notice how the balloon is getting smaller and smaller, and your body and emotions are getting lighter and lighter.
6. Continue using your exhale to move the balloon away, just let it all float away. If your balloon doesn't move any farther, that's OK. Notice how far you did make it go, and if you feel inclined, try again another time.
7. Continue exhaling your balloon away until it either completely disappears into the sunset or stops moving altogether. If your balloon does reach the sun, imagine it burning up and releasing all your old stuff to help the sun burn brighter.
8. Be pleased with your progress and slowly return to the room.

Stimming exercise

The other day I was with a new client and explaining an exercise to them. Having had an education in psychology, the client responded, "It sounds like stimming and using our natural stims to move into a more positive energy space." I responded emphatically, "Yes! That's brilliant, that's exactly what we are doing."

WebMD explains stimming as a term for repetitive behaviors that are a response to overstimulation, those simple fidgeting habits we all do. People on the autism spectrum experience frequent stimming, but everyone can experience it to a lesser extent. We have two documented examples of our historical Sensitives stimming. Tesla is known to have curled his toes 100 times before bed each night. It is easy to imagine him having many others with his possible obsessive-compulsive behavior.

We can also see Lady Diana stimming each time she bit her lower lip. Rick Hanson's book *Buddha's Brain* suggests pursing your mouth (and other mouth-based habits) is a physical activity pointing to the emotional need for comfort, tracing the behavior back to nursing as a baby.[7]

We have already discussed how HSP traits are very similar to those on the neurodivergent scale. Therefore, it comes as no surprise that HSPs may use stimming as a comfort/coping technique.

The technique I teach uses four levels of the human experience—the physical, emotional, mental, and the energetic—and consists of three steps.

1. IDENTIFY

Identify your repetitive habit. Perhaps it is fidgeting with something, like a necklace, your phone, or your hair. Then identify an emotion you wish to experience, such as peace, calm, or joy. Then mentally identify what activity you will be doing when you finally feel this desired emotion. Bring in as many details and senses as possible. What will you smell, touch, taste, etc? Will the sun be shining? Or will it be the quiet of the night? Really develop the scene.

2. CREATE A NEW NEUROPATHWAY

Once you have the physical habit and your emotional/energetic end result identified strongly in your mind, it's now time to connect the two with a visualization.

A. Move into a place where you are comfortable (but still able to perform your repetitive habit). Take a few deep breaths, inhaling relaxation, exhaling stress or physical tension.

B. Once you feel calm and relaxed, begin to visualize your end-result movie in your mind. Let it play, expand, and change if you are so moved. Allow your body to feel your end-result emotion, let it wash over you.

C. Once you have your end-result movie playing and your end-result emotion flowing, begin to perform your repetitive physical habit slowly and gently, just a little bit.

D. Stop your repetitive physical habit and focus on your end-result movie.

E. Repeat your repetitive habit again, letting your movie play on and on, filling in even more details, or starting your movie over.

F. Once again, stop your repetitive movement for a moment and play your end result movie.

G. Then resume your repetitive movement, fully engaging with the sensation in your body—perhaps noticing the muscles you're using—while allowing your end-result movie to play and your end-result emotion to flow.

H. Allow the emotion and the movie to run through you for a few moments while noticing your physical repetitive movements. Give your mental, emotional, and physical selves time to connect. Notice how calm you feel (or whatever your end-result emotion is). Take the time to let this moment soak into every part of you.

I. Slowly and gradually, begin waking up, and return to the room. Wiggle your toes, move your shoulders, open your eyelids, stretch your arms.

3. PRACTICE

Now, this is the most challenging part of the technique. Practice. To reach your end-result emotion you must follow the same path as Carnegie Hall. Practice. Practice. Practice. Run your end-result movie when you notice your body performing the repetitive habit. You may want to practice at the beginning or end of the day. You may want to set a reminder on your phone. You'll reach your end-result emotion faster the more often you put these two habits together. At first, this may take some effort, but relax and give yourself some credit for trying something challenging, caring for yourself, and engaging in a healthy practice. Eventually, your end-result emotion will become automatic whenever you perform your repetitive habit.

CHAPTER 23

Energetic Care

We have talked a lot about energy, mostly emotional energy. We've seen moments in history where I referred to swirling energy, times like the Italian Renaissance, the American Civil War, and the Industrial Age at the end of the 19th-century. We've also seen our historical sensitives get caught up in the energy of their time. Some like Frederick Douglass and Tesla work to improve their energy for their time period. Some individuals, such as Stalin and Hitler, became entangled in the swirl of energy. Instead of channeling their abilities and energy for good, they seemingly went with the flow of their current energy, possibly feeding off it and using it for their personal gain rather than the higher good. The actions of Stalin and Hitler indicate the importance of healthy energetic care for Sensitives. As we have stated previously, self-care is a very good coping mechanism. When your world begins to spiral or swirl out of your seeming control, I offer a few techniques to try for your self-care.

The Postulate for Fear

But before we get into a few suggested techniques for self-care, let's back up a bit and look at some concepts about energy. I love postulates. I first learned of them in my high school geometry class. Remember, A+B=C means that when statements A and B are both true, combining them results in a third true statement, C. But instead of finding the angle of a triangle, I use them for more philosophical concepts. One of my favorite postulates is:

A. God is Love (the Bible verse, 1 John 4:16).
+ B. I am loving.
= C. I am godlike.

These kinds of word and thought play have often kept my mind focused and my heart open. Recently, I wandered into an interesting area of thought that I hope will clarify my perspective on energy, helping you better understand me and offering some comfort during challenging times. I get more into the science in Chapter 25 when I discuss the soul, but here's an introduction. It goes like this:

    A. Atoms are the building blocks of everything tangible, physical.
+ B. Atoms are energy.
+ C. I am tangible, physical, and made of atoms.
= D. Therefore, I am energy.
    E. Energy cannot be destroyed, only change forms.
+ F. Energy is malleable and adaptable.
= G. Therefore, I cannot be destroyed—only change forms—and I am malleable and adaptable.
+ H. If energy is adaptable and changeable, then it is finite in its current form, temporal.
    I. My current form, as energy, is temporary/momentary (similar to the Buddhist belief of Impermanence and the Christian Science theology).
    J. If my current form is merely temporary/momentary anything I experience (pain, fear, or joy) is also temporary.
+ K. If everything is temporary, This Too Shall Pass, and whatever I experience in this current form (pain, fear, joy) will also pass and is also temporary/momentary.
= L. Therefore: fear and pain are mere moments in the grand scheme of my physical form, which is also momentary in its energetic form.

I know it's a long one, but I think it's a pretty good postulate. Not only can we consider the soul eternal but the physical body only temporary. I realize this is not a new concept. Many of us, if not all, have experienced at one time or another, the idea of time running out. However, when you recognize that whatever you're experiencing is temporary—whether it's a headache or heartache—that feeling, which may seem endless, will indeed come to an end. But like Celine Dion sings, your heart and soul "will go on."

Cleansing and Protection Techniques

One key self-care tool for Sensitives is learning how to keep your energy field clean. Even if you choose to not get dirty by shielding, protecting, or cleansing, keeping your energy clean is essential to a healthy Sensitive. After all, a Knight's shield gets dirty and needs to be shined up once in a while.

When we look at our historical Sensitives, we see some of them removing themselves from the hustle and bustle of swirling energy and spending time in nature, namely George Washington Carver, Monet, and Adolph. Professor Carver spent the bulk of his life in nature, getting his hands dirty, and learning from and loving plants. Monet chose to live approximately 65km, or 40 miles, from Paris. Adolph's home, Berghof, was nearly a 7-hour drive from Munich where he spent a great deal of time. First Lady Roosevelt went for long walks outside to clear her head and calm down. Stalin read to escape and be alone for a bit. This practice of moving away from crowds and into nature is a tried-and-true practice of energetic care.

There are a myriad of ways and techniques (about 8 billion of them, one for each human) for cleansing and protection. The following is intended for you to use as a starting point. Try what feels comfortable to you, discard the rest. Take what you wish and make it your own.

Grounding/Calming

I consider Grounding to be a synonym for protection or shielding. They all have the same goal: being calm and staying calm. Many of these terms are modern and postdate our historical Sensitives' lives, however we've seen them doing similar activities. Walking, playing, or just spending time in nature all bring about a sense of calm, an energetic grounding. The difference between the practices and habits of our historical Sensitives and today is adding intent and awareness. Like our historical Sensitives, you may now be aware of some habits and behaviors that calm and comfort you. Perhaps, all you need is to become more aware of when you feel calm and to fully indulge in and soak up that calm feeling. Here are a few techniques to begin or deepen your calm grounding sensation.

Breathing techniques

There are many breathing techniques out there. In my research, I have found that many alternative healing modalities, from reiki to mindfulness, begin with the breath. The Latin word for "breath" is *spiritus*, which suggests that purposeful breathing can theoretically bring one closer to Spirit. Caroline Myss offers a nice simple prayer, "Let my breath be Grace."

You breathe all the time, in out in out. It is a mandatory practice. So, what do I mean by "breathing techniques"? I mean conscious breathing, breathing on purpose, or in other words, focusing on your breath. We can easily imagine some of our historically Sensitives public speakers taking a deep, cleansing exhale before delivering their Gettysburg Address, their "I have a Dream" speech, or even just stepping in front of television cameras for a press announcement. We actually see the deep exhale, a form of conscious breathing, often in movies and television shows.

When I was working in the corporate world, my breath was shallow and stayed high in my body, around my shoulders. My body would barely move. Many times, I found myself holding my breath. When I was in high school, my dance teacher insisted we learn to hold our breath; no one wants to see you belly heaving, she would say. Conscious breathing is the deep reviving breaths that fills the belly instead of the shoulders.

Deep breathing brings in loads of new clean oxygen for your body, wakes up the brain, and gets things moving. Take a moment, right now, and just breathe deeply. Exhale slowly. Breathe in slowly through the nostrils. Gently exhale through the nostrils. One more time and ah! How do you feel? Imagine feeling like this more often. Can you feel your muscles relaxing? Are your shoulders dropping? Your stomach rising and falling, maybe even your heart beating a little easier?

Mindfulness
The practice of Mindfulness begins with focusing on the breath. Bring your attention to the cool air the inhale brings and warmth of the exhale. Mindful breathing can be done anywhere anytime. When you are driving. When you are shopping. When you are working.

Even count In, Hold, Even Count Out
This practice was taught to me in the late nineties around the same time I discovered Dr. Elaine Aron's book and has brought me great calmness during stormy times. The key to this practice is keeping your inhale and exhale even by counting. The count may be changed of course to fit your needs and abilities. The technique looks as follows:

1. While breathing through your nostrils, Inhale 2, 3.
2. Hold 2, 3.
3. Exhale 2, 3.
4. Some add a Hold after the exhale.

This technique of even breathing can stop an anxiety attack in its proverbial tracks. I have been known to add the Anchoring Technique, once I am calm and grounded, to remind my body and mind to breathe evenly. Genius!

Earth Rocks!

Some of us Sensitives love rocks. When I worked retail in a rock shop, I loved watching the kids run to touch the rocks. My theory was that the quicker they touched the rocks, the more sensitive they were. Mother Earth has provided, in her infinite wisdom, lovely tools to help us live on her. She has given us rocks to calm us, to wake us up, to connect with spirit, and even to help us physically. It is easy to imagine Tesla picking up rocks when he was young and playing in the hills of his home. I can even picture him saying hello and chatting with the rocks, making friends with them, although I have no documented reports of such; I could just be projecting my love and fun with rocks onto Tesla.

When looking to be grounded and calm, black or earth-colored stones are usually recommended. While Obsidian is the most widely used, jet, lava, and smokey quartz are all wonderful stones for grounding/calming. But truth be told, any stone you are drawn to can support you. In fact, you can even program the stone for your own needs.

When you are out rock hunting, be it in a store or in the woods, pay attention to what falls at your feet. Rocks have a funny way of getting so excited when you are near, they often will jump off the shelves. It's pretty neat.

Choosing a rock can be overwhelming, especially in a rock shop. You may want them all. But there is a good way to see if a rock is right for you, if it wants to come home with you. I usually teach this exercise to kids, so bear with me.

1. Take a moment to cleanse your energy. Shake your tail feathers or imagine you are standing under a beautiful waterfall.
2. Pick up a stone and hold it in your hand.
3. Wait a few breaths and notice how the rock feels. Does it feel warmer? Cooler?
4. Notice how you feel. Do you feel calmer? Do you feel giggly?
5. Do you like the way you feel? Do you want to feel it more often? If yes, then you've found your rock. If no (or you feel no change) try again with another rock. Remember to cleanse and shake your tail feathers first.

Additionally, amethyst and selenite are great stones for Sensitives. Both are known for their calming properties and clarity. Selenite under your pillow is known to help with healthy deep sleep. Amethyst can be used many ways for calming the mind and body. I keep a piece of amethyst in my water glass, so I am always as calm as possible. Some rocks can be used as elixirs—water infused with rocks—but not all. I love this technique of keeping rocks in my water bottle, it is a great passive way to stay present and clean. However, not all rocks are safe to ingest. If you are interested in working more with rocks in water, I suggest the book *Gem Water* by Michael Gienger and Joachim Goebel.

Essential Oils/Aromas

Smell is the strongest of the human senses for creating a shift in energy and mood. Mother Earth is simply amazing; not only has she provided us with rocks, but also plants to assist us. When the plants are distilled down to their essential being, we obtain essential oils. There are plenty of oils to explore and with which to play. Classic grounding essential oils are frankincense, myrrh, sandalwood, white angelica, cedarwood, and of course the quintessential calming essential oil lavender. Essential oils distilled from the roots of the plant are typically good for grounding and calming, but any aroma you find comforting, especially if you have a strong personal connection, will help ground and calm you. Some sensitives find aromas that are not essential oils, such as vanilla or baked bread, equally effective. These scents can evoke memories of childhood when they felt safe.

One of the reasons I chose the historical figures I did was for the abundance of information available. For example, we know Princess Diana's favorite scents. Apparently, the Princess of Wales loved, not surprisingly, florals mixed with the grounding woodsy aromas. She, reportedly, "always always always" wore perfume.[1] With Lady Diana being a known fashion icon, we can see how "smellin' purty" (as my grandfather used to say) is an extension of that archetype. But we can also conjecture that she wore the scents she did for protection, grounding, and strength. By choosing scents she felt most comfortable with they may have assisted Lady Diana to be the person she was expected to be and her most authentic self.

Currently, popular culture is trending toward natural products, including products branded with Hildegard's name. Essential oils are no exception. Scientific studies are looking into Saint Hildegard's writings on herbal remedies and finding surprising accuracy.[2] Essential oils were a large part of her suggestions for healing; lavender for chest colds, a clear mind, and deep sleep, chamomile to detoxify the body, and clary sage for digestive issues. In her book *Physica*, Hildegard recommended frankincense for clearing the brain and mind. Today, studies have shown pure frankincense to be effective in fighting cancer cells, as well as being a grounding aroma.[3] An interesting side note, frankincense is more efficacious when the plant has gone through some kind of trauma, supporting the phrase that which doesn't kill you makes you stronger.

My current favorite essential oil is peppermint. It is great for headaches and tummy aches. The FDA recommends peppermint oil to be the number one solution for headaches and migraines.[4] Cypress essential oil is also helpful to Sensitives. Cypress is known to increase circulation; therefore, it helps Sensitives move extraneous energy out of the body.

Grounding Visualizations

Given the fact that HSPs think a lot, using your mind for your good and balanced health can be quite helpful to feeling calm and grounded. Thus, we include some visualizations, or meditations, to get you started on creating your own grounding visualization.

ROOT VISUALIZATION

1. Move into in a comfortable position.
2. Begin your deep belly breathing and relax.
3. Imagine you are standing barefoot in a beautiful ancient forest, surrounded by huge wise trees.
4. Take a moment to really feel the imagined environment. Feel the warmth of the sun and the cool breeze. Notice the smell of the forest, the trees, and the soil.
5. Imagine roots growing out of your feet and down into the forest floor. Witness moss growing over your feet.
6. Allow those roots to grow down further and further into the earth. Watch and feel those roots growing stronger and deeper.
7. At this point, you may feel a unique kind of tingling. Allow or draw the tingling up your legs, hips, and spine. If you don't actually feel a tingling, that's ok, not everyone does.
8. Imagine the moss on your feet growing upwards, over your legs, hips, and spine. Allow the sensation of the earth's energy to go as high as you are comfortable.
9. Let the roots grow down and the moss grow up. Notice how calm you feel becoming part of nature. Really let this calm grow within you.
10. You can add the anchoring technique, explained earlier, to train your body to return to this feeling of calm anytime.

11. When you are ready, begin to come back to your room. Wiggle your toes and fingers. Open your eyes. Shrug your shoulders. Give your whole self some time to return.

SHIELDS UP VISUALIZATION

A variation of grounding is shielding or protecting. The concept of shielding can be quite fun, especially if you are a Star Trek fan. Play with the idea of you being on the starship Enterprise and put your Shields Up. I add sound effects from the original Star Trek to trigger this technique when I'm in public. You could also use the Medieval knight's shield or any other metaphor you wish.

SHIELDS EXERCISE WITH FRIEND

To test your shields or simply to enjoy a fun evening, try this exercise to learn how to recognize the feeling when your shields are up. When I taught this to a client of mine, they could feel my presence across the room when their shields were down. However, when their shields were up, they didn't sense my energy until I stood three feet behind them.

Begin by standing on opposite sides of a room, facing the same direction.

One friend, the sender, walks toward the other, the receiver, with hands out, sending their energy toward the receiver.

The receiver focuses on their body and when they can feel the sender's energy, say stop.

The sender stops moving and the receiver turns around to see where the sender is.

Now repeat the exercise but this time with the receiver's shields up and notice the distance difference.

Experiment with different shielding techniques to find your favorite or the most effective. I'm betting that the strongest technique will also be your favorite.

Develop an Early Warning System

I think we can all agree that strong energy is very easy to identify, feel, and notice. For example, it could be the evening news, something shocking, a sudden strong shift, seeing an old boyfriend, or meeting your grandchild for the first time. I'm betting many of us remember where we were on September 11, 2001, or some similar event. But it is the slow-building "sneaky" energy that is tricky for us to notice. The baby steps of some energy that allows you to adapt and accept then ask much later, "How did I get here?" That's the energy we Sensitives need to be most aware of.

One of my favorite tools I like to teach—and one that my clients enjoy working with—is developing a positive trigger that warns them when something is coming that they need to protect themselves against. For instance, I was working retail in an antique shop (no easy task for Sensitives in itself). The shop was hosting a holiday party, and it was all hands on deck. As a Sensitive working in a shop with all kinds of varying energies, I routinely shielded myself, and I strengthened them especially for the party. Even with all that protection, I still kept hearing a warning sound, a klaxon. It was a sound like a fire alarm, continuing in my head. As the evening wore on, I gradually got more and more tired. About 4 hours into the event, I asked my supervisor if I could go home. Thankfully, I was allowed; the party was wrapping up anyway. The next time I returned to the store, I was greeted with questions like, "Do you know what happened?" Obviously, I didn't and was regaled with stories of a "big blow up" between two co-workers later at the party. "You missed it by about an hour." I realized the fire alarm I heard in my head was a message to leave the building, and boy, was I grateful I did. As a result, I have strengthened that technique so it will alert me more often. I have found it incredibly helpful, as have some of my clients.

Here's how it works:

Choose a color, a sound, or a sensation that means danger or warning. I use a fire alarm, but even something like Lucy from *Despicable Me 2* making her "Mee maw, mee maw, mee maw" sound would work. You might also choose seeing the color red repeatedly or even visualizing an animal as your trigger. I do recommend when using items seen often you set a number to repeat (like 3) to make sure it is a message and not just a pretty red car.

Then when you are in a quiet place, set/create the program. Ask that these set of circumstances be an early warning system from now on. Something along the lines of "When I hear this sound (or see three red cars) my protective energy will strengthen automatically."

You can add additional protective layers to your program, such as a new layer of titanium or whatever means safety and security to you.

Cleansing

If grounding (i.e. shielding or protecting) is not your bag, you can choose cleansing. I actually do both grounding and cleansing. Let's face it, you can ground all you want, but sometimes the outside energies can be very stubborn and persistent. So, cleansing is needed.

Florence Nightingale is a prime example of the importance of cleansing, calling for more cleaning practices in hospitals. George Washington Carver insisted on cleanliness and immaculate manners from everyone when teaching at Tuskegee. Our obsessive-compulsive Tesla was a well-known germaphobe, most likely due to all his near-death illnesses when he was a child.

In my viewpoint, everything is a metaphor. I love metaphors. In case you somehow missed it, I use them almost constantly, for practically everything. Cleaning my house or body is a metaphor to set my intention for cleaning my energy field. Whether it's brushing my teeth or scrubbing the tub, I'm cleansing.

As with everything else we've discussed, there are countless ways to cleanse your energy field. Here are merely a few suggestions for you to begin creating your own cleansing practice. One client liked to use the metaphor of a car wash, another being inside a disco ball (for the younger generations, google disco ball), and yet another envisioned wearing mirrored gloves like Michael Jackson. (Again, young'uns, look it up. I can't teach you everything). The point being this is your life, your visualization—make it your own. Walk clean and proud.

BRIGHT LIGHT VISUALIZATION

Many Sensitives begin their cleansing practice with the Bright Light Visualization, and I know I did. Many have found that with practice they can summon the visualization at will, at any time.

1. Imagine yourself surrounded with the most beautiful and vibrant light.
2. Feel the light move through you, completely filling you with light.

The color of the light is completely up to you, but the idea is light does not cast a shadow. Shadows are created when one moves into the light or gets between you and light. Light is the source of warmth and life. When we shine light by being our best and brightest selves no darkness or lower energies can remain.

THE STEAM CLEAN CLEANSING PRACTICE

Your mind is the original Star Trek Holodeck. You can do anything in a meditation, that's the fun of it. No laws of physics or reality to hold you back. You are completely free to do whatever you wish. But this meditation actually takes place in your shower, in your real actual shower. I first learned this as a meditation from my friend, teacher, and author of *Belief, Being and Beyond,* Granddaughter Crow, who was taught by Michael Smith, author of *Navigating the Shift* and founder of the Empath Academy, but I have since brought it into my daily practice of actually showering. I have found it to be very helpful to combine my mental practices with my physical life. Should you choose to incorporate this practice, feel free to make it your own. You do not need to memorize my words or exact steps; focus instead on the underlying concept.

This practice may have a big impact on you, so I suggest experimenting with it when your schedule allows time to rest afterward. I've been doing this practice for over eight years and there are times when I cleanse so deeply, I need a nap afterwards. Sometimes I think the dirt was keeping me together.

1. As you remove your clothing, think "I remove and release all roles and responsibilities. Dissolve my weaknesses for infinite peace."
2. Step into the shower. As your body begins to touch the water, think "Clean, clean, clean," washing away all the surface dirt.
3. Make the water a little hotter and as you shampoo your hair, think "Steam, steam, steam," allowing the heat of the water to open your pores and move deeper into your body, your bloodstream, your organs.
4. While you are rinsing your hair think "Clean deeper, clean deeper, clean deeper." Imagine the hot water moving into the spaces the steam just opened and cleaning them out.
5. Make the water a little hotter and, as you condition your hair, think "Steam deeper, steam deeper, steam deeper," opening you up even deeper.
6. When rinsing the conditioner think "Clean deepest darkest depths. Clean deepest darkest depths. Clean deepest darkest depths." At this point, I imagine the hot water has opened my body completely all the way down to my atoms, quarks, and photons.
7. Make the water a touch hotter as you wash your body and think "Deepest darkest depths, deepest darkest depths, deepest darkest depths."
8. Once all practical tasks are completed and your body is completely clean, make the water a little cooler—just a tap will do.
9. Face east (or at least close enough) think "Seal my East."
10. Face South, think "Seal my South."
11. Face West, think "Seal my West."
12. Face North, think "Seal my North."
13. As you are toweling dry, think "Shine bright like a Diamond."
14. Now you are all clean on all levels and nicely sealed and all shiny.

Recycle It!

Another metaphor you can add into your daily life is the trash can—or the recycle bin, if you prefer. I like the metaphor of the recycle bin myself because it supports the idea of transforming energy into something good or helpful somewhere else. Just because the energy may be detrimental or too much for me, it can still be helpful or needed elsewhere. This is why Sensitives need to cleanse.

Sensitives are a curious bunch. We can simultaneously believe we are worthless and saviors. Two diametrically opposed concepts can live within the same mind at the same moment. I know, I've done it. When I realized it, I was dumbfounded. Sensitives, as previously mentioned, will hold onto energy and emotions, thinking something bad will happen if they release it. We feel like we are the only ones equipped to handle whatever we carry. When we recognize that energy itself is neither good nor bad, but simply exists, we begin to shift toward discernment without judgment. Some energy may not be to your liking, but this understanding fosters a more objective perspective.

We can, and should, be particular about what energy we allow into our environment. It is perfectly acceptable to recycle unwanted energy. Consider the metaphor of junk mail. We all get it (if you've found a way to stop junk mail, please let me know). We all throw it away. We don't judge the advertisement; we merely decide we don't need new windows right now and put it in the recycle bin. Same thing with energy. Let it go. Let it find a place where it does belong. Put your unwanted energy in the recycle bin, compost pile, or a brightly glowing tree stump. Put it anywhere, but let it go. What is unwanted to you may be exactly what someone else needs. (Maybe your neighbor needs new windows.) Holding that unwanted energy may be preventing someone else from getting what they need. But you need to let it go before it can be recycled. Do the universe and yourself a favor, recycle it.

Focal Points

While chatting with a friend about HSPs and tools to help them, as I often do, she oh so wisely stated, "Everything you are talking about is Focal Points." My eyes got big, and my jaw dropped. She was absolutely right. Whatever you choose, be it stones or visuals, are focal points, something for you to focus on. Something ELSE for you to focus on, instead of spinning around worrying in your head. It doesn't have to be traditional or even conventional, it just needs to have meaning to you. The deeper the meaning, the stronger the emotion, and the more effective it will be for you.

We Sensitives think being human is hard, and sometimes it is. But it doesn't have to be, nor, I believe, is it meant to be. Life is meant to be enjoyed and embraced. So, find your focal point, make it strong, and enjoy. Be the most Sensitive caring being you are meant to be.

CHAPTER 24

Spiritual Care

I grew up in a Christian Science household. I was often told to watch my thoughts and if I wasn't feeling well to work with my Higher Self to feel better. I was taught that working with Spirit is the first place to start and everything else, similar to President Reagan's Trickle-Down theory for economics, trickles down with the physical body being the last place energy would present itself. If you are spiritually clean and pure, so the theory goes, the rest of you will remain clean and pure. So, all this watching your thoughts and manifesting stuff is natural to me. If it is not natural or comfortable for you, feel free to take what does feel comfortable and leave the rest. You can even skip this section if you wish, but there are a few interesting concepts here so perhaps just skim.

Nearly all of our Historical Sensitives, with a few notable and telling exceptions, had strong spiritual lives and practices. From Hildegard de Bingen's drawings, writings, and teachings to Tesla's work with the natural powers available, the bulk of them believed in a higher power of some sort. Some of these individuals, as Sensitives, worked with that "power." As we've seen, many, like Florence Nightingale, felt a strong calling, a mission that pushed them forward. I believe it was this calling that helped them through tough times, bumps, and challenges. Call it whatever you wish, God, The Great Creator, Source of Love, believing in some higher level has provided comfort to many through the ages, including our Sensitives, and may do the same for you. For Sensitives, believing we are doing something for the higher, greater good is enough to keep us working on our mission. Consider Lincoln and Tesla: both gentlemen felt a strong calling to improve the world and positively impact humanity.

Now for the "notable exceptions" in our group of historical Sensitives. Monet was an atheist. President Grant, while raised Methodist, prayed privately but is considered an agnostic. Machiavelli is considered to have been "profoundly anti-Christian."[1] Stalin, a follower of Marx and the originator of the quote

"Religion is the opiate of the people," strove to stamp out religion throughout his country, establishing an atheistic country. Hitler—well, we know what he did—but it seems his personal religious views are still hotly debated. Neither the Christians nor the atheists wish to be aligned with him, understandably. Some say he was very into the occult, pointing to his use of runes in his symbols for support. Others say he hated all contemporary religions and attempted to revive the ancient pagan beliefs. I believe—though this is based solely on my intuition and not on concrete sources—that Himmler was likely behind the bulk of the occult interests, while Hitler, as a master marketer, was open to using anything to achieve his goals. Incidentally, I find it both fascinating and somewhat ironic that Himmler was likely homosexual, yet Hitler overlooked this "flaw" because Himmler was so effective. This actually contradicts Hitler's theory of Jewish people and homosexuals being of no use. I also find it fascinating that it's highly possible Hitler himself would not have passed his own purity laws.

In our historical Sensitives, we see a marked difference; they either helped humanity or hurt humanity (and deeply). We see the impact of forcing beliefs on others. I believe in letting people come to and have their own belief systems. Humanity runs into trouble when we insist that everyone should think or believe the same as we do and force others to conform, as seen in events like the Crusades of the Middle Ages and World War II. Many of our historical Sensitives held definite beliefs, and many of them worked toward their goals attached to their beliefs, sticking to their principles rightly or wrongly. When we see our historical Sensitives with a lack of spirituality, we see them landing on the "wrong" side of history, known for their nightmarish actions.

Love and Light

Energy workers like Reiki Masters use the phrase "Love and Light," a lot. It is practically the core of the healing modality. As Sensitives, on some level, we are energy workers. It is our core being; our core energy is love and light. People respond to this loving energy. It may be why complete strangers will confess things to you and why people want to be around you. Consider the popularity of Lady Diana and her heart-based work with children and HIV patients and the response to her death.

But Love and Light can be used by anyone, not just certified Reiki Masters, and in a myriad of ways for all sorts of reasons. You can use Love and Light to release energy. You can fill a room with Love and Light to cleanse it. You can envision Love and Light surrounding your car for a safe road trip or preventative car maintenance. You can think Love and Light before you eat. You can call

Love and Light to you, let it fill you up. Try it. Go on. I'll wait. "Love and Light, fill me now, here, completely." Feels good, right?

You can imagine or think Love and Light all the time, anywhere for anything.

Highest Good

A second phrase we energy workers use is "Highest Good." Like Love and Light, it can be used for many reasons, but primarily to ensure whatever you are doing is for the Highest Good. Reiki Masters add Highest Good when working with clients—at least I do—to ensure we are only doing good, the client's highest good. When I'm asking for help for myself or someone else, I ask for the Highest Good. This helps me keep things in perspective, after all, a quick healing may not be in the person's highest good. There may be a lesson in the person's challenging moment or repercussions that I can't possibly be aware of. Therefore, asking for their highest good releases me from the pressure of the outcome and gives it over to Universal energy.

Master of Light

As a Sensitive, you are a bundle of loving energy and a Master of Light. I often use this phrase when a global tragedy occurs. "I am a Master of Light. I shed Light, I send Love and Light to . . ." anyone you wish or "anyone who is suffering," (which is everyone). I sometimes combine it with, "Bless the Suffering. Bless the Inflictors. Bless the Witnesses." In this simple way, I send love and light to every being and consequently myself. The concept that I am helping every being, even in some small way, brings me comfort and peace. It's worth a try—you might actually feel better or make your world a more loving and compassionate place.

I recently came across Gary Zukav's latest book, *Universal Human*, where he describes the Universal Human as someone who has respect for all life. This comes naturally for most Sensitives. But remember to include yourself as part of all life. Sure, we sensitives help usher spiders outside or allow bees to buzz around us or tiptoe around ants. You are a living being as well. You deserve as much respect as anyone.

Grey Lives

For those who believe in reincarnation, you may find this technique helpful and fascinating. But a little backstory first. As a Highly Sensitive Person, I struggled to put myself out there; promoting my services was scary and when I dug deeper, it felt life-threatening. I called a good friend of mine, a professional intuitive/

psychic, Kami Blackwell Lichtenberg. When she got a hit, "Oh, this is good," she said, getting very excited, "I may even use this in my personal practice."

"What? What?" I asked, getting excited myself.

"Grey lives," she said. With the concept new to both of us, we talked back and forth to understand and flesh out the idea better.

Grey Lives are those boring past lives when nothing karmic or spectacular occurred, but you lived a nice quiet life. Getting in touch with that Grey boring past life energy can help you learn more about yourself and work with that energy for more clarity on how to live your life.

For example: in one of my grey boring lives I was a teacher named Michael, a professor near the end of the Middle Ages in what we now know as Germany. During this life, nothing much happened. I taught, I went home, I lived. By working with this "do nothing" grey life, I learned about protection—doing my own thing quietly. When I have a day where I am particularly scared, I call on Michael, the Medieval Professor me, for strength and protection. I imagine putting on his professor cloak and glasses and holding a classic book. Immediately, I feel calmer, composed, and ready for whatever I need to do.

Grey Lives is a technique of working with your past self. The understanding that I did it once and was ok, and I can do it again is very powerful. History is knowledge and knowledge is power. Knowing that everything turned out ok before gives me confidence and power that everything will turn out ok again. It's more data, more evidence to support you on this life's journey.

Guides—Essence of Emotions and Energy

If you spend any time in the metaphysical world, it is likely you have heard about Guides or guardian angels working with ancestors. Yes, working with Guides (whatever you choose to call them) is a biggie. It is a biggie because they help, and they work. In my studies of gods and goddesses, I've found many crossovers from culture to culture. For example: Mother Mary, Kwan Yin, and Isis are different names that different cultures use for nurturing energy. Christians pray to Mother Mary to provide mothering comfort. Kwan Yin is called to help with children and mercy. The same goes for Isis. Different names, same result, same emotions, same energy, same essence. In my mind, (and forgive me if I offend) the name you use to work with is not important. It is not the name specifically you are working with but the energy, the essence that the name represents. Call Archangel Michael for protection, sure. But what you are really doing, I believe, is conjuring the emotions and energy known to be associated with that name. You can even call on one of your favorite historical persons to guide and assist you. The energy is there, just ask for it.

One word of caution: if at any time you receive a message about hurting yourself or another being, that is NOT a guide. Guides of any kind will only offer positive assistance and comfort. If you feel you are being told to do something against the law or life, expel that energy immediately and clearly.

Animal and Ancestor Essence

An offshoot of working with Guides/Essence is working with animals and/or ancestors. They both provide insight and guidance in the same way as Guides. As a Highly Sensitive Person, you may be drawn to work with either of these types of energies. I have found animals to be very helpful as signs or messages. For example, when I see a deer (or three) I work on being and walking with grace. When I see a hawk, I believe it is a sign I am going in the right direction.

I often work with the essence of the coyote, the intelligent trickster, and much of the suggestions I make in this book are "coyote energy." Coyotes are known to be very intelligent and quite wily, thus the appropriately named *Looney Tunes* character Wiley Coyote. Since Sensitives often prioritize others, I "trick" myself into self-care by reminding myself that I can't help anyone if I don't feel well or take care of myself first. While this is very logical thinking, it is also coyote thinking.

There is coyote energy running all throughout this book. For example, some of our Historical Sensitives, like Saint Hildegard, Florence Nightingale, and Frederick Douglass all had a strong purpose for being where and when they were. This mission would carry them through their challenges. Their work wasn't for themselves; it was for others, the higher good, making the world a better place for everyone. In the cases of Hildegard and Florence, when they experienced physical limitations, they kept working. Their life missions would spurn them on, "tricking" them, so to speak, into continuing their work. Many of the techniques offered here hint at taking care of yourself for the higher, greater good or for your family. Coyote energy.

If you need a reason to take care of yourself, coyote energy is a great way to start. It can help you trick yourself into doing something your self-esteem may not consider important. If we can reason a way for the higher, greater good to be involved, boy howdy can we Sensitives muster the effort—coyote energy. For example: I must take good care of my physical health so I can continue to take care of my family—coyote energy.

Ancestors, especially ones you've known (like grandparents or great-aunts and uncles) are great to work with. They know and love you and want the best for you. If you are wondering if your ancestors, especially your immediate family, are ok on the "other side," they are. If you're wondering if they forgive you, they do. If you're wondering if they love you and are available to help and guide you, they are. Working with your ancestors can be as easy as hanging up their photos on your stairway wall. Saying hello to them anytime you see something that reminds you of them. When you are in a quiet moment, you may even smell them or feel them hugging you. Your physical relationship may have changed since their crossing, but the emotions and energetic connection remain. You feel it every time you miss them. But saying hello, asking them for guidance, or smiling when you think of them is a great way to stay in touch.

The three big topics in the metaphysical world are health, wealth, and relationships. We are used to working with guides for these three areas of our lives. But guides can be used for anything. Anything! If I need a little clarity on how to help someone, I ask for my Clarity Guide, the essence of clarity. If I need help with increasing my vibration, I call my Vibration Guide. If I need help dealing with ascension sickness, I call my Ascension Guide. Get the idea?

Sure, I may need help with increasing my finances, but to me, that's a tall order. When I dig deeper, I find what I really need is more clients. I call my Client Magnet guide to make me a magnet for potential perfect clients, ensuring I am specific about who my clients are. When I dig even deeper, I find I need business savvy and confidence in my abilities. So, who am I going to call? That's right! My Business skills/manager guide. When I dig even deeper, I recognize my fear of success. So, I call on my Success guide.

Once I've figured out what energy I think I need, I call that energy to me and play with it. I anthropomorphize it, giving it shape and a name. We become friends. If you don't know where you need help, you can call the Guide/Energy for my Highest Good.

If you want a more tangible sign your Guides are nearby, ask them. Ask for a sign. Sometimes it's a literal stop sign. Sometimes it's a feather. (I see feathers EVERYWHERE.) Sometimes it's a color you see everywhere. Sometimes it's a number repeating itself. Ask and look for a pattern. They are there. When you finally see the pattern or sign of your Guides, give a big smile and thanks.

By now you may be asking "How do I call my Guides?" The answer is . . . Ask.

Ask for Assistance

It is a long-held belief that humans have free will, it's the core of the American way. Therefore, to receive help from the higher realms, we need to ask for it. Now, Sensitives are not used to asking for help. We think we can handle it on our own, it may be the only way our ego presents itself. Asking for help is one of those life lessons I believe all Sensitives need to learn. The energy is there, use it. Ask it to help. It wants to help but since humans have free will, it is our choice (perhaps even duty) to ask.

Being Empathic

One of the greatest gifts we Sensitives have been given is the ability to empathize. We can read someone and know exactly what they need. Some of us empathize so much, that we can feel their pain, literally. Sensitives on that level of the spectrum are considered Empaths. The Nickerson Institute defines an empath as a Sensitive with a spiritual purpose.[2]

It is highly likely Saint Hildegard was an empath. It is also just as likely President Lincoln was an empath. It is possible many of our historical Sensitives were so sensitive, they were empaths. A lesson all of our historical Sensitives could've benefitted from greatly is that just because you are an empath, it doesn't mean you need to take on everyone else's pain and suffering. I wonder how much more work Saint Hildegard would've accomplished if she had not taken on the suffering energy of all she met. Would the Civil War have been shorter if Lincoln had stayed in his own energy, not bogged down with the grief of his constituents? If Hitler had been aware of his empathic abilities, refused to take on everyone else's hatred and blaming tactics, and learned cleansing or grounding techniques would the Second World War have been so unbelievably brutal?

Oh, yes. You have free will; you can choose to take or leave their energy. Of course, as a heart-based being, you will probably take it thinking it helps them. But what if it doesn't? What if by taking their pain you are inadvertently removing an opportunity for them, a lesson they need to learn? What if you are only multiplying the painful energy?

In my experience, this is exactly what happens. We fully believe in the spreading power of love, we send love to anyone who needs it, anyone who is suffering from trauma. We hear this in Dr. King's words. He speaks of love being a creative, capable force. He encourages us to be like Jesus, to love our enemy to transform them into a friend. Therefore, we believe the energy of love is contagious and expandable. If love is contagious, why should any other emotion be different?

I have experimented with taking on someone else's physical pain, only to find out that both of us felt icky. I have also experimented with helping someone with emotional pain, removing it so they don't have to experience it. Come to find out, I only extended the pain. They learned nothing. My enabling, nurturing self inadvertently increased their pain down the road. Oops! Not my intent. While they may not have learned anything, I did. Be picky about who you help. Just like you have to ask for help from your Guides, wait for someone to ask you for help. Wait for your skills to be valued. When this occurs, both parties can party with abandon.

Have fun!

I am a firm believer that life is meant to be enjoyed. The concept of suffering is long gone, over, kaput. However, as a Sensitive, I find this hard to achieve. Humans have long been told to suffer for our sins, Sensitives taking this training to heart. We can only guess about any fun activities our historical Sensitives may have done. We do know President Grant liked to draw and paint and was fairly good at it. He also loved his horse, Cincinnati. We also know Dr. King loved to play Monopoly as a child (and seemingly tortured his sisters). There are many reports of Rasputin partying in his day, drinking and carousing till the sun came up. But other reports suggest his partying, similar to President Grant's and most Sensitives, was an escape tactic, a coping mechanism to deal with his depression. My inability to find fun in these historical Sensitives' lives could be a sign of their times or of being human. We really can't know for sure.

We do know Sensitives tend to be serious and responsible, making fun an afterthought, if any thought at all. We Sensitives get bogged down with responsibilities, other people's energy, and caregiving. In our effort to avoid rocking the boat and making waves, we often forget to have fun. We turn our fun into an exercise that needs to be performed perfectly, becoming arduous. Not fun. Everything we do seems like work, pulling teeth.

A friend of mine spoke of getting a massage. I applauded her self-care. But wait, there's more. During her massage, she felt a hook, an old energetic belief being pulled out and released. She talked herself through releasing it completely. Again, I applauded her awareness and self-care, but then I realized, we can't even have a massage without working. Ugh! This being human stuff can be tough. Such is the life of a Sensitive.

I recently came across an immensely helpful video of inspirational speaker, Abraham-Hicks. They reminded me that we are Source material. That we, humans, chose to incarnate for the experience, for the fun of it. I know many Sensitives who are just biding their time, waiting for the next level, and pushing through the best they can. When being human gets heavy, Abraham-Hicks would say release the resistance and enjoy the ride of being in the flow. They would encourage you to let go of your oars and let your canoe point you downstream. When I feel myself "pushing the river" I say to myself, "Lift oars, point downstream," and take a deep cleansing inhale, relaxing my shoulders on the exhale. Ah, I feel lighter. It is especially effective when actually driving downhill.

On those days, and you know the days I mean, the days when you aren't getting anywhere, days when everything is work, days when everything is heavy, and nothing gets accomplished. On those days, take a moment to realize you are pushing the river, forcing yourself to do something that either you are not ready for or is not ready to be done. It's just not the right time. Honor your body and the energy by doing something that does feel right. Maybe that means leaving work, rescheduling your day, going home, or taking a nap. Whatever feels more like "downstream" to you, allow it and let it carry you and enjoy the ride.

In all honesty, I am uncomfortable with the term God. It carries such weight and history, and much of it is unkind. My concept of an omniscient being is far greater than an old white guy sitting on a throne judging and watching everyone. Sometimes humans need a visual to grasp a concept, and if that is your version that's fine and understandable. But my concept of an all-powerful being is more akin to the First Nation's Great Creator, a natural all-pervasive energy that may be called upon to assist and create more ease and joy.

Why, you may ask, do I bring this up now? Because if God is more like a Creator than a Judge, God is everywhere. God is life and love and all the things that go with it, including happiness, beauty, and joy. There is beauty and joy everywhere, look for it. You'll find it. Then you'll see more of it. And even more.

Being spiritual doesn't mean you have to suffer or be serious, nor does being Sensitive. Being Sensitive is natural, wondrous, Divine, and can be easy. The practice of cleansing can be as easy as saying, "I'm Clean." The idea of growing a business can be as easy as thinking of all the people you could help. The technique of increasing your vibration can be as simple as drinking water.

Being Sensitive doesn't have to be hard—humans make it hard. We think if something is worth having, it's worth fighting for. Therefore, we think living a lovely balanced and healthy life needs to be difficult to attain. Not so! Being Sensitive is lovely and easy. You are already lovely, balanced, and healthy, you just need to jettison the idea that you are not.

Hopefully, this work has offered you some techniques and ideas on how to lighten up and have fun. Remember, Joy is one of the highest vibrating emotions. Wallow in your joy instead of the other stuff.

CHAPTER 25

Soul Curricula and Why Highly Sensitive Persons Should Care about Self-Care?

We've already discussed self-care extensively—what it is, how it can look, and how it works. But why should a Highly Sensitive Person even care about taking care of themselves? In short, it's about your soul curricula.

Soul curricula are the agreements a soul makes before incarnating into a new physical life, including lessons to be learned. Soul families are a collection of souls that vibrate at similar rates and have theoretically gathered in multiple incarnations to assist and support each other. Healing or renegotiating your soul curriculum may help your soul family by increasing your vibrations and, thereby, the soul family's group vibrations. Working toward fulfilling or healing your soul curriculum is the most impactful work a human can do. Consequently, self-care is the most important lesson in that curriculum and the easiest way to cope as a Sensitive and grow as a human.

I understand the content of this writing may be a little "out there" for some. So, as with all things, like Dr. Martin Luther King, take what resonates with you and leave the rest. But I respectfully invite you to continue reading with an open mind; you may find something new to explore further.

We use some terms interchangeably, such as healing the soul and soul work or soul contract and soul curriculum. I believe any work with the soul is healing the soul, and therefore the terms are synonymous. The term soul curriculum is my personal term for what others define as soul contracts.

With our gift of hindsight, long-term perspective, Sensitive sleuthing, and some conjecture, we have seen that many of our historical Sensitives possessed clear and important soul curricula. All of our historical Sensitives changed their world to help create our world. They seem to have had huge soul curricula which, fortunately for us, was accomplished and completed. President Lincoln's soul curriculum was presumably to write the Emancipation Proclamation and guide America toward the path of abolishing slavery. Frederick Douglass' soul agreed to help convince President Lincoln with his soul curriculum through his life in slavery and therefore writing, speaking, and influencing the President about the said horrors. This connection between our two historical Sensitives points to them possibly being part of a soul family, one which may have included Harriet Tubman and President Grant. We of course cannot know, but we can conjecture. Given that these four people existed at the same time and place and worked toward the same goal, it is easy to conclude their souls were entwined to support and teach each other—the very nature of a soul family. We can also consider the leaders in the South who supported slavery as possible soul family members—those who agreed to play the role of the opposition to offer opportunities for the soul growth of our historical Sensitives.

We can also consider the possibility of the Roosevelts, Churchill, Mussolini, Stalin, and Hitler as soul family members. I realize this seems a bit far-fetched, but as we'll see, soul family members are not always your best friend; sometimes, they're your most challenging relationships or even your enemies. Some soul family members have agreed to help you learn a lesson, which is not always easy or pretty. Let's hope the souls involved in the Second World War and all of humanity learned their lessons so we can all grow and evolve.

The concept of a Soul Curriculum has been argued for centuries although under a different guise, namely the argument of free will vs. destiny. Soul curriculum can be regarded as a compromise between the two, providing a general outline of lessons to be learned while allowing the individual to choose how and when to learn them. Thus, soul curricula don't limit an individual but rather provide an outline or a to-do list. Consider, purely theoretically, the soul curriculum of Claude Monet. Let's say, hypothetically, Monet's curriculum included learning the lesson of appreciating the beauty of nature. With this broad lesson to learn, Monet could have taken various paths—becoming a tour guide (highlighting beauty to tourists), a botanist (exploring the inner workings of nature), or a flower shop owner (creating beautiful bouquets for others). Instead, Monet chose to learn his hypothetical lesson through painting.

The basic concept of soul curricula has comforted me for nearly a decade. When I hear of a seemingly senseless act or tragedy, I remind myself that on some level the souls involved consented to participate in the event. When I introduce the concept of soul curricula to friends, family, or clients they usually ask, "Why would anyone consent to that?" After explaining the difference between short-term and long-term perspective, the ultimate good, and potential growth that can result from a senseless event, I usually turn to my family history to further explain.

My grandfather was a farmer in Michigan with a wife and two children. In 1953, his son, Freddy, was age 9 and his daughter, Carol Ann, my mother, was 6. One day in early November of that year, Freddy got sick and died. As you can only imagine, this caused tremendous trauma and heartache for the family. The trauma of my uncle's passing was so painful my family never spoke of it—that was how they dealt with things in those days. I didn't even know I had an uncle until I was in college. My grandfather had planned on leaving the farm to Freddy to continue the family business. When that was no longer possible, my grandfather's life path took a major turn. He sold the farm, moved to the city, and took a job in aeronautics, specifically non-destructive testing.

Flash forward approximately 15 years to sometime during the Vietnam War. The landing gear on F-4 fighter jets was randomly failing, causing the loss of several planes and crew. Everyone was baffled, no one could figure out what was happening until my grandfather (can you hear my pride?) stepped in with his non-destructive testing. He tested the planes, located the weakness, and saved the planes, and the crews were able to continue their duty.

Flash forward again to sometime during 2002, I was at a birthday party for a friend on the Space Coast of Florida. "It just so happens" an astronaut, Frank Culbertson, was in attendance. Recently returned from the International Space Station as Captain on September 11th, 2001, he was on a press tour. Eventually, I was able to have a few words with him. I asked him how he started on his path of becoming an astronaut. He replied he was a pilot during the Vietnam War.

"Really?" I asked, "Do you remember when the landing gear was failing on the planes?"

"Of course, I lost a few friends because of it."

"My grandfather found the problem so it could be fixed."

"Wow, your grandfather saved my life!"

"Yes, yes he did," I said smiling with immense pride.

The astronaut handed me a window decal of his mission as a thank you.

Reflecting my grandfather's dry sense of humor I replied, "My grandfather saved your life. I don't get an embroidered patch of the mission?"

He chuckled and said, "They don't make those anymore."

The next time I visited my grandfather, I gave him the mission decal and told him the story. He said, humbly and with a twinkle of pride, "Well, what do you know?"

Now . . . if my uncle had not crossed over in the 1950s, my grandfather would have remained a farmer, and that International Space Station Captain and others would not have survived the Vietnam War. Knowing that, I can understand why my Uncle Freddy would agree to crossover at such a young age, why he would agree to that soul curriculum.

Sacred Contracts

On this planet, we create agreements, and we call them contracts. We make contracts for leasing a place to live, employment, confidentiality, marriage, purchases, and much more. Contracts can be straightforward, such as an agreement to purchase a car, or complex, like corporate or intercompany contracts. Dr. Sheldon Cooper, a fictional character on the television show, *The Big Bang Theory*, uses contracts to clearly define requirements between the two parties, such as in the event that Sheldon becomes a zombie, his roommate, Leonard, is not allowed to kill him. Contracts can include clauses and, as Perry Mason—a fictional lawyer created by Erle Stanley Gardner—would say, even loopholes. Contracts can also be renegotiated, perhaps for better terms or merely updated to reflect current situations.

Throughout human history we see some "higher level" contracts; consider the Magna Carta, the Declaration of Independence, and even the 10 Commandments, the covenant between God and the Hebrew people. These contracts were agreements for peace and freedom. They were not about ownership but rather the higher needs of humans, a more sacred contract. These kinds of contracts allude to the idea of soul contracts, i.e. soul curriculum.

If we consider life on earth as a metaphor for our inner or Greater Life and extrapolate the concept of contracts out into the spiritual, the idea of soul contracts becomes both understandable and natural.

The concept of soul contracts may be referred to by many names. Writer Caroline Myss calls them "Sacred Contracts." Other authors use the term "pre-birth planning." Still others refer to them as "soul agreements." I prefer the term Soul Curriculum.

Soul Curriculum

The term Soul Curriculum connotes the feeling of taking classes, learning lessons, choosing a degree program, and taking the required classes for graduation. Consider life on earth to be like a school, the Universal University, with each grade equaling one life. A soul would need to learn the basics, starting in 1st grade with the alphabet. Many people can teach the alphabet, but a person, or soul, will learn easier if taught by a like-minded individual, someone whom the student admires or with whom they have an easy rapport. With this in mind, one can understand why a soul family member would agree to teach a soul the deeper or harder lessons.

If we continue with the metaphor and think of the archetypes of the Dunce and the Egghead or the Fool and Scholar, we can begin to understand the concepts of the Old Soul and its opposite. These archetypes suggest the theory that one soul (the scholar) may have learned more in those "school years" compared to others (the fool), leading to different rates of progress. Consequently, some souls advance to the next class or lesson, while others may need to repeat a class. One can perhaps understand the metaphor better when we consider some of our historical Sensitives and their schooling. Dr. King, Stalin, and Tesla all completed their schooling ahead of schedule, taking three years to graduate from four-year institutions. Eggheads, Old Souls, or Scholarly souls may apply themselves to their studies, grow and learn faster than Dunces, Fools, or "slow learners."

Soul Families

I like to imagine when a soul is between lives a Hugh Jackman-like character appears as the Greatest Showman presenting all the many options that a soul can choose from before incarnating. "We have a lovely little family over here who will help you experience and understand unconditional love. While this family and life path over here will teach you more about forgiveness." With Soul Curriculum, one can imagine, you can even choose your classmates, study pals, and teachers, i.e. your soul family, or soul tribe. These are souls you have a previous relationship with, the souls you resonate with, and souls you want to spend more time with. And so, you agree to reincarnate and support each other once more, learning from one another again.

In the material world, soul family members can be actual biological family, perhaps your favorite uncle, a sibling you are particularly close to, or a cousin who is your best friend. A soul family member may even love you so much that they agree to be the one to teach you the harder lessons, with the idea it will somehow soften the blow.

When your rebellious teenager yells, "I didn't ask to be born. I didn't ask to be part of this family."

You can chuckle and reply, "Oh yes you did! And you're welcome."

Perhaps, President Grant and General Lee were soul family members, with Grant agreeing to help Lee learn the use of power and when to relinquish control.

Soul family members can be your best friends, people, or even animals, you choose on a higher level to be in your life. I personally have a very deep connection with my dog, Bear; he is definitely part of my soul family. He has taught me so much about unconditional love, patience, other humans, and myself.

So, what does a soul curriculum "look" like? Purely conjecture of course, but I believe a soul's curriculum looks something like this:

> I agree to learn more about love and all its facets.
> I agree to support Soul A.
> I agree to learn from Soul B.
> I agree to be challenged by Soul C.
> I agree to be with Soul D when they are released from the material world.

With this type of agreement, you can begin to see how wide-open a soul curriculum can be. There is both free choice and predetermination woven into a soul curriculum.

The Science of the Soul

Let's look at what others have written over the ages about souls, contracts, soul families, and even the idea of increasing your vibration. This is where we get a little "science-y." Tesla and Dr. King would probably love this part; they really would. Both of them had an interest in the universe and its secrets.

When discussing soul curriculum, one naturally questions or considers the soul—I mean it's right there in the title. While we won't go into too much depth, we will look into the question of the soul's existence.

Finding a definition of the soul is surprisingly challenging considering we use the term a great deal these days. Many use it, such as advertisements like "Massages for the Body, Mind, and Soul" to conjure rest and relaxation. The Bible refers to the soul, "He restores my soul" (Psalms 23:3) but nowhere does it say what the soul IS. In Matthew 22:37, a passage reads, "Love the Lord your God with all your heart, and with all your soul and with all your mind." Like the massage advertisements, this passage separates the soul from the body and the mind, suggesting the soul is "something else" other than the physical or mental. Mary Baker G. Eddy, in her book *The Science and Health with Key to the Scriptures*, considers the soul to be a synonym for God,[1] stating no difference between the individual and Source but alluding to a difference from the physical body. Perhaps the difficulty in defining the soul arises because we all understand the general concept of the soul, but the specific definition varies by individual, similar to the phrase, "I'll know it when I see it."

According to the Oxford online dictionary, the word soul, as we consider it today, refers to the soul as "the spiritual or immaterial part of a human being or animal, regarded as immortal."[2] But the concept of immortality has touched the minds of humans since Ancient Egypt and nearly every culture and religion since. However, for most of us, the idea of a soul has not changed since Plato wrote *The Republic* in 375 B.C. "The soul of man is immortal and imperishable ... there is no difficulty in proving it."[3]

In her book, *Soul Contracts*, Danielle MacKinnon describes the soul as "the beautiful brilliant, an unconscious energy within you, connected yet amorphous."[4] Lovely words indeed, especially when paired with Cyndi Dale's definition of energy, in her book *Illuminating the Afterlife*, as "information that moves."[5] Cyndi Dale separates Spirit and Soul, describing the soul as "a sloweddown version of your essence. Whereas your spirit cannot be injured, your soul can. While your spirit does not require instruction, your soul does. Your spirit knows it is loved, but your soul has a choice."[6] This description suggests the need for healing the soul and working on soul lessons. When we bring all these concepts together, we can conclude that the soul is eternal information with the capability to improve, learn, and grow.

Putting Science and Souls Together

While scientists have yet to prove or locate the soul, I believe, with a little help from science, we can theoretically prove its existence. Albert Einstein famously said, "Everything is energy and that's all there is to it ... This is not philosophy. This is physics." These words speak to the idea that everything is made up of atoms, the building blocks of the universe and powerful sources of energy. This is reflected in the 1927 poem, *Desiderata*, where Max Ehrmann writes, "You are a child of the universe no less than the trees and the stars; you have a right to be here."[7]

Energy cannot be created or destroyed; it can only be changed from one form to another,[8] which suggests and supports the Hindu, Buddhist, and even Christian traditions of reincarnation (the Christian belief is more restricted about the resurrection of Jesus), the idea that a soul lives many lives.[9] This quote is known as the Law of Conservation of Energy, or the first law of thermodynamics, and refers to the concept that the same amount of energy always exists, balanced; it cannot be taken away or added to. Therefore, we can easily conclude what has existed, still exists merely in a different state and what is "new" is merely "old" in a different form, evolved as it were (anyone who has lived through a few decades to see your old clothes on teenagers understands this concept). Hence, while one's physical body may have an expiration date, the essence of a person, their soul, continues on in another form.

When we combine these two ideas we arrive at the following conclusion: if everything is energy, and energy can not be destroyed the opposite postulate is also true; everything is eternal. Pretty cool, eh? If everything is eternal, then the concept of souls and reincarnation is a simple extrapolation. For our purposes we will define the soul as an eternal cluster of energy creating a core essence of life.

Soul Growth

Since the total amount of energy in the universe remains the same, only changing forms, then we are all the same eternal "age" energetically. How then do we get old souls? In his book, *Your Soul Contract Decoded*, Nicholas David Ngan writes, "A soul's 'job' is to learn, grow, evolve. By doing so, the knowledge of the Creator learns, grows, expands."[10] This idea alludes to a definite connection to "All That Is" and suggests the reliance of the growth of "All That Is" is dependent on the growth of the individual. We can easily conclude every soul's purpose is to learn, grow, and evolve, thereby assisting the growth of "All That Is." We accomplish this purpose through our soul curriculum, taking classes, studying, passing tests, and graduating to the next grade or level. Given all the lessons he learned, we can surmise that President Lincoln's soul grew during his lifetime. He likely advanced to a higher grade, or possibly even graduated.

In their book *CosMos: A Co-Creators Guide to the Whole World*, Drs. Laszlo and Currivan write, "The ultimate aspiration of an evolved consciousness is to attain balance and wholeness."[11] This supports the concept of growth and the goal of achieving balance and wholeness in consciousness, suggesting that consciousness itself can be improved upon. I think we can all agree, that while humans have improved since Hildegard's time and even since Frederick Douglass' time, humans can still use a little improvement.

In the book *You Are The Universe*, authors Deepak Chopra and Dr. Menas C. Kafatos write, "Everything in the Universe is either conscious or unconscious . . . an object is either participating in the domain of mind or it isn't."[12] With respect to one's soul curriculum, how can one be unconscious, not participating? That's an easy one, "the veil of forgetfulness."

The Veil of Forgetfulness

Humans are very forgetful. I've often forgotten why I walked into a room, let alone why I am here on this planet in this body at this time. Those who believe in reincarnation agree with the idea of the veil of forgetfulness, the amnesiac effect of incarnating. In between lives, we assess, plan based on our lessons already learned, make agreements, and choose our curriculum for our next life. Then . . . we incarnate, and we forget. Dolores Cannon, in her book, *The Three Waves of Volunteers & the New Earth*, explains, "The main problem is the forgetting or amnesia process that affects souls when they come to Earth."[13]

Many of us wonder why we forget. Sometimes it feels like the deck is already stacked against us and forgetting makes our jobs harder. Dolores Cannon continues, "it is best to have all memory erased and to allow us to rediscover ourselves, as well as our mission . . . it would not be a test if we knew the answers."[14]

Our historical Sensitives seemed to have planned their soul curricula well. Consider George Washington Carver's life. Born at the end of the Civil War, he was enslaved by people who reportedly opposed slavery but needed the labor. His ill health and weak body allowed him to spend time in nature, learning and playing, which put him on a direct path of changing farming practices in the South. Professor Carver definitely "hit the ground running" on his soul curriculum. Or Florence Nightingale. In her teens, she felt a definite calling—she just wasn't clear on what that mission was or how it was to be undertaken.

Dr. Richard Gerber's book, *Vibrational Medicine,* explains that the veil of forgetfulness allows us to start fresh, free of any hang-ups we may have accrued in previous lives. He writes, "If we were to have the knowledge and personality of our previous lives, we would have the same prejudices and biases that we had previously left. Each lifetime is a chance to start anew with a clean slate, so to speak, with the mistakes of the past behind us."[15] How many times have you wished you could have a "do-over?"

Karma

We've looked at soul curriculum, but where and how does karma fit in? Is karma different than soul curriculum? Karma, I've come to understand, is created while you are working on your soul curriculum. Similar to the saying, "Life is what happens when you are busy making plans," karma is what happens when you are busy working on your soul curriculum. Continuing with the metaphor of the Universal University: hypothetically, if you incarnated and were tested without having studied, choosing instead to goof off, that is a choice you made and is considered "allowed" in terms of your soul curriculum. You just need to take the test another time. But what if you cheat on that test? That's when karma is established. In this example, not only would you need to retake the test to complete your soul curriculum, but you would also have to make amends for cheating. Karma.

One of my teachers, Kami Blackwell Lichtenberg, describes the soul curriculum by comparing it to a "vacation itinerary" with karma as the souvenirs you bought on the trip. Another teacher of mine, Mavis Salazar, described it as the need to see a situation from all sides. For example: if I punched someone, next time I will get to feel what it is like to be punched. Incidentally, can you imagine Dr. Joseph Mengele's karma, or the karma of our historical Sensitives Stalin and Hitler? Or another example would be if I give a gift, I need to feel how it would be to receive a gift. This idea of karma is supported by Dr. Gerber's explanation of karma in *Vibrational Medicine*. He writes, "By experiencing life from all possible viewpoints, the reincarnational scheme allows us to see the world from all possible perspectives."[16]

Gary Zukav, in his book *The Seat of the Soul*, writes, "The law of karma governs the balancing of energy within our system of morality and within those of our neighbors. It serves humanity as an impersonal and Universal teacher of responsibility."[17] Dr. Gerber explains karma as, "the true meaning of the expression, 'as ye sow, so shall ye reap.'"[18]

In the mainstream world, karma has gotten a bad rap. With sayings such as "karma is a bitch" we've come to think of karma as a bad thing. However, when we consider karma as a balancing force of nature and that nature is neutral, karma becomes more like a snowstorm. Some snow here, more snow there, neutral in where it falls, and based solely on the natural atmospheric conditions.

What seems to be the deciding factor of karma is intent, thus answering the question, "Is it ok to do the wrong thing for the right reasons?" Buddhists would say yes. If your intent is to bring about goodness in the end but in the process you cause harm, no karma is created. If you intend to cause harm and you act on that intent, karma is created. Dr. Fred Alan Wolf writes in *The Spiritual Universe*, "Karma means, rather specifically, willful action, not all action."[19]

With this theory, what would Hitler's karma be? One can easily imagine lifetime upon lifetime of hardships and challenges. He maintained that his actions were to bring about a stronger human race. I can understand wanting humans to be better and kinder, but Hitler's ultimate goal implies a judgment on his part (and his followers) that, I believe, is beyond a human's responsibility. His actions, and those made in his name and by his order, are way beyond acceptable karmic levels. He must've been held accountable for his actions. In my twisted imagination, I visualize him stuck in a Groundhog Day version of the tasks of Hercules, repeating the mucking of horse stalls day after day after lifetime. Then, I send him love and work on forgiving him. It's a process.

Soul Families

According to Alethia Luna in "12 Signs You've Met Someone From Your Soul Family," soul families are, "comprised of a group of people that your Soul energetically resonates with on a mental, emotional, physical, and spiritual level." She continues, "your Soul Family is often described as being comprised of Souls that are cut from the same 'energetic cloth' as you."[20]

Your Soul Family can include your parents, your best friend, lover, or soul mate. A soul family member is someone to whom you are drawn, and with whom you bond tightly. Alison Wem writes succinctly in *Finding Your Soul Family*, "Your soul family can consist of blood family, adopted family, in-laws, friends, colleagues and neighbors. They are the important people in your life."[21]

As we alluded to earlier, a soul family member can be someone who you are equally repulsed by, the equal but opposite force. These family members are in your life for a reason; there is a lesson to be learned from them. At this point, we can better understand how President Lincoln agreed to experience great loss in his life. With the wider, long-term perspective, we can begin to understand how (and why) his soul family agreed to cause him such grief and loss. We can conclude he took his grief and sorrow and turned it into a unified slavery-free country.

Soul Entanglement

The entire concept of soul curriculum becomes even more interesting when considering the "physical phenomenon" of quantum entanglement. CalTech Science Exchange explains entanglement occurs "when two particles, such as a pair of photons or electrons, become entangled, they remain connected even when separated by vast distances."[22] That's a big fancy way of saying tiny particles can be connected, even across long distances and still share similar, if not exact, characteristics. Mind-blowing, no? It becomes even more astounding when you discover if one entangled particle changes a characteristic, the other particles will change to match that characteristic, again regardless of distance. Therefore, it is possible to think, a soul family member may not be in your immediate world, but rather somewhere "out there," on a different continent, a different planet, or even a different galaxy.

If a soul consists of energy particles that are entangled with other souls, any change in that soul will also affect all entangled particles of other souls. In other words, when a soul heals or works on its soul curriculum, it grows, learns, and changes its state, increasing its vibration as well as the vibration of its soul family regardless of proximity. Can you imagine the far-reaching changes in the soul family of Lincoln? He went from anti-slavery to abolitionist to establishing a free country. The soul growth that man experienced is staggering as is the possible ripples and growth of his soul family. With this theory, that means any soul particles that were entangled with Lincoln also evolved and grew.

Another mind-blowing theory that supports the idea that "all boats float" is entrainment. The website, *Frontiers in Psychology*, defines entrainment as a "temporal locking process in which one system's motion or signal frequency entrains the frequency of another system."[23] For example, if I play a C note on the piano and someone else plays an E note on another piano across the room, the vibrations will synchronize, or entrain, to a common pitch, such as a D note. One vibration will adjust upwards while the other adjusts downwards to reach a shared frequency. This concept explains why you may experience tiredness around certain people, places, or things. If their energy is very different than yours, you work harder at pulling up their lower level. The phenomenon of entrainment supports the concept of increasing your soul family vibrations. If you increase your vibration, you will entrain others around you to that higher vibration, along with the souls with which you are entangled.

Photons and Color

Here comes even more science-y stuff. I remember my third-grade teacher, Mrs. Burns, teaching us about the atom and its components. When she said, "If you could vibrate at the same rate, you could put your hand right through this table," my mouth just dropped open, my eyes got big, and my breath was taken away. To find how or if atoms can indeed increase their vibration, I had to go back to my third-grade class and remember what else Mrs. Burns taught us. NASA's website was tremendously helpful in bringing my memory back.

Atoms are made of protons, neutrons, and electrons. Electrons spin around and around the nucleus, which is made of protons and neutrons. When an electron is close to the nucleus, physicists call that a ground state. When an electron moves farther away from the nucleus to a higher energy level, that is called an excited state. When electrons move from a grounded state to an excited state, the electron increases in energy, called absorption. When the electrons move back to its grounded state, it releases energy, called emission. The released energy is called photons. Therefore, an electron emits photons when returning to its grounded state. Photons are little "packets of light." This back and forth between absorption and emission (adding and shedding photons) changes the atom's frequency, or vibration, and the light the atom emits. Different colors of light are associated with different photon energies. For example, a photon of red light has less energy than a photon of blue light. The red light has longer wavelengths than the blue which results in less energy. If the photon energy, and therefore its color, has less energy and energy is data, then the color red would have less data than the color blue and a lower vibration.[24]

In *Seat of the Soul*, Gary Zukav writes, "Emotions are currents of energy with different frequencies. When you choose to replace a lower-frequency current of energy such as anger, with a higher-frequency current, such as forgiveness you raise the frequency of your light."[25] This corresponds to the theory that emotions correlate to colors, the photon energy. For example, red, with its longer wavelengths and less energy may be associated with lower-frequency emotions, such as guilt, anger, or shame. And by extension, blue may be associated with the higher vibrating emotions.

David R. Hawkins', M.D., Ph.D., work takes this concept a step further in his book *The Map of Consciousness Explained: A Proven Energy Scale to Actualize Your Ultimate Potential*. Dr. Hawkins has researched the level at which emotions vibrate. Using muscle testing, Dr. Hawkins "documents the first time that levels of consciousness have ever been calibrated. On this chart, we find the entire spectrum of human experience."[26] With Love rated high on Dr. Hawkins' charts at an energy level of 500, Joy at 540, Peace at 600, and Enlightenment ranging from an energy level of 700 to 1000, his work confirms the insights of ancient healers: a state of peace brings even greater peace.

To summarize the "science-y stuff," everything is made of vibrating particles of energy, some of which are connected and are affected by each other. When a particle increases its vibration, the connected particles increase as well. The longer a particle remains at the higher vibration, the more it is likely to entrain, or change, other particles around and connected to it. By remaining in a higher emotional state, such as love, an individual will vibrate at the level of love, emanating and spreading that higher emotional state, regardless of distance.

Soul Work

What IS Soul Work? How do I complete my soul homework? How do I heal my soul? How do I renegotiate my contract? What are the down-and-dirty details? And how does it relate to self-care?

Author Gary Zukav suggests working with your emotions is a great place to start, in fact, as Sensitives, I believe, it is the place to start, stay, and finish. As we have shown previously, higher vibrating emotions will increase your vibrations. Increasing your vibrations by being in a state of love, joy, gratitude, or peace IS soul work. It involves engaging with your soul curriculum and healing both your own soul and those of others. When we are in the flow of higher vibrating emotions, we feel better, lighter. Abraham-Hicks calls it "downstream." Rupert Sheldrake termed this flow as a "morphic field." In her book, *The Evolutionary Empath*, Rev. Stephanie Red Feather, Ph.D., explains a morphic field as "a field that influences the pattern or form of things . . . A morphic field is a type of consciousness that shapes form, pattern, and organization."[27] She further explains that a morphic field is the energy of thought and is strengthened by repetition. According to her, "The evolution of a morphic field can be likened to a habit where a specific energy or frequency is reinforced by doing the same thing over and over."[28] Therefore, the more you experience high-vibrating energies or emotions, the more you connect with the morphic field, the more you contribute to the growth of the said field, and the greater the morphic field becomes. Consequently, the cycle continues, reinforcing the connection and further expanding the morphic field.

Perhaps the metaphor of a river is a good example of being in the flow of the morphic field. When you first discover a river, you cautiously dip your toe in. However, as you gradually immerse yourself, get to know the river, and acclimate to its temperature, you can wade deeper and eventually swim with the current. Adding Archimedes' principle of displacement, as you flow with the river, its level rises, symbolizing how your presence contributes to its growth, growing as you are flowing. I believe Tesla was "in the flow." When he was young, he initially tried to control his abilities, but at some point—namely in Budapest—he embraced them, allowing them to flow naturally. By accepting his abilities as a gift, he learned to work with them. He learned to let his mind go and find the flow. Look where it carried him: vast inventions, most of which we are only beginning to develop today, some of which, when implemented, may help ease our use of the earth's resources.

Neurobiologists would describe this as similar to creating and strengthening neural pathways. Very simply put, neural pathways are created when you do something new. The more you perform that new action, the stronger the neural pathway is developed and therefore the new behavior eventually becomes habit. Put even simpler, stay in the emotions of love, gratitude, and peace, and those higher vibrating emotions will become second nature. Surround yourself with beauty. Become aware of all the good things and how you feel when you are in a beautiful place. Turn off the news, or at least be selective and aware of what you are allowing in your world.

With that said, being a sensitive human can be challenging, and there may be moments when love or beauty is hard to find. I often hear from friends and clients that "this planet is so dense." When those moments come, it is helpful to take a moment, breathe, and remember it is just a moment. Somehow in the grand scheme, this emotion serves to help and heal not only you and your soul but also your soul family. This collective healing radiates outward, positively impacting the world and the universe as a whole. Consider quirky Tesla, Rasputin, or First Lady Roosevelt. When situations became too challenging for them, they went on walks and sought out fresh air to revitalize themselves and clear their heads (and thus their energy fields).

After Fight Flight Freeze

Many of us react without thinking. It is a natural response to stimuli; we Sensitives are constantly in a physical state of survival, the fight, flight, or freeze mode. When our bodies are in this state, we do not think—literally. We are working off survival instincts. The online paper titled "The Science of Fight or Flight" written by Roberta Scherf and Chris Bye explains the phenomenon well: "During 'fight or flight' blood drains from the prefrontal cortex, so there's no rational thought. This makes it virtually impossible to learn new things, focus on small tasks, or engage with other people as the lower parts of the brain are focused on survival and escape."[29]

Candace Pert, in her book *Molecules of Emotions*, explains that our bodies react physically first, even before we know if we are in trouble or what threat we are experiencing. Our bodies will jump at a loud sound, for example, when a smoke detector goes off in the middle of the night and release chemicals (which Candace Pert states are emotions) to help us out of danger even before we've had a chance to process the situation.

The physical response is so natural and immediate that there isn't time to evaluate the situation. But once we have established safety, that is the time to evaluate, question, and work with our emotions. Asking ourselves questions, like "What emotion did I feel then?" or "Why did I feel fear then?" helps us to process the emotions, releasing the stress-released chemicals, cleaning out our cells, and keeping them healthy. Processing your emotions is essential to your physical, mental, and emotional health, along with the health and growth of humanity.

Processing emotions is KEY to soul homework, healing the soul.

Soul work can be accomplished through meditation and introspection, but it can also be done by merely asking ourselves, "What am I feeling now? Why?" Just posing this question turns our focus onto our emotional layer and encourages inward reflection. I know several times I've felt "blah" and had no idea why.

Or as Holly Golightly calls them in the 1961 movie *Breakfast at Tiffany's*, they are the "Mean Reds." "You're just sad that's all," Holly says, "Suddenly you're afraid, and you don't know what you're afraid of." While Miss Holly Golightly chooses to deflect or deny her emotions by "jumping in a cab and going to Tiffany's," this would be a perfect time to go deeper and explore why you're afraid and sad, moving just a little out of your comfort zone.

Yes, moving out of your comfort zone takes courage. After all, you don't know what you'll learn about yourself. Once you begin this journey of self-discovery, you may find that your burdens lighten, even dissipating the lower energy. The trigger, whatever is causing your current emotion, is in the past and can no longer hurt you. The behaviors or responses that once served you may no longer be needed or pertinent to the person you currently are. They can be released and healed, leading to a lighter and more empowered self and soul, even increasing your vibration.

Soul Healing Techniques

We have already discussed several options for self-care, a.k.a. coping mechanisms and soul care/work, but there are always more ways. Here are a few more ideas to consider.

Establishing a relationship with your soul is another way to work on your soul curriculum or heal your soul. While in a quiet meditative state, talk to your soul. Introduce yourself, and ask your soul questions like, "What is your name, how would you like me to refer to you?" Have a conversation with your inner self, your soul.

When you are ready, you can even "call back" parts of your soul that have been shattered in the past due to a particularly traumatic event. When I am preparing for a remote reiki session, I will ask my conscious mind and any "trickster" archetypes (for example, drama queen, saboteur, or martyr) to leave and find the next part of my soul that is ready to come home. I ask them to make all the preparations needed for us to return at a designated time. This helps in two ways: it allows my inner self to come forward easier so I may help my client during the reiki session, and it sets up a separate time for my soul to feel more whole and healed. Lesson learned.

The Mirror Effect

Another technique useful for soul homework is called the Mirror Effect, introduced by Gregg Braden. It is also referred to as Psychological Projection, a concept explored by Dr. Sigmund Freud, who believed behaviors you find upsetting in someone else are really behaviors within yourself that you do not like. For example, suppose you find someone, anyone, exasperatingly chatty. This could be a signal to yourself that you are uncomfortable with your own chattiness.

Gregg Braden's Mirror Effect is very similar to Dr. Freud's theory. In his audiobook *Awakening the Power of a Modern God*, Braden suggests using the world around you as a mirror to examine yourself and the work that needs to be done. For example, look around your room, your world, what do you see? Do you see beauty? Do you see hate, fear, chaos? Do you see disorganization? Do you see calm and peace? A personal example would be after a tough breakup, I found myself in a "hate men" mode, perceiving all men as bad and hurtful. I began to notice examples that reinforced my feelings everywhere I looked. Now, after a great deal of processing, I see many men doing many loving things: holding a door open, pushing a child on a swing, playing with dogs, and even remaining calm and patient until those dogs are ready to play with them. I see kindness, both large and small, everywhere, a signal my soul is healing and vibrating higher.

God Goggles

Using the outer world as signals to your inner world is a great place to start doing soul homework. You can even shift what you see by practicing a technique from spiritual teacher Dr. Masters, who advises to "feel that it is your God-Self that is seeing through your eyes."[30] My variation on this technique is what I call "God Goggles."

Dr. Masters suggests imagining that God is seeing through your eyes, with your inner divinity moving through you and seeing the world alongside you. With my variation, in the morning when I'm outside with my dogs, I imagine putting on my God Goggles. I imagine they are similar to the first pilot glasses made of leather, brass bolts, and little windshield wipers on the lens. My image of my God Goggles makes me giggle, a shift in energy itself. Then I add a little sparkle to everything I look at through my God Goggles, the trees, the rocks, even my toes. When I practice putting on my God Goggles, I see beauty, kindness, and love everywhere. My vibration increases and the energy of love emanates.

My Favorite Things

Another technique I have recently discovered is identifying my favorite things. In the words of Julie Andrews from the 1965 movie *Sound of Music*, "When the dog bites, when the bee stings, when I'm feeling sad, I simply remember my favorite things and then I don't feel so bad." It may sound trite and too easy, but thinking about your favorite things, the things that fill you with love, will create an energetic shift, lifting your mood and vibration. This technique has worked so well for me, some mornings I will wake up with the song in my head, reminding me to do the work.

Suitcase Meditation/Exercise

This is a fun technique to incorporate the lessons learned while releasing the weight and energy of the past. I recommend working with one suitcase (year) at a time.

1. Get into a comfy place, breathe deep, relax your body, and quiet your mind.
2. Once your mind is calm and your body relaxed, imagine a row of suitcases, one for each year of your life. Some suitcases may be larger than others, filled with all the memories of that year. Others smaller, less busy years.
3. Visualize stickers symbolizing and summarizing the year on the outside of the suitcases.
4. Imagine yourself in your "observer" mode/clothing. I usually imagine myself as a reporter from the 1940s, wearing a fedora hat with a press pass in the hatband and a long khaki raincoat.
5. As your Observer, pick up one of the suitcases, but do not open it. Just set it apart from the others.
6. On your Observer notepad, imagine writing down brief notes, the lessons learned, from that year. It's not necessary to actually be able to read the notes, but just visualizing the act of making the notes is enough.
7. Visualize tearing the note off the notepad, and place it over your heart (or head, wherever feels right to you). Allow the note to dissolve into your soul.
8. Imagine the suitcase dissolving into sand and blowing away, allowing the energy of that year to be reincorporated back into the universe.
9. Come back to the room.

Soul Curriculum Renegotiated

If you have studied soul contracts, you may have come across the lesser-known concept of renegotiating a soul contract. I first heard of soul contracts and the possibility of renegotiating from a metaphysical teacher, Mary Grady. She shared that she had come to the realization that she had accomplished everything in her soul contract and was nearing her time to discarnate. But she was not ready to leave yet. So, she renegotiated her contract to add more lessons, or in the soul curriculum metaphor, more classes.

What some people forget is humans have free will. We have the gift of choice. While we are between lives we are choosing our next life and its path. However, what happens when you incarnate and find the circumstances too hard? In the metaphor of the Soul Curriculum, this is similar to how many feel about taking a college Statistics class. In my freshman year at college, many of my friends registered for Statistics only to find it really challenging. Many of my friends said "I just don't get it" or "This is just too hard. I didn't sign up for this."

If that is truly the case, if you honestly can't take the class and you can't learn the lesson in this lifetime, you can drop the class, postponing the lesson for a different life. You can renegotiate your contract. After all, it's your contract, your choice.

Consider the possibility that Lady Diana decided to drop her soul class. She may have renegotiated her contract, decided her lesson was too difficult for this lifetime, and wanted out. She may have felt standing up to her nemesis, Camilla, was enough to learn (it is a hard lesson for a Sensitive) during this lifetime and was released from her class/contract. Remember, when Charles proposed she heard a voice telling her it would be difficult, and she agreed anyway. It is possible that when she found out just how hard it was to be Queen in Waiting and Charles' wife, she chose to renegotiate her soul contract and drop the class. By doing so, she changed her life path and soul. Her choice.

By opting to renegotiate your contract, the pressure to learn the agreed lesson lightens, freeing you up to possibly learn other lessons. For example, let's say you agreed to teach a soul family member about asking for help. Perhaps that means you, as the teacher, must stand by, watching your soul family member struggle, waiting until they finally ask for help. But for you, watching the struggle may be too much, too hard. You just can't stand to see them hurt. In fact, it hurts you so much it causes you pain and darkness and lowers your vibration. In a case such as this, you can renegotiate your contract and ask to not be a witness any longer. Once you drop that class and your contract is renegotiated, you will feel lighter and freer to work on other agreed lessons, which perhaps come to you more easily. Remember how good and light you felt once you dropped that statistics class? While you didn't complete one particular lesson, you did open yourself up to learning others. In doing so, you raised your vibration and that of your soul family, including the soul family member you couldn't teach, and ultimately helped that soul family member after all. Lady Diana may not have finished her class in being Queen in Waiting, but once she dropped that class, she learned to stand up for herself more and harness her celebrity to highlight the causes she was passionate about. Thus, a new lesson was learned.

The concept of renegotiating a soul contract, or dropping a soul class, may initially feel like a you are a "quitter" or is taking the easy way out. But when we consider the overall goal of the conscious universe is to learn, grow, and expand, perhaps one lesson would be to say "no," "enough," and "not right now." This is in fact a hard lesson to learn for some Sensitive souls, the lesson of setting boundaries or self-care. One could argue that self-care, while the hardest lesson, is the most important lesson to learn.

Self-Care and Its Importance

If you are a mother on this earth, you understand sacrifice and putting others first. "But my family needs me, my children need help. How can I possibly work on self-care?" you may ask. Allow me a moment to explain. If, as a mother, you do not remain healthy and able how can you continue to help your family and loved ones? If you continually put others first, sacrificing your health and well-being, you will get tired and burn out, possibly even to the point of being unable to help anyone. But if you find time for yourself to relax, rest, and restore regularly, then you can happily assist others. Remember, when flying the flight attendant reminds us that "in the case of a drop in air pressure, secure your oxygen mask first before helping others." Same principle. You can't help anyone with their mask if you can't breathe.

Therefore, self-care is pivotal in the soul's development. It is not selfish. It is not vain or egotistical. It IS essential.

Doing your Soul Homework

There are countless ways to work on your soul curriculum. A quick search on Google shows 536,000,000 books on the subject. Sonia Choquette, Sanaya Roman, and Sandra Ingerman are just three authors who write soul how-to books. The key to soul homework is finding out what works best for you. This means experimenting with new and different techniques, like ones I have offered. There is no one way or a single answer for everyone; you must find your way, your own answer. While this may be frustrating, the payoff is worth the effort.

A Historical Soul Family Curriculum Example

The Freedom Summer in 1964, as documented in the 1994 film, *Freedom on My Mind*,[31] beautifully explains how the concept of the soul curriculum and soul family may improve the world. Many people interviewed for the documentary reported a "pull" or a "call" to join the movement toward equality. One woman, a northern white student, when deciding to go to Mississippi that summer, explained that if she went, then her parents, brothers, and sister would care about the struggles of inequality in Mississippi. "

The Freedom Summer of 1964 was an effort to get black citizens of Mississippi registered to vote. To say they encountered difficulties would be a vast understatement. The local leaders of the movement recognized early on that they needed more help, particularly cross-cultural assistance, involving not just Black individuals but also white allies. 1,000 students from the North traveled to Mississippi to "get the word out" on registering to vote not only to locals but also the media, which then spread the word to the nation.[32]

The people involved in the Freedom Summer movement were forever changed, some finding their soul purpose in life, that of developing programs to support those in need, seeking PhDs and teaching, or remaining politically active. Some interviewed in the documentary reported feeling a sense of finding their family or home during that summer.

When we consider the concept of Soul Curriculum and Soul Family, the Freedom Summer Movement is an excellent example. Strangers felt compelled, and pushed and pulled to join the movement for change and were met with loving grateful people, their soul family. In the end, progress was made via the signing of the Civil Rights Act of 1964. Admittedly, more work still needs to be accomplished. Still, the work of the souls in Mississippi in 1964 was a huge step for the evolution of humanity and society, the ultimate goal of the soul curriculum.

To summarize, self-care, developing coping mechanisms, and working with your emotions IS working on your Soul Curriculum. Working on your soul curriculum increases your vibration. Increasing your vibration provides the opportunity for those around you and your soul family to do the same. Higher vibrations become contagious, spreading across the universe. So, while spending time getting to know yourself will definitely help you it may also help others, maybe even those you don't know.

Self-Care and the Ego

This may seem like an obvious statement but one must have a healthy ego in order to have healthy self-care. Consider; if you don't care about yourself, i.e., low self-esteem, low self-image, and a deflated ego, you won't care what your hair looks like or if your clothes are clean. Sensitives commonly have low self-esteem and low self-confidence. We tend to be quieter looking and less flashy like Harriet Tubman or the simple style of Eleanor Roosevelt.

The word ego is understood to mean the self or self-worth. Over time, the word ego has become almost synonymous with egotistical, meaning an over-inflated ego or selfish, translating to a negative term. However, the word ego in Latin simply means I, neither good nor bad, but merely the self. The ego is what helps us to want to brush our teeth, make our hair look nice, and dress appropriately. It helps us to move forward, achieve, and strive for goals. For Sensitives, sometimes just showing up is challenging enough, let alone putting energy into how we look. We can get too caught up in what other people will think of us, and it can scare us into not going to a party and choosing to stay home.

But here's the kicker. In order to have healthy self-care, a Sensitive needs a healthy balanced ego, or any ego. Why would you take care of something you don't care about? HOW do you care for something you don't care about? And there, my friends, is the lesson: learning to care for yourself as much, or more, as you care for others. Learning you are just as worthy of love and care as any other being. Understanding and believing you are as much a part of the Universe and deserving of love. Believing you are a divine creation, as divine as a beautiful sunrise or any sweet-faced creature on this planet.

Here's a suggested first step to building a healthy ego and therefore self-care.

1. Look for the beauty around you. Focus on the beauty around you. The more beauty you look for, the more beauty you will see.
2. Realize (and believe) your world is a reflection of you. The beauty you see is a reflection of you.
3. Understand (and believe) that you are beautiful, just as beautiful as everything around you.

A great and easy example of this is your home. Everything in your home is a reflection of you. You chose that couch. You chose those pillows. You chose those clothes. And presumably (hopefully), you chose them because you thought they were lovely. Those things in your home are a lovely collection and expression of you, and therefore of your beauty. Look around your space. Notice all the beautiful things you choose to surround you. Consider your most prized possession, perhaps it's your grandmother's china, or simply a rock you found on a summer vacation when you were young. Whatever it may be, realize how you treat that item: with care and tenderness. Remember how careful you are when you are near it or if it ever needs to be packed and moved. THAT level of care and consideration is exactly what YOU deserve and require. THAT is the beginning of a balanced and healthy ego and the first step to self-care.

Self-Care in an Uncaring World

At this moment in Earth's history, we are experiencing a challenge to all humans. Many humans have transformed and crossed over. Some were Warriors for Good—Betty White, Sidney Poitier, and most recently Thich Nhat Hanh. With my belief in the theory of soul curriculum, I take a moment to thank these souls, realizing that their jobs are done and their lessons are learned. However, many humans are sad, angry, and filled with fear about what tomorrow will bring. I choose to believe that this is an important time in the evolution of humanity; some would call it a bifurcation moment. We are offered the opportunity to grow, releasing stuffy old traditions that no longer serve our species or the universe. However, this transition is challenging for many humans and can cause great fear, leading some to react defensively, much like toddlers throwing tantrums. Silly young souls.

During such tumultuous times, love and kindness for yourself and others is important, even key. Even if your sole soul purpose is to love all and be kind, that in itself is a HUGE and important task. It proves to others that living lovingly is possible and even perhaps profitable. You are a role model for the next generation, a generation of loving, kind, and honorable humans—a generation that will then pass that style of living onto the next generation.

Doing self-care, or soul curriculum work, may feel selfish, egotistical, or even narcissistic. After all, you are working on your soul and yourself, what could be more self-centered than that? Self-care and engaging with your soul curriculum are essential to the evolution of humanity. This important work not only benefits the individual but also contributes to the growth of humanity and the expansion of universal consciousness. In fact, in the words of the 1985 movie *Real Genius*, "It's a moral imperative."

Soul Purposes

If you are here, it means you agreed to be here, which signifies that you have a purpose. You are important. You are needed, for what or why I don't know. But I thoroughly believe that you are here, we are all here, for the good and advancement of All and All That Is. If you need permission to take time to rest, remember, you are doing self-care for all sentient beings, not just yourself. Even if I'm completely crazy and wrong and this whole book is filled with bunk, living lovingly is still a very good and honorable way to exist. How can that be wrong?

I believe a quote from the 2011 movie *The Help* sums up my point succinctly and beautifully:

"You is kind. You is smart. You is important."

CHAPTER 26

Conclusion

We have discussed a lot in our journey together. We have looked at several historical characters and discovered that they were most likely Highly Sensitive. We have seen how their sensitivity made them who we know. We have learned how our historical Sensitives coped and cared for themselves, offering us suggestions for our own self-care. We have discussed some ideas of what to try, and possibly what not to try. We have offered many self-caring ideas to give you a starting point as you find your way as an empowered empath.

My Top Tools for HSPs

I realize we have already discussed these items, but they are so crucial to becoming an empowered being that they bear repeating.

AWARENESS AND TRACKING

Being aware of your thoughts, emotions, energy, and environment is the strongest and most powerful thing a Sensitive can do. As discussed earlier, you can't improve something if you are unaware of its need for support. Being self-aware helps you realize what is yours, what needs attention, and what can be jettisoned. In order to identify what is yours or what your strengths are I suggest tracking your emotions, energy, and even your physical body. This may be even more effective with a partner or a friend, a more neutral observer, who can maintain some distance. Tracking can be quite helpful; for example: my emotions when Russia invaded Ukraine. Tracking can be as easy as making a note in your calendar, assigning a number to your emotions or energy, or creating your own scale of how you feel. On those "off days" when your assigned number is different than your usual, consider peeking at the headlines (but quickly and merely as an observer) to see if anything highly charged occurred recently. Take note of this. Over time, a pattern may emerge that can help you better understand your sensitivities.

INTENT
Adding in your intention for peace, joy, love, or the Highest Good is an easy way to increase your positivity, bring in healthy energy, and lessen the pressure of an expected outcome. Remembering that the Highest Good may not be what we expect allows us a little wiggle room. If we leave the outcome to the Highest Good, then the goal is out of our hands, and we can relax and help the best we can. Adding in the intention of helping ourselves or others before an activity, such as eating or sleeping, helps us enter a mindset with the energy of our requested goals.

FOOD AND WATER
As an Earthling, we need sustenance. Making a healthy and aware choice can help you feel empowered while understanding your body and what it needs. Eating natural foods can bring in lovely Earth energy—the more natural the food, the more healing and loving its energy.

All Earthlings need water, it is essential to all life here. As a Sensitive, water helps move toxins and any stuck energy out of our bodies, keeping us clean and vibrant. Drinking even more water after conscious energy work, getting a massage, or sending love to an emotionally charged area of the world, can be an easy (and inexpensive) way to recover quicker or avoid "energy hangovers" altogether. Water can also alleviate headaches and tummy issues so common to us Sensitives.

ME TIME, SELF-CARE
Allowing yourself time to rest and recharge is essential to all Earthlings, but especially HSPs. Sensitives need downtime. We need our alone time, time to be in our own energy, time for our nervous system to rejuvenate and our bodies to heal. This helps us reconnect with and better know our own energy, enabling us to recognize energy that is not ours and choose whether to let it in.

A Brief Word About Parenting Sensitive Children
I am not a parent. This has been drummed into my head multiple times. As a result, I'm a little gun-shy about the subject. But as a sensitive child, I have two suggestions.

BELIEVE THEM

When your sweet innocent child tells you they saw great-grandma at the end of their bed last night—believe them. When they say their imaginary friend is real and their name is *Whatever*—believe them. (Their imaginary friend just may be an angel or guide to help them.) When they say something "crazy," and you inquire further; whatever they say—believe them.

In 1981, when I was 11 years old in elementary school, I had an unnerving experience. I was on the playground, and I had an out-of-body experience. I could see the kids playing, even myself playing, I rose until I could see the roof of my school. To this day, I can still visualize where the HVAC units are. When I "came to," I was in my classroom writing and instead of writing my name at the top of the paper, I'd written "Moon Doggie." Weird.

My world was very typical middle class, with my family being non-practicing Protestants. Very typical family. I had no contacts with the mystical world, it wasn't even on my radar as a possibility. I had no idea what happened and no way of finding out. I was so scared, mostly that if I told anyone, they would lock me away in an awful place. So, I kept my mouth shut and began reading psychology books to figure out what happened. My remaining school years were filled with sick days and extreme emotional discomfort. I never told anyone until I was nearly fifty. When I finally told my mother more than 30 years later, after she got over her shock, I asked what she would've done if I had told her back in the 80s. She said she probably would have sent to me to a psychiatrist.

As a result of my fear, my meta-abilities shut down and didn't open back up until I was around 44 years old, when I began learning about the mystical world and more about Sensitives. My life would've been very different had I learned I was Sensitive with meta-skills or if my mom had taken me to a psychiatrist. When I see my friends who were born into families that were aware of their special skills and have lived their lifetime in the mystical meta-world, I do have moments of jealousy and regret my decision to shut down my abilities. But the phrase "If it could've been different, it would've been," and my belief in soul curricula offers me comfort and acceptance. Now, I love who I am, who I have become, and who I continue to become.

I mention my story only to illustrate how your child may be feeling. Scared. Alone. Out of place. Weird. Vulnerable. Creating a safe environment and letting your child know that they are always wonderfully loved, and everything is ok is the best thing you can do for your lovely child. Believe them, support them. Ask them what they want to do about their special skills. Do they want to explore them, learn to work with them, or control them? Or do they want to shut them down? Help them to feel that either way is ok.

LEARN MORE ABOUT YOUR ABILITIES

Since the Sensitive trait is inherited, learning about your sensitivities and your abilities will go a long way to support your sensitive child. A household filled with aware Sensitives is a wonderful thing. It creates an Orchid environment for your child. It supports the child's feeling of normalcy; they aren't weird, they're unique, special, and amazingly loving. The more you know about yourself and your abilities, the more capable you are to talk to your child about their abilities. While your special skills may be different and your child's sensitivity increased, you can still support them on their journey of discovery.

I know many parents who are struggling with their young Sensitive child and are just learning about the HSP trait. They find themselves in a whole new world, having to catch up and learn quickly. From my personal experience, I recommend regular reiki sessions. Reiki helps the child release all outside emotions they soak up at school or wherever they go. I also recommend that the whole family learn about the trait and how it manifests in each sensitive family member together, kinda like family game night but focused on energy and abilities. Can you imagine your Friday night family night being filled with fun experiments of energy and intuition? Oh, what fun!

Sensitive Revolution Revisited

Our world is changing, and as hard as it may be to believe, for the better. Our society is transforming into a more sensitive society. Insensitivity is "out," kindness, consideration, and sensitivity are "in." We see this in products for sensitive skin, sensitive teeth, and even foods for sensitive digestion. We have the Black Lives Matter movement and the Me Too movement—even a "new" pronoun, all designed to create equality for those demographics. We see celebrities and other high-profile people being called out for their insensitive remarks, some even losing their jobs due to their lack of sensitivity. Add a dollop of pandemic and quarantine, which feels like a prison sentence for extroverts but a welcome respite for HSPs, and we have a recipe for true change and evolution. And now we have the Ukrainian War and the Israel-Hamas War resulting in global support for those in need.

Yes, the world seems crazy and full of fear and anger. As an HSP, it can be overwhelming, especially if you sense the emotion-infused energy. All of this is to say, the world is evolving into a more sensitive society. The turmoil we are currently experiencing stems from non-HSPs clinging to the life they once knew. (Remember The Stone Child story) But with love and understanding, a kinder, more peaceful, and more heart-based society will prevail.

In Conclusion

We have seen how our historical people were indeed highly sensitive persons. We have learned the importance of these historically highly sensitive persons and their impact on their world, our society, and our future. We have also expanded our understanding of what highly sensitive persons can be; we are more than just Nerds or Nurturers. We can be Rebels, Leaders, Champions, and complete and total Game-Changers. We can be Freedom-Fighters, Activists, and Rebels for a Cause. We can change the world!

So, if you are in need of finding your purpose or calling, establish a relationship with Florence Nightingale, Martin Luther King, or Hildegard de Bingen.

If you need assistance with protection, grounding, or clearing, call on Frederick Douglass, George Washington Carver, President Grant, or Eleanor Roosevelt.

If you feel you need conviction of justice and equality, call on Abraham Lincoln, Frederick Douglass, Eleanor Roosevelt, or Martin Luther King.

If you need help righting a wrong, an injustice, or inequality peacefully, work with Harriet Tubman, President Grant, Martin Luther King, or Eleanor Roosevelt.

If you feel you need to take better care of yourself, develop your relationship with Eleanor Roosevelt, Saint Hildegard, Nikola Tesla, or Florence Nightingale.

If you need help just being comfortable with who you are, work with the quirky Nikola Tesla or the nature-loving George Washington Carver.

Or . . . find your own historical HSP role models. Develop a relationship with your favorite historical hero. If you are an HSP and find yourself gravitating toward them, there's a good chance that they were an HSPs as well. Read and learn about your favorite historical figures. Hang their picture on your wall like the rock stars of history that they are. They are out there, just waiting to be of assistance. They can continue to improve humanity as energy, just as they did in their physical form.

By now, we have spent quite a bit of time together. Thank you for your time and attention. My hope is that by establishing the idea of historical sensitive persons, we expand the definition of the character trait and learn even more from them. If we can become more impactful like them, we, too, can make the world a better place. With their help, we can be empowered empaths. I sincerely hope you found some insight and ideas on how to be more empowered. I hope I have impressed upon you the importance of your own self-care and that you've found some techniques to make your own or developed your own ideas about how to care for yourself. I hope I have expressed how experimenting with your self-care (and your Sensitivities) can be essential to learning about yourself, remembering you learn just as much with something that doesn't work as you do with something that does.

And I sincerely hope you had fun and continue the fun of shifting your energy toward positivity, self-care, and empowerment. Just because you may be doing serious soul-healing work with serious impact, you can still whistle, giggle, and smile while doing it.

Above all, I hope our time together has revealed how amazing, loving, and wonderful you are and has opened you up to a world of possibilities for making a compassionate and loving impact on the world.

Now go be you through and through. Take good care of yourself and THEN others.

Onward and upward!

BIBLIOGRAPHY

Allione, Tsultrim. *Feeding Your Demons: Ancient Wisdom for Resolving Inner Conflict*, (New York, Little, Brown Spark, 2008).
"Archetype." *NewWorldEncyclopedia.org*. Web. November 3, 2021.
Aron, Elaine, Ph.D. *The Highly Sensitive Person*. (New York: Three Rivers Press, 1998.)
Braden, Gregg. *Awakening the Power of a Modern God: Unlock the Mystery and Healing of Your Spiritual DNA*, (Carlsbad, CA: Hay House, 2006).
Byrne, Rhonda. *The Secret*, (New York: Simon and Schuster, 2006).
Cendrowski, Mark, director. *The Big Bang Theory*. Warner Bros. Television, 2007. TV.
"Champion Archetype." *KnowYourArchetypes.com*. Web. 2022.
Cloud, Henry and Townsend, John. *Boundaries: When to Say Yes, How to Say No to Take Control of Your Life*, (Grand Rapids, MI: Zondervan, 1992).
Conet. "Machiavellianism: What it is, how to recognize and cope with Machiavellians." *Cjku.net*.
Estés, Clarissa Pinkola. *Warming the Stone Child*, (Boulder, CO: Sounds True, 1990).
"FAQ: You talk about DOES as a good way to summarize all the aspects of high sensitivity: Depth of processing, overstimulation, emotional responsivity/empathy, and sensitive to subtleties. But what is the evidence that these actually exist?" *HSPerson.com*. Web. 2022.
Gienger, Michael and Goebel, Joachim. *Gem Water: How to Prepare and Use More than 130 Crystal Waters for Therapeutic Treatments*, (Baden-Baden: Germany, Earthdancer Books, 2008).
Kanew, Jeff, director. *Revenge of the Nerds*. 1984. Film.
"Knight Archetype." *KnowYourArchetypes.com*. Web. 2022.
"Leader Archetype." *KnowYourArchetypes.com*. Web. 2022.
Oslie, Pamala. *Life Colors: What the Colors in Your Aura Reveal*, (Novato, CA: New World Library, 2020).
Palmer, Laura. "The Weird Kids - A Letter to Sensitive Kids Everywhere." *Creating Love*. Self-published by Jeannette Folan and Dr. Michael Smith, 2021.
Pert, Candace. *Molecules of Emotions: The Science Behind The Mind-Body Medicine*, (New York: Simon and Schuster, 1999).
"Rebel Archetype." *KnowYourArchetypes.com*. Web. 2022.
Selig, Paul. *Beyond the Known: Realization*, (New York: St. Martin's Essentials, 2019).
"Sensory Processing Disorder Checklist: Signs And Symptoms Of Dysfunction." *Sensory-Processing-Disorder.com*. Web. March 16, 2022.
Shunya, Acharya. *Roar Like a Goddess*, (Boulder, CO: Sounds True, 2022).
The Bible; New International Version. Colorado Springs, CO: Biblica, Inc., 1984. Print.
"The Tale of Two Wolves." *NanticokeIndians.org*. Web. 2011

Virtue, Doreen. *Earth Angels,* (Carlsbad, CA: Hay House, 2002).
Zukav, Gary. *Universal Human: Creating Authentic Power and the New Consciousness,* (New York: Atria Books, 2021).

NOTES

Part 1: The Highly Sensitive Person

CHAPTER 1 – THE HIGHLY SENSITIVE PERSON CHARACTER TRAIT

1. Gary Zukav, *The Seat of the Soul*, (New York, NY: Simon & Schuster, Inc., 1990), 26.
2. G.J. Tortora and B. Derrickson, *Principles of anatomy and Physiology* (15th ed,), (Hoboken NJ: J Wiley, 2016).
3. "Nervous System," *Better Health Clinic*, August 31, 2014, https://www.betterhealth.vic.gov.au/health/conditionsandtreatments/nervous-system.
4. "6 Ways A Highly Sensitive Person's Brain is Different," *Dr. Elayne Daniels*, September, 12 2021, 6 Ways a Highly Sensitive Person's Brain is Different - Dr. Elayne Daniels (hspglow.com).
5. "Sensory Processing Disorder Checklist: Signs And Symptoms Of Dysfunction," *Sensory Processing Disorder*, (No date listed), https://www.sensory-processing-disorder.com/sensory-processing-disorder-checklist.html.
6. F. Lionetti, A. Aron, E.N. Aron, et al. "Dandelions, tulips and orchids: evidence for the existence of low-sensitive, medium-sensitive and high-sensitive individuals," *Transl Psychiatry* 8, 24 (2018), https://doi.org/10.1038/s41398-017-0090-6.
7. "Highly Sensitive Person (HSP) Certification Course," *Nickerson Institute*, https://nickersoninstitute.thinkific.com/courses/hsp-certification-training-program?ref=1eb6cd.
8. Melody Wilding, "About," No date listed, Executive Coach for Sensitive High-achievers — Melody Wilding.
9. "Archetype." *New World Encyclopedia,* 12 Aug 2023, 06:17 UTC. 26 Aug 2024, 16:37, https://www.newworldencyclopedia.org/p/index.php?title=Archetype&oldid=1119876.
10. Caroline Myss, *Sacred Contracts*, (New York NY: Harmony Books, 2001), 410.
11. Myss, *Contracts*, 396.
12. Ibid., 397.
13. Clarissa Pinkola Estés, *Mother Night: Myths, Stories, and Teachings for Learning to See in the Dark*, (Lousville, CO, Sounds True, 2010), Chapter 1.
14. Myss, *Contracts*, 386.
15. Vanesse Van Edwards, "The Charismatic Personality: 12 Traits You can Master," *The Science of People*. June 13, 2024, https://www.scienceofpeople.com/charismatic-traits/.

Part II
SECTION 1: RELIGIOUS FIGURES AND ARTISTS

CHAPTER 2 – HILDEGARD VON BINGEN
1. Dorsey Armstrong, PhD, "Great Minds of the Medieval World," *The Great Courses,* 2014, https://www.thegreatcourses.com/courses/great-minds-of-the-medieval-world.
2. Regine Pernoud, *Hildegard of Bingen: Inspired Conscience of the Twelfth Century,* (New York, NY, Marlowe & Company, 1998), 7.
3. Ibid., 7-8.
4. Ibid., 8.
5. Ibid., 14.
6. Ibid., 10.
7. Ibid., 168.
8. Ibid., 18.
9. *The Highly Sensitive Person,* https://hsperson.com/.
10. Barbara Newman, "Hildegard of Bingen: Visions and Validation," *Church History,* 54, no. 2 (1985): 163–75.
11. Byron Katie, *A Mind at Home with Itself,* (San Francisco, CA: HarperOne, 2017), Audio book. Disk 2 track 15.

CHAPTER 3 – FREDERICK DOUGLASS
1. David W. Blight, *Frederick Douglas: Prophet of Freedom,* (New York, NY: Simon & Schuster, 2018), xiv.
2. Ibid., 23.
3. Ibid., 22.
4. Ibid., xx.
5. Ibid., 28.
6. Ibid., 27.
7. Ibid., 46.
8. Ibid., 47.
9. Ibid., xvii.
10. Wills, Shomari, *Black Fortunes: The Story of the First Six African Americans who Survived Slaver and Became Millionaires,* HarperCollins Publishers, New York, 2019. Pages 10-11.
11. Blight, *Douglas,* 21.

CHAPTER 4 – CLAUDE MONET
1. Ross King, *Mad Enchantment: Claude Monet and the painting of the water lilies,* (New York: Bloosmbury, 2016), 39.
2. King, *Monet,* 38.
3. Ibid., 39.
4. Ibid., 195.

5. Ibid., 107–108.
6. Ibid., 86.
7. Ibid., 87.
8. Ibid., x.
9. Ibid., 37.

CHAPTER 5 – MARTIN LUTHER KING
1. Carson Clayborne, *The Autobiography of Martin Luther King Jr*, (New York, NY: Grant Central Publishing), 2.
2. Ibid., 2.
3. Ibid., 5.
4. Ibid., 2.
5. Ibid.
6. Ibid., 9.
7. Ibid., 11.
8. Ibid., 9-10.
9. Ibid., 13.
10. Ibid., 14.
11. Ibid., 17.
12. Ibid., 14.
13. Ibid.
14. Ibid., 20.
15. Ibid., 15.
16. Ibid., 16.
17. Reverend Dr. Martin Luther King, Jr., *The Strength to Love*, (Boston: Beacon Press, 1981), 1-11.

SECTION 2: INVENTORS AND INNOVATORS

CHAPTER 6 – FLORENCE NIGHTINGALE
1. Gillian Gill, *Nightingales: The Extraordinary Upbringing and Curious Life of Miss Florence Nightingale*, (New York, NY: Ballantine Books, 2004), 100.
2. Ibid., 97.
3. Ibid., 354.
4. Ibid., xxi.
5. Ibid., 157.
6. Ibid., 105.
7. Ibid., 92.
8. Ibid., 105.
9. Ibid.
10. Ibid.
11. Ibid., 133.
12. Ibid.

13. Ibid.
14. Ibid., 134.

CHAPTER 7 – GEORGE WASHINGTON CARVER
1. Elizabeth MacLeod, *George Washington Carver: An Innovative Life*, (Tonawanda, NY: Kids Can Press Ltd, 2007), 4.
2. Gene Barretta, *The Secret Garden of George Washington Carver,* (New York, NY: Katherine Tegen Books, 2020), 6.
3. MacLeod, *Carver*, 9.
4. Ibid., 10.
5. Barretta, *Secret*, 15.
6. MacLeod, *Carver*, 4.
7. Ibid., 10.
8. Barretta, *Secret*, 26.
9. MacLeod, *Carver*, 16.
10. Barretta, *Secret*, 27.
11. MacLeod, *Carver*, 12.
12. Barretta, *Secret*, 4.
13. MacLeod, *Carver*, 17.
14. Ibid., 25.
15. Documentary *George Washington Carver: An Uncommon Life*, dir by Ken Carpenter and Mark Schlicher, 2010.
16. Barretta, *Secret*, 1.
17. MacLeod, *Carver*, 24.
18. Ibid., 28.

CHAPTER 8 – NIKOLA TESLA
1. Richard Munson, *Tesla: Inventor of the Modern*, (New York, NY, W.W. Norton & Company, 2018), 9.
2. Ibid., 2.
3. Ibid., 4.
4. Ibid., 15.
5. Ibid.
6. John J. O'Neill, *Prodigal Genius: The Life of Nikola Tesla,* (Kempton, Illinois: Adventures Unlimited Press, 2008), 34.
7. Munson, *Tesla*, 19.
8. Ibid., 20.
9. Ibid.
10. O'Neill, *Genius*, 53.
11. "Highly Sensitive Person (HSP) Certification Course," Nickerson Institute, https://nickersoninstitute.thinkific.com/courses/hsp-certification-training-program?ref=1eb6cd.

SECTION 3: LEADERS

CHAPTER 9 – ABRAHAM LINCOLN
1. "The Rail Splitter," *Abraham Lincoln*, directed by Malcom Venville, aired Feb 20, 2022, (New York: History Channel).
2. Thomas L. Carson, *Lincoln's Ethics*, (New York, NY: Cambridge University Press, 2015), 424-425.
3. Carson, *Ethics*, 306.
4. Ibid., 326.
5. Ibid., 304.
6. Aron, *HSP*, 198.
7. Michael Burlingame, *The Inner World of Abraham Lincoln*, (Champaign, IL, Board of Trustees of the University of Illinois, 1994), 92.
8. Ibid., xvii.
9. Ibid., 104.
10. Ibid.
11. Ibid., 96.
12. John Lobb, *Frederick Douglass: From 1817-1882*, (London: Christian Age Office, London, 1882), https://www.whitehousehistory.org/frederick-douglass-and-abraham-lincoln).
13. Ibid.

CHAPTER 10 – HARRIET TUBMAN
1. Elizabeth Lowry, *Harriet Tubman; Imagining a Life*, (New York: Doubleday Publishing Group, 2007), 238.
2. Kate Clifford Larson, *Harriet Tubman; Portrait of an American Hero*, (New York: The Random House Publishing Group, 2003), 303.
3. Ibid., 304.
4. Lowry, *Imagining*, 47.
5. Ibid., 48.
6. Ibid.
7. Ibid., 99.
8. Ibid., 52.
9. Ibid., 99.
10. Catherine Clinton, *Harriet Tubman; The Road to Freedom*, (New York: Back Bay Books, 2005) 20.
11. Ibid., 19–20.
12. Clinton, *Road*, 20.
13. Lowry, *Imagining*, 68.
14. Larson, *Portrait*, 43.
15. Ibid.
16. Clinton, *Road*, 20.
17. Lowry, *Imagining*, 63.

CHAPTER 11 - ULYSSES S. GRANT
1. Ron Chernow, *Grant*, (New York, NY: Penguin Press, 2017), 4.
2. Ibid., 11.
3. Ibid.
4. Ibid., 10.
5. Ibid., xxiii.
6. Ibid., 84.
7. Ibid., 68.
8. Ibid., xxi.
9. Ibid.
10. Ibid., 11.
11. Ibid., 10.
12. Ibid., 11.
13. Ibid., 10.
14. Ibid., 11.
15. Ibid., 7.

CHAPTER 12 - ELEANOR ROOSEVELT
1. Blanche Wiesenthal Cook, *Eleanor Roosevelt: The Early Years Volume 1 1884-1933*, (New York, NY: Penguin Books, 1993), 38.
2. Cook, *Early Years*, 39.
3. David Michaelis, *Eleanor*. (New York: Simon & Schuster, 2020), 7.
4. Cook, *Early Years*, 48.
5. Ibid., 69.
6. Michaelis, *Eleanor*, 35.
7. Ibid., 42.
8. Ibid., 51–52.
9. Cook, *Early Years*, 16.
10. Ibid.
11. Ibid.
12. Ibid.
13. Michaelis, *Eleanor*, 273–74.
14. Cook, *Early Years*, 15.
15. Ibid., 16.
16. Ibid., 17.
17. Michaelis, *Eleanor*, 273.
18. Ibid., 273–74.
19. Harold Ivan Smith, *Eleanor: A Spiritual Biography: The Faith of the 20th Century's Most Influential Woman*, (Louisville, KY: Westminster John Know Press, 2017).
20. Jan Jarboe Russell, *Eleanor in the Village*. (New York: Scribner, 2021), 68.
21. Russell, *Village* 68.

CHAPTER 13 - PRINCESS DIANA
1. "Diana In Her Own Words" directed by Tom Jennings and David Tillman, 2017, DVD. (https://www.imdb.com/title/tt0257545/?ref_=nv_sr_srsg_2)

SECTION 4: THE LESS THAN LOVING HISTORICAL SENSITIVE PERSONS

CHAPTER 14 - NICCOLO MACHIAVELLI
1. Annette, Towler, PhD. "Machiavellianism: What it is, how to recognize and cope with Machiavellians," *CQ Net*, 31.12.2020, https://www.ckju.net/en/dossier/machiavellianism-what-it-how-recognize-and-cope-machiavellians.
2. Erica Benner, *Be Like the Fox: Machiavelli in His World*, (New York: Norton & Company, Inc., 2017), 1.
3. Christopher S. Celenza, *Machiavelli: A Portrait*, (Cambridge MA: Harvard University Press, 2015), 49.
4. Benner, *Fox*, 12.
5. Ibid.
6. Ibid., 143.
7. Ibid., xvii–xviii.
8. Ibid., xx.
9. Ibid., xxi.
10. Ibid., 139.
11. Ibid.
12. Ibid., 97.
13. Ibid., 151.
14. Ibid., 142–43.
15. Ibid., 148.
16. Ibid., 150.
17. Ibid., 148.
18. John M. Najemy, *Between Friends: Discourses of Power and Desire in the Machiavelli-Vettori Letters of 1513–1515*, (Princeton, NJ: Princeton University Press, 2019, ISBN 978-0691656649.
19. Harvey Mansfield, "The Prince of Niccolo Machiavelli," *Britannica*, https://www.britannica.com/biography/Niccolo-Machiavelli/The-Prince.

CHAPTER 15 - RASPUTIN
1. Douglas Smith, *Rasputin: Faith, Power and the Twilight of the Romanovs*, (New York: Farrar, Straus and Giroux, 2016), 5.
2. Smith, *Faith*, 3.
3. Ibid., 16.
4. Ibid., 17.
5. Ibid., 18.
6. Maria Rasputin and Patte Barham, *Rasputin: The Man Behind the Myth*, (Englewood Cliffs, NJ: Prentice-Hall Inc, 1977), 61.

7. Ibid., 201.
8. Ibid., 168.
9. Ibid., 237.
10. Smith, *Faith*, 23.
11. Ibid.
12. Ibid., 104.
13. Rasputin, *Myth*, 193, 219.
14. Ibid., 213.
15. Baroness Sophie Buxhoeveden, *The Life and Tragedy of Alexandra Feodorovna, Empress of Russia: A Biography*, (London and Toronto, 1928), 15.
16. Candace Fleming, *The Family Romanov: Murder, Rebellion and the Fall of Imperial Russia*, (New York, NY: Random House Children's Books, 2014), 4.
17. Ibid., 22.
18. Ibid., 42.
19. Ibid., 98.
20. Ibid., 138.

CHAPTER 16 - JOSEPH STALIN

1. Stephen Kotkin, *Stalin: Paradoxes of Power, 1878-1928*, (New York: Penguin Press, 2014), 21.
2. Ibid., 117.
3. Ibid., 21.
4. Ibid., 33.
5. Ibid., 54.
6. Ibid., 20.
7. Ibid., 17.
8. Ibid., 602.
9. Ibid., 155.
10. Ibid., 620.
11. Ibid., 55.
12. Ruwan M. Jayatunge, "*Joseph Stalin - Psychopathology of a Dictator*" Colombo Telegraph, last edited May 23, 2014, https://www.colombotelegraph.com/index.php/joseph-stalin-psychopathology-of-a-dictator/.
13. Timothy Snyder, *Bloodlands: Europe between Hitler and Stalin*, (New York: 2010), 384. ISBN 9780465002399.

CHAPTER 17 - ADOLPH HITLER

1. August Kubizek, *The Young Hitler I Knew*, (St Paul, MN: MBI Publishing Co, 2006), 14.
2. Ibid., 27.
3. Ibid., 73.
4. Ibid., 78.
5. Ibid., 33.
6. Ibid., 32.

7. Ibid., 14.
8. Ibid., 39.
9. Ibid.
10. Ibid., 40.
11. Tsultrim Allione, *Feeding Your Demons; Ancient Wisdom for Resolving Inner Conflict*, (London: Hay House UK LTD, 2009).
12. Robert Moore and Douglas Gillette, *The Warrior Within: Accessing the Knight in the Male Psyche*, (New York: William Morrow and Company, Inc., 1992), 135.
13. Alice Miller, *For Your Own Good; The Hidden Cruelty in Child-rearing and the Roots of Violence*, (London: Virago Press, 1987), xi.
14. Alice Miller writes Hitler was beaten by his father pages 153-55. Beatings began presumably at age 3 or 4. Alice Miller page 155, "my thesis that Hitler's justifiable childhood hatred of his father found an outlet in hatred of the Jews."
15. Moore, *Warrior*, 135.

CHAPTER 18 – J EDGAR HOOVER

1. Paul Letersky, *The Director: My Years Assisting J. Edgar Hoover*, (New York: Scribner, 2021), 20.
2. Kenneth D. Ackerman, *Young J. Edgar: Hoover, the Red Scare, and the Assault on Civil Liberties*, (New York: Carroll & Grad Publishers, 2007), 3.
3. Letersky, *The Director*, 21.
4. Ibid.
5. Ackerman, *Young Edgar*, 3.
6. Anthony Summers, *Official and Confidential: The Secret Life of J. Edgar Hoover*, (New York: Open Road Media, 2013), 33.
7. Ibid., 33.
8. Ibid., 73.
9. Ibid.
10. Ibid., 71.
11. Ibid.
12. Ibid., 48.
13. Ibid., 60.
14. Ibid., 45.
15. Ibid., 51.
16. Letersky, *The Director*, 19.
17. Summers, *Official*, 38, 48.
18. Ibid., 49.
19. Ibid., 48.
20. "The Hoover Legacy, 40 Years After. Part 5: A Day In the Life," *FBI News*, September 25, 2012, https://www.fbi.gov/news/stories/copy3_of_the-hoover-legacy-40-years-after.
21. Esther Bergsma, *The Brain of the Highly Sensitive Person: Why you shouldn't judge a fish by its ability to climb a tree*, (Woodstock, NY: Booklight Publishing 2020), 38.
22. Marian Keyes. *Rachel's Holiday*, (New York: William Morrow Paperbacks, 2002).

23. Letersky, *The Director*, xiv.
24. Ibid., 127.

Part 3: Being and Thriving as a Highly Sensitive Person

CHAPTER 20 – PHYSICAL CARE

1. Grace Mannon, "15 of Abraham Lincoln's Favorite Foods," *Taste of Home*, last edited 2/21/2024, https://www.tasteofhome.com/collection/abraham-lincolns-favorite-foods/.
2. "Coping Mechanism," *APA dictionary of Psychology*, last edited 4/19/2018, https://dictionary.apa.org/coping-mechanism.
3. "Dopamine." *Cleveland Clinic*, last edited 3/23/2022, https://my.clevelandclinic.org/health/articles/22581-dopamine.
4. Katherine Marengo, LDN, R.D., "7 Foods that could boost your Serotonin: The Serotonin Diet," *Healthline*, 2/16/23, https://www.healthline.com/health/healthy-sleep/foods-that-could-boost-your-serotonin#food-and-mood.
5. Dany Paul Baby, MD (reviewer), "Health Benefits of Beta Carotene," *WebMD*, last edited 9/14/2022, https://www.webmd.com/diet/health-benefits-beta-carotene.
6. Autumn Enloe, MS, RD, LD, "The 13 Healthiest Leafy Green Vegetables," *Healthline*, last edited 2/15/2024, Healthline.com/nutrition/leafy-green-vegetables.
7. David Hawkins, MD, PhD, *The Map of Consciousness Explained*, (Carlsbad, CA: Hay House, 2020), 78-81.
8. Tansy Rodgers, FNTP, "Practicing Daily Gratitude to Enhance Health," *Moravian Manor Communities*, last edited 11/25/2020, https://www.moravian-manorcommunities.org/practicing-daily-gratitude-to-enhance-health/.
9. Amanda Logan, APRN, C.N.P., "Can Expressing Gratitude Improve Your Mental, Physical Health?" *Mayo Clinic Health System*, last edited 4/8/2021, https://www.mayoclinichealthsystem.org/hometown-health/speaking-of-health/can-expressing-gratitude-improve-health.
10. Summer Allen, "Is Gratitude Good For Your Health?" *The Greater Good Magazine*, last edited 3/5/2018, https://greatergood.berkeley.edu/article/item/is_gratitude_good_for_your_health.
11. "Forest Bathing: What it is and Why You Should Try It," *Kaiser Permanente*, last edited 12/16/2022, https://thrive.kaiserpermanente.org/thrive-together/live-well/forest-bathing-try.
12. "Phytoncides: The Science Behind Forest Bathing Benefits," *Forest Bathing Central*, last edited 12/8/2020, https://forestbathingcentral.com/phytoncides/.
13. Rupert Sheldrake, *Science and Spiritual Practices: Transformative Experiences and their Effects on our Bodies, Brains and Health*, (Berkeley, CA: Counterpoint, Berkeley, CA 2018), 55.
14. G. Chevalier, ST. Sinatra, JL. Oschman, K. Sokal, and P. Sokal, "Earthing: health implications of reconnecting the human body to the Earth's surface electrons,"

J Environ Public Health, 2012;2012:291541. doi: 10.1155/2012/291541. Epub 2012 Jan 12. PMID: 22291721; PMCID: PMC3265077, https://www.ncbi.nlm.nih.gov/pmc/articles/PMC3265077/.
15. Ralph Waldo Emerson, "Nature." *Emerson Central*, 1836, https://emersoncentral.com/texts/nature-addresses-lectures/nature2/chapter1-nature/.
16. G.J. Tortora, and B Derrickson, "Electrolytes," *Principles of anatomy and Physiology* (15th ed, J Wiley, 2016).
17. Jacob Berman (reviewer), "Electrolytes," *MedlinePlus*, last edited 11/19/2023, https://medlineplus.gov/ency/article/002350.htm.
18. "Rules of life according to Hildegard of Bingen" *Maria Adam Natural Products*, https://www.maria-adam.com/rules-of-life-according-to-hildegard-of-bingen/.

CHAPTER 21 – EMOTIONAL CARE

1. Joe Vitale, *Zero Limits*, (Hoboken, NJ: John Wiley and Sons, 2007).

CHAPTER 22 – MENTAL CARE

1. "Rules of life according to Hildegard of Bingen," *Maria Adam Natural Products*, https://www.maria-adam.com/rules-of-life-according-to-hildegard-of-bingen/.
2. John J. O'Neill, *Prodigal Genius: The Life of Nikola Tesla*, (Kempton, Illinois: Adventures Unlimited Press, 2008), 47.
3. O'Neill, *Tesla*, 47.
4. Ibid., 15.
5. Harold Byers, "The Miracle Mind of Nikola Tesla," *Tesla Universe*, July 1949, https://teslauniverse.com/nikola-tesla/articles/miracle-mind-nikola-tesla.
6. Michaelis, *Eleanor*, 274.
7. Rick Hanson, *Buddha's Brain: The Practical Neuroscience of Happiness, Love, and Wisdom*, (New South Wales: ReadHowYouWant, 2012).

CHAPTER 23 – ENERGETIC CARE

1. Juliana LaBianca, "The Perfume Princess Diana Never Left Home Without," *Reader's Digest*, last edited Jul 19, 2021, https://www.rd.com/article/princess-diana-perfume/.
2. S Melino S, and E Mormone, "On the Interplay Between the Medicine of Hildegard of Bingen and Modern Medicine: The Role of Estrogen Receptor as an Example of Biodynamic Interface for Studying the Chronic Disease's Complexity," *Front Neurosci*, 2022 May 25;16:745138. doi: 10.3389/fnins.2022.745138. PMID: 35712451; PMCID: PMC9196248, https://www.ncbi.nlm.nih.gov/pmc/articles/PMC9196248/.
3. MK Farahani, FS Bitaraf, A Atashi, and Z Jabbarpour, "Evaluation of anticancer effects of frankincense on breast cancer stem-like cells," *Cancer Rep*, (Hoboken). 2023 Feb;6(2):e1693. doi: 10.1002/cnr2.1693. Epub 2022 Aug 8. PMID: 36806721; PMCID: PMC9939999. https://www.ncbi.nlm.nih.gov/pmc/articles/PMC9939999/.

4. "Peppermint Oil." *National Center for Complementary and Integrative Health*, https://www.nccih.nih.gov/health/peppermint-oil.

CHAPTER 24 – SPIRITUAL CARE

1. "Niccolo Machiavelli," *Stanford Encyclopedia of Philosophy*, last edited Dec 6, 2023. https://plato.stanford.edu/entries/machiavelli/.
2. "Highly Sensitive Person (HSP) Certification Course," *Nickerson Institute*, https://nickersoninstitute.thinkific.com/courses/hsp-certification-training-program?ref=1eb6cd.

CHAPTER 25 – SOUL CURRICULA AND WHY HIGHLY SENSITIVE PERSONS SHOULD CARE ABOUT SELF CARE?

1. Mary Baker Eddy, *The Science and Health with Key to the Scriptures, Writings of Mary Baker Eddy*, (Boston, 1994), 115.
2. "What does Soul mean?" *Oxford English Dictionary*, https://www.oed.com/dictionary/soul_n?tab=factsheet#218084753.
3. Plato, *The Republic*, (Scotts Valley CA: *CreateSpace Independent Publishing Platform*, 2021), Book X.
4. Danielle MacKinnon, *Soul Contracts*, (New York, Atria Books, 2014), 1.
5. Cyndi Dale, *Illuminating the Afterlife*, (Boulder, CO: Sounds True, 2008), 9.
6. Ibid., 37.
7. Max Ehrmann, *The Poems of Max Ehrmann*, (New York: Dodge Publishing Company, 1910).
8. "What is Energy? Laws of Energy," *US Energy Information Administration*, last edited Aug 16, 2023, https://www.eia.gov/energyexplained/what-is-energy/laws-of-energy.php.
9. Meg Blackburn Losey, *The Secret History of Consciousness: Ancient Keys to Our Future Survival*, (Newburyport, MA, Weiser Books, 2010), 69.
10. David Ngan, *Your Soul Contract Decoded*, (London: Watkins Publishing, 2013), 13.
11. Ervin Laszlo, and Jude Currivan, *CosMos; A Co-creator's Guide to the Whole-World*, (Carlsbad, CA: Hay House, Inc, 2008), 114.
12. Deepak Chopra, M.D., and Menas Kafatos, Ph.D., *You are the Universe; Discovering Your Cosmic Self and Why it Matters*, (New York, NY: Harmony Books, 2017), 153.
13. Dolores Cannon, *The Three Waves of Volunteers and the New Earth*, (Huntsville, AR: Ozark Mountain Publishing, 2011), 24.
14. Cannon, *Three Waves*, 24.
15. Richard Gerber, M.D., *Vibrational Medicine; New Choices for Healing Ourselves*, (Santa Fe, NM: Bear & Company, 1988), 168.
16. Gerber, *Vibrational Medicine*, 168.
17. Gary Zukav, *The Seat of the Soul*, (New York, NY: Simon & Schuster, Inc., 1990), 41.

18. Gerber, *Vibrational Medicine*, 168.
19. Fred Alan Wolf, Ph.D., *The Spiritual Universe; How Quantum Physics Proves the Existence of the Soul,* (New York, NY: Simon and Schuster, 1996), 247.
20. Alethia Luna, "12 Signs You've Met Someone From Your Soul Family," *LonerWolf,* last edited 6/5/2021, https://lonerwolf.com/soul-family/.
21. Alison Wem, *Finding your Soul Family: A guide to personal development,* (London, UK: Alison Wem Publishing, 2018), 20.
22. "What is Entanglement and Why Is It Important?" *CalTech Science Exchange*, https://scienceexchange.caltech.edu/topics/quantum-science-explained/entanglement.
23. Michael H. Thaut, Gerald C. McIntosh, and Volker Hoemberg, "Neurobiological foundations of neurologic music therapy: rhythmic entrainment and the motor system," *Frontiers In Psychology*, 2015, https://www.frontiersin.org/journals/psychology/articles/10.3389/fpsyg.2014.01185/full.
24. "Understanding The Atom," *NASA, Imagine The Universe!*, Nov 2013, https://imagine.gsfc.nasa.gov/science/toolbox/atom.html.
25. Zukav, *Seat of Soul*, 94.
26. Hawkins, *Map*, 1.
27. Rev. Stephanie Red Feather, Ph.D., *The Evolutionary Empath,* (Rochester VT: Bear & Company, 2019), 8.
28. Red Feather, *Evolutionary*, 8.
29. Roberta Scherf, and Chris Bye, "The Science of Fight or Flight," *Prio Health*, last edited 10/12/2022, https://www.priohealth.com/blog/blog-category/the-science-of-fight-or-flight/.
30. Paul Leon Masters, *Bachelor's Degree Curriculum.* 4 vols. (Burbank, CA: Burbank Publishing, 2012), 3:15.
31. Directed by Connie Field and Marilyn Mulford, *Freedom on My Mind,* (Tara Releasing, 1994).
32. Ibid.

Index

A
Abraham-Hicks, 51, 195, 210
alcoholic, 67, 70, 98
Alexandra, Tsarina, 91–92, 94–97
Archetypes, 14, 16
Aron, Dr. Elaine, vii, 6–7, 9, 11–14, 81, 121, 138, 179, 227
aware, 16–17, 21, 34–35, 41, 47, 60–61, 80–81, 109, 112, 124, 127, 137–38, 146, 160, 166, 168, 178, 183, 190, 194, 210, 221–24

B
Boundaries, 148
Braden, Greg, 46, 111–12, 212–13, 227
breathing, 103–104, 142, 153, 161, 163, 171–72, 178–79, 182
Byrne, Rhonda, 37, 166, 227

C
Carver, George Washington, 48–51, 116, 118, 121, 128, 130, 149, 178, 184, 205, 225
Chakra, Brow, 132, 161
Chakra, Crown, 132
Chakra, Heart, 127, 130–31
Chakra, Root, 128
Chakra, Sacral, 129
Chakra, Solar Plexus, 130
Chakra, Throat, 131–32
Character traits, 4, 7, 9, 11, 13, 16–17, 24, 43, 57, 71, 75, 78, 81, 85–86, 101, 109, 116, 131, 224, 225

clairaudience, 79
clairaudient, 19, 63, 65, 79
Clairaudient, 18
Claircognizant, 18
clairgustance, 19
clairsalience, 19
Clairsentient, 18
clairvoyant, 18–19, 65, 79, 94
Clairvoyant, 18
cleansing, 19, 47, 135, 177, 179, 181, 185–86, 188, 205, 218, 222
communication, 88, 92, 153
Communication, 153
contracts, soul, 197, 200, 209, 214–16
coping mechanisms, 36, 40, 49, 67–69, 71, 73–74, 121, 123, 146, 160, 173, 176, 195, 212, 217

D
Dale, Cyndi, 128, 203
detached, 79, 95, 99, 151
Diana, Lady, 76–83, 131–32, 134, 146–47, 149, 151, 173, 181, 189, 215–16
Divine, The, 28, 32, 35–36, 135–36, 146, 196
Dopamine, 126
Douglass, Frederick, 29–32, 37–39, 49, 56, 60, 79, 108, 115–17, 121, 128, 131–32, 160, 176, 192, 198, 204, 225

E
Earthing, 136
Eddy, Mary Baker, 32, 202
ego, 57, 94, 130, 194, 217–19

Electrolytes, 139
empath, 7, 43–44, 56, 75, 80, 105, 115, 117, 122, 127, 147, 194, 221
Empathy, 19
entanglement, quantum, 207
Exercise, 134, 183, 214

F
fear, 32, 41–42, 64, 80–81, 95, 97–98, 105, 109–12, 117, 128, 130, 146, 158, 168, 170, 177, 193, 211, 213, 219, 223–24
Forest Bathing, 135
forgive, 64, 66, 76, 156, 159, 191, 193
forgiving, 45, 66, 156, 159, 206
fun, 19, 25, 51, 127, 130, 140, 150, 152, 165, 167, 169, 170–71, 180, 183, 185, 195–96, 214, 224, 226

G
Grant, President Ulysses S., 57, 67–69, 116–17, 121, 123, 126, 134, 137, 146, 188, 195, 198, 201, 225
grounding, 49, 118, 122, 124–25, 129, 136–37, 157, 178, 180–84, 194, 225

H
Hawkins, David R., 133, 209
Highest Good, 134, 190, 193, 222
Hildegard, Saint, 23–28, 39, 44, 46, 49, 65, 72, 79, 114, 118, 121, 123–24, 134, 136, 139, 143–44,

147, 160, 163, 165, 181, 188, 192, 194, 204, 225
Hitler, Adolph, 101–104, 109, 117–18, 135, 143, 146–47, 176, 189, 194, 198, 206
Ho'Oponopono, 159
Hoover, J Edgar, 106–13, 146

I

injustice, Sensitives and, 16, 31, 38, 59–60, 65, 67, 115–16, 225
intelligence, 31, 38, 63, 108, 110, 115
intelligent, 11, 14, 29, 43, 63, 111, 117, 192
intention, 80, 90, 127, 129–30, 133, 144, 147, 169, 185, 222

J

joy, 50, 53, 71, 127, 133–34, 146, 149, 169, 174, 177, 196, 209, 222

K

karma, 205–206
King, Dr. Reverend Martin Luther, 33, 37–41, 93, 115, 169, 194

L

Laughter, 154
Lincoln, Abraham, 29, 31, 56–61, 67, 100, 115–16, 123, 125–26, 128–32, 134, 146–47, 149, 160, 168–69, 188, 194, 197–98, 204, 207–208, 225
Luther King Jr, Dr Reverend Martin, 17, 37, 39, 106, 115, 197, 225

M

Machiavelli, 85–90, 121, 124, 148, 151, 188
meditation, 34, 73–74, 117, 142, 158, 170, 185, 211

migraines, 11, 15, 68, 72, 96, 139, 182
Mindfulness, 179
Mirror Effect, 212–13
Monet, Claude, 33–36, 101, 114–15, 129, 137, 143, 146, 149, 168, 178, 188, 198
morphic field, 210
Myss, Caroline, 14, 178, 200

N

nervous system, 10, 122, 124, 126, 136, 138, 155, 222
neural pathways, 210
neurodivergent, 12, 173
Nightingale, Florence, 43–47, 59, 65, 107, 111, 114, 121, 123, 165, 184, 188, 192, 205, 225

O

Observer Mode, 89, 151–52, 159
open-minded, 45, 59–60
Oprah, 125
Orloff, Judith, 18, 156
overstimulated, 10, 124, 146, 161

P

Pert, Candace, 211, 227
Pinkola Estés, Clarissa, 3, 15

R

Rasputin, Grigori, 91–95, 97, 123, 126, 134, 146–47, 195, 211
Roosevelt, First Lady Eleanor, 70, 72–75, 97, 106–107, 116–17, 121, 123, 125, 130, 135, 139, 149–50, 160, 162, 164–65, 170, 178, 211, 218, 225

S

self-aware, 221
self-care, 6, 55, 71, 74, 113, 117, 122–23, 128, 143,

159, 176, 177, 192, 195, 197, 209, 212, 216–21, 226
Sensitives, 3, 7, 11–12, 14, 19, 25–31, 39–41, 43, 45–47, 50–51, 53–55, 59–60, 65–66, 69, 71, 74–75, 79, 81–82, 89, 94–95, 97, 102–103, 108–10, 113–14, 118, 121–25, 128–29, 131, 133–36, 138, 140, 143–44, 146–51, 153, 155–56, 159–62, 166, 168–71, 173, 176–78, 180, 182–85, 187–90, 192–95, 197, 201, 205–206, 209, 211, 218, 221–24
Sensory Processing Disorder (SPD), 13, 227
sleep issues, 26, 54, 74, 134, 136–39, 143–45, 158, 160, 162, 180–81
soul family, 197–98, 201–202, 207–208, 211, 215, 217
Soul purpose, 5, 7, 16, 46, 51, 72, 97, 100, 114, 128, 131, 168, 178, 192, 194, 204, 217, 219, 225
Stalin, Joseph, 98–100, 109, 143, 146, 176, 178, 188, 198, 201, 206
stimming, 173

T

Tesla, 52–55, 116, 121–22, 124, 135, 137, 146, 149, 160–61, 163, 173, 176, 180, 185, 188, 201–202, 210–11, 225
tryptophan, 126
Tubman, Harriet, 62–66, 69, 71, 98, 108, 112, 114, 121, 123, 144, 168–70, 198, 218, 225

V

Vampires, Energy, 61, 90
Virtue, Doreen, 19, 125, 228

visualization, 40, 141,
    161–63, 170, 172, 174,
    182–83, 185
visualizations, 170, 182
visualizing, 72, 160, 162,
    168, 184, 214
von Bingen, Hildegard,
    23–26, 143

W

warrior, 44
weight issues, 45, 71, 80,
    123–25, 141, 147, 164,
    196, 214

Z

Zukav, Gary, 8, 190, 206,
    209, 228

ABOUT THE AUTHOR

DR. REV. LAURA PALMER holds a PhD in Holistic Life Counseling from the University of Sedona and is a Reiki Master Teacher. She enjoys helping Highly Sensitive Persons to be and feel strong and empowered by assisting them to find their inner strength and remember how amazing they are. She is the owner operator of Sacred Science Energy located in Evergreen, Colorado, where she lives with her mother, and her dog Sofie.

www.ingramcontent.com/pod-product-compliance
Lightning Source LLC
Chambersburg PA
CBHW011956150426
43200CB00016B/2916